TRUE KNOWLEDGE
OF THE CHRIST

Theosophy and Rosicrucianism—The Gospel of John

TRUE KNOWLEDGE OF THE CHRIST

Theosophy and Rosicrucianism—The Gospel of John

Fourteen lectures given in Kassel between 16 and 29 June 1907
and eight lectures given in Basel between 16 and 25 November 1907

ENGLISH BY ANNA MEUSS

INTRODUCTION BY URS DIETLER

RUDOLF STEINER

RUDOLF STEINER PRESS

CW 100

The publishers gratefully acknowledge the generous funding of this publication by the estate of Dr Eva Frommer MD (1927–2004) and the Anthroposophical Society in Great Britain

Rudolf Steiner Press
Hillside House, The Square
Forest Row, RH18 5ES

www.rudolfsteinerpress.com

Published by Rudolf Steiner Press 2015

Originally published in German under the title *Menschheitsentwickelung und Christus-Erkenntnis, Theosophie und Rosenkreuzertum—Das Johannes-Evangelium* (volume 100 in the *Rudolf Steiner Gesamtausgabe* or Collected Works) by Rudolf Steiner Verlag, Dornach. Based on shorthand transcripts and notes, not reviewed by the speaker. This authorized, editorially abridged translation is based on the latest available (third) edition of 2006 edited by Urs Dietler

Published by permission of the Rudolf Steiner Nachlassverwaltung, Dornach

A catalogue record for this book is available from the British Library

ISBN 978 1 85584 415 5

Cover by Mary Giddens
Typeset by DP Photosetting, Neath, West Glamorgan
Printed and bound by Gutenberg Press Ltd., Malta

CONTENTS

THEOSOPHY AND ROSICRUCIANISM

LECTURE 1

KASSEL, 16 JUNE 1907

The nature of our time; theosophy—Religion dying out—Richard Wagner and the world of myths—Reincarnation taught by the Druids—Origin of legends and myths—Egyptian astronomy—The materialism of industry and technology as a necessity in evolution—Christian Rosenkreutz paving the way for a new spiritual culture—Paul and Dionysius the Areopagite—Christianity and Rosicrucianism in accord—Fichte's words—Du Bois-Reymond and his limits of knowledge—The nature of spiritual science—spiritual insight and logic—Theosophy and practical life.

LECTURE 2

KASSEL, 17 JUNE 1907

Paracelsus and Goethe on the subject of the lecture—The nature of man, the physical body, the mineral world—The upper devachan—characterization of the ether body—Two human genders—The plant's level of consciousness—Wisdom of the ether body, thigh bone—Sentience as the essential characteristic of the astral body—The astral body in sleep—The harmony of the spheres for Pythagoras and Goethe—Quotes from *Faust*—The fourfold nature of man.

new life on earth—Assumption of an astral body—Souls of nations helping with integration of ether body—Fritz Mauthner's *Kritik der Sprache*—Relationship between abilities brought into the world and heredity, Bach and Bernoulli families as examples—A mother's love—Parents—Example of five judges in a Vehmic court for powers of attraction and balancing out between people—The ennobling of man through his incarnations—Esoteric interpretation of Lord's Prayer—Objections to the interpretation refuted.

LECTURE 7

KASSEL, 22 JUNE 1907

The law of karma—Examples of the law of karma in action—The law of karma and the beginning of the Old Testament—Karmic law as solution for life's riddles—Astral experiences affect the consistency of the ether body, etheric qualities that of the physical body—Things done in the outside world come back in next life as destiny—Materialistic view of cause and effect and its refutation—Weeping—Nature of leprosy—The European peoples' fear of the Huns was cause of leprosy—Harmful effect of materialism, especially on religious life—Development of mental diseases—Wrong view of karma and its refutation—The Christ's death for redemption in line with karmic law—Other examples of the effects of karma—Fabre d'Olivet's words—Question of sin against the Holy Spirit.

LECTURE 8

KASSEL, 23 JUNE 1907

Previous incarnation of present-day humanity—Problem of equality—Progress of the sun through the zodiac—Reflection of this in periods of civilization—Length and nature of human incarnations in those periods—Review after death and preview before birth—Possible consequences of preview—Characterization of the human bodies—Man at the midpoint of evolution—Nature of old Moon, Sun, Saturn—The seven incarnations of the earth—Their names reflected in days of the week—Connection between the human bodies and the earth's stages of evolution.

Lecture 12
KASSEL, 27 JUNE 1907

Separation into two genders—close and distant marriage—The writer Anzengruber—Nature of close marriage—Memory through generations in age of patriarchs—Blood experience as prime love—Individual, spiritual love of the future—Christianity as mystic fact—The ancient mysteries as precondition for Christianity—Words of Augustine—Details of ancient initiation—Its relationship to the Christ spirit—Richard Wagner and the blood mystery—The Christ's blood sacrifice—The uniqueness of Christianity—Response to Strauss, Drews and others—Transformation of the earth through the Mystery of Golgotha—Nature of the gospel of John and the prologue's power to awaken us—The first five stages of Christian initiation—Goethe's words on the sun and the eye—The Christ organ.

Lecture 13
KASSEL, 28 JUNE 1907

Vision of the future and predetermination—Dionysius the Areopagite and the doctrine of 'the word'—The larynx as the future reproductive organ—Christian Rosenkreutz and his school—The first three stages of training—Study as the first stage—Computing machines—Reference to *Philosophy of Spiritual Activity*—Vision in images as the second stage—Goethe and the earth spirit—The dewdrop—The doctrine of the Holy Grail—Man as upside-down plant—The larynx as the organ of the future—Fly, ladybird, fly!—Story of the stork, butterfly chrysalis—Learning the occult script as the third stage—The process of evolution—Correspondence between periods of civilization and signs of the zodiac.

Lecture 14
KASSEL, 29 JUNE 1907

Preparing the Philosophers' Stone as the fourth stage—Betrayal at the end of the 18th century—Breathing process in man and plant is opposite—The Golden Legend and its explanation—The Tree of Life and the Tree of Knowledge—Training to gain the Philosophers' Stone—Difference between evolution of soul and of race—Legend of Ahasver—Correspondence between microcosm and macrocosm as fifth stage—Etheric and physical body coming to coincide in post-Atlantean time—Entering deeply into macrocosm as sixth stage—The human being's love for all creatures—Seventh stage of training—Nature of the occult teacher—Thought control and positivity—Eduard von Hartmann and the dispute with his contemporaries—Invention of the postage stamp—Arguments against railways—Spiritual science as a fact of life.

The Gospel of John

Lecture 1

BASEL, 16 NOVEMBER 1907

Natural science and religion—The nature of theosophy and how it relates to the religious documents—Four standpoints relating to religious documents—The relationship of the Gospel of John to the other gospels—The dispute between Karl Vogt and Professor Wagner—The Christ as the spirit encompassing the whole earth—The beginning of the Gospel of John—Dionysius the Areopagite and the doctrine of hierarchies—The word as form and configuration—Larynx and heart.

Lecture 2

BASEL, 17 NOVEMBER 1907

The nature of the physical and etheric body—The pentagram = The ether body in man and in woman—Nature of the astral body—About getting tired—Astral body and general astral world—The I of human beings, of animals, of plants, of minerals—Stages in human evolution—Francis of Assisi—Transformation of the human bodies into Manas, Buddhi, Atman.

Lecture 3

BASEL, 18 NOVEMBER 1907

Agreement between beginning of the Bible and of the Gospel of John—The seven embodiments of the earth—The nature of pralaya—Atman on Saturn—Sun–air, Moon–water—Separation of sun and moon from earth—Jehovah and the I—The teaching of Dionysius the Areopagite—The 'children of God' or 'sons of god'.

LECTURE 4

BASEL, 19 NOVEMBER 1907

Wisdom and love—Passage of Mars through the earth—The integration of the I through Yahweh—Breathing fire and breathing air—Sun spirits, Yahweh, Lucifer—Humanity on Atlantis—No awareness of reproduction on Atlantis—Transition from love within blood bond to the universal love of Christianity.

LECTURE 5

BASEL, 20 NOVEMBER 1907

Mosaic law and its replacement—Pre-Christian initiation—Initiation through the Christ in the physical body—Initiation of Lazarus—The three women at the foot of the cross on Golgotha—The 'children of God'—Mary and Mary Magdalene—Nathaniel—The I of the different bodies in relation to the individual I—Inner harmony through the Christ—Goethe's words about the eye and light—The symbolic and historical significance of the Gospel of John.

LECTURE 6

BASEL, 21 NOVEMBER 1907

The numbers secret of the Gospel of John—The school of Pythagoras—The figure five—Atlantis and the Atlanteans—Richard Wagner and his *Rheingold* opera—Rise and fall of post-Atlantean civilization—Leprosy—Nervous diseases of our time—Christianity and the healing element—Interpretation of the figure five—The Christ and the Samaritan woman—The three women at the foot of the cross—Historical facts as symbols for future evolution of humanity.

LECTURE 7

BASEL, 22 NOVEMBER 1907

Europeans and native Americans—The problem of human descent—The rule of the ether body over the physical body in Lemuria—Origins of apes—Haeckel's genealogical tree—The nature of the Holy Spirit—Man as upside-down plant—The hermaphrodite—Sexual organs, brain, larynx—The heart—The Holy

Grail—The nature of plants—The Christian spirit and the earth—The atmosphere is the same for all—The earth as the true body of the Christ.

pages 202–210

LECTURE 8
BASEL, 25 NOVEMBER 1907

The Judaism of the Old Testament—Individualization of the I through the Christ—The Golden Legend—Red and blue blood—Man and plant—The Tree of Knowledge and the Tree of Life—Nicodemus—Way, Truth, Life—The Gospel of John and repeated lives on earth—The man born blind—The adulteress—Karma and freedom—The wedding at Cana as an image of the future—Changing water into wine—The feeding of the five thousand—The Gospel of John as initiation document—Mother Sophia.

pages 211–221

INTRODUCTION

At the beginning of his talks on St John's Gospel Rudolf Steiner spoke of a 'deep conflict in the souls' of his contemporaries, a conflict originally laid down in their young days. He said it arose because young people were not presented with a single but with two philosophies of life—a religious one and a natural-scientific one that cast doubt on the religious one. In this situation theosophy was given its particular mission, which did not, however, make it a sect or indeed a new religion.

One hundred years later we find ourselves in a very different situation. The approach represented by anthroposophy is clearly something that is urgently needed, though the emphasis has changed. The sciences—Rudolf Steiner greatly valued their method, closely following their results—have made the most rapid advances, extending their researches like wildfire into the sphere of ever smaller particles and that of expanding cosmic spaces. Natural sciences are progressively taking over areas of research belonging to the humanities and reducing them to the commonplace. The religious question, on the other hand, continues at the same level as before, despite the expanding secularization that follows the scientific way of thinking. There is now talk of 'religious revival' and there is evidence that many are looking for spiritually broadened insight into the nature of man and world. The gulf between the 'two cultures' of natural and spiritual science still has not been bridged, and ethics commissions, consulted more than ever, point out that the technological advances in the established natural-scientific sense are raising questions which scientific methods do not serve to answer.

Rudolf Steiner's approach, a natural science broadened by comprehensive spiritual science which consciously and systematically intensifies thinking and perceptions, changing their quality, is presented from different viewpoints in the two lecture courses included in this volume.

In Kassel Rudolf Steiner sought to deepen insight into theosophy and Rosicrucianism, showing the relationship to science and religion as he went on. In Basel he spoke about the most mysterious of the Gospels, the Gospel of John. Although the focus was on the Gospel and reference to science and religion was based on this, it is possible to see connections with the Kassel lectures. The basic tenets of theosophy—the levels of human existence and world evolution—are considered, as is the concept of karma and the nature of Christianity. In essence the connection may be seen to lie in the fact that Rudolf Steiner gave the prologue to the Gospel of John in his own translation in both lecture courses—the meditative approach to gain insight into the Gospel and, in a wider sense, Christianity.

In present times it is difficult to envisage the situation and atmosphere in which those lectures were given. It does, however, seem necessary, if we want to understand what Rudolf Steiner was saying at the time, to take a closer look at the situation. It has often been said that Rudolf Steiner used different forms of address and style when speaking to people in different places.

The Kassel lectures were given in the beautiful Wilhelmshoehe hillside park, which is near Kassel, Germany. Rudolf Steiner, accompanied by Marie von Sivers, his future wife, her sister and mother, was staying in Villa Elsa, specially rented for him, and gave the lectures in the hall of a nearby guest house. His audience, numbering about 40, would take the tram up the hill in the evening, as Ludwig Kleeberg wrote, and would afterwards walk down into the town engaged in lively discussion. Among them were several physicians, the director of the court orchestra, the 'open-minded' pastor Hollstein, members of the Theosophical Society including its Kassel branch (founded that year), and also non-members who were interested. Ludwig Kleeberg described the atmosphere as open, lively and full of reverence and profound gratitude. Rudolf Steiner gave the lecture course as an 'introduction', proceeding in much the same way as in the lectures on *The Theosophy of the Rosicrucian* given shortly before in Munich. Taking a closer look at seeming repetition of parts of these and also of elements found in his fundamental works *Occult Science, an Outline* and *Theosophy*, one finds that they take things further. Rudolf Steiner was never interested in providing information, not even in the form of new revelations. The insights, always seen in a new way, had their own grounds and origin, with new illustrative examples. Taking this point of view, we reap great benefit from reading and studying these lectures on the basic tenets of theosophy/anthroposophy.

A few months later Rudolf Steiner spoke at the invitation of the Paracelsus Branch in Basel to an audience of about a hundred about the Gospel of John. The authorities permitted the great hall of De Wette School in the Augustinergasse to be used for a public lecture on 'Science at the Crossroads' on 23 November of that year, which was attended by about three hundred people. Those who attended the Basel lectures for members on the Gospel of John also referred to a warm atmosphere and sense of community. A 'Prologue' by member Oscar Grosheintz opened the course with hymnic words and rhythms:

> To all of you, whom noble search for wisdom
> Has brought to us from far and near,
> Basel's Paracelsus Lodge now offers
> A joyful, cordial welcome.
> Thank you for coming to join us
> To share our joy, our happiness,
> And in so doing adding to our joy.
>
> . . .

Such things are not easily entered into at a much later time, but it is important to know that we are here dealing with the *spoken* word and the lectures must be read with this in mind, all the more so as they are here given in a shortened form (see also 'Text sources' on page 243).

New additions in this edition are the (lightly edited for style) question and answer sessions in Kassel recorded by Ludwig Kleeberg. The subject matter relates only to some degree to that of the lectures, as was often the case in such sessions. Being brief and aphoristic, they need deepening on the basis of Rudolf Steiner's collected works.

Urs Dietler, 2006

TRANSLATOR'S NOTE

In German, every noun is given an initial capital letter. In English we have some extra room for play as initial capital letters are only used to dignify titles and institutions, and much less so in modern times. To help comprehension, I have in the case of sun, moon and earth used an initial capital for Sun and Moon when the text was referring to the 'old Sun' and 'old Moon', and no initial capital when it referred to the present-day sun and moon. The earth, accordingly, was not given an initial capital.

For the quotes from St John's and other Gospels I have used the translation by Kalmia Bittleston (published by Floris Books), but adapted this where Rudolf Steiner was giving his own interpretation and this differed from the Bittleston translation.

Anna R. Meuss, January 2015

THEOSOPHY AND ROSICRUCIANISM

LECTURE 1

KASSEL, 16 JUNE 1907

THE aim of this lecture will be to present an overview of the philosophy we are in the habit of calling theosophy. This theosophy must in the most comprehensive sense develop into a new cultural impulse; it is something for which humanity has been longing for a long time and it must answer the question asked by humanity which is in every respect a burning one. At the present time it still tends to be something which people not only want to refute but which is considered questionable, and in fact something quite mad, like the fantasies of a handful of dreamers.

Of course if we were to ask those dreamers what their aim is with theosophy and what they think it will do for them, the answer will be fairly comprehensive. Above all these supposed fantasies of today are seen as something which in 20 to 50 years is bound to be of tremendous importance for human sentience, thinking, will and doings.

Nothing exists in the world which cannot be shone upon by this theosophy as an impulse and which theosophy is not called upon to shine on.

There are all kinds of questions in this day and age—health and social issues, questions concerning women and education, as you know. And there is an even greater number of answers. An objective look at all these questions and their answers will make us aware, however, that whilst the questions are right to arise in our civilization—they are posed by present-day conditions—they cannot be so easily answered in our present time.

People who do not close their eyes and ears to the questions of our time will understand that they meet with obstacles everywhere. A time will come when people realize that there are many more questions—the fact that there are internal and external wars, pain and suffering, shattered hopes in all spheres is giving rise to them. And only theosophy can provide the answers.

More and more people keep their heads down today, meeting their obligations but not knowing why they are doing all the work they do, with this muddle-headedness leading to despair, even affecting their physical health in the phenomena seen in neurasthenics.

I just want to touch on this briefly. The main idea we should have in mind is that theosophy is not something for just a few people who have nothing better to do, but that it should be part of practical life.

In the 30 years of its existence the Theosophical Society has of course had its teething troubles and gone through all kinds of things that might have cast doubt on its significance, but it will work its way through all this and show what it is capable of achieving. Theosophy will have to become an all-embracing affair, something universal, for it has to provide answers to the questions that ultimately are the fundamental questions concerning all existence, and show how people of today should see these questions, and understand why there are such things as religions and sciences in the world. Whatever we do, we must refer to certain basic questions if there is to be art, science and practical work, and ways must be found to solve these basic questions. All religions have been attempts to find answers to these questions, answers which were, however, in accord with the intellect and level of civilization of the different nations.

Theosophy is not meant to be a religion; it has nothing to do with a sect and does not agitate for or against anything.

As you know, religion is as old as human endeavour. Looking at the different religions among different peoples we are convinced that all the different religions tried to answer the questions as to what, firstly, is the very core of the essential human being, secondly, what is the destination of man, and thirdly, what lies beyond this physical existence.

With regard to these questions we, the people of today, have a strange time behind us which has caused many to grow confused about religion. Let us ask ourselves how many people there are today who do need religion but are unable to have it. Some of us can still look back on times when religion had much greater validity, indeed to a much higher degree than is the case today with individuals who are particularly religious by nature. They still have something of the warm feeling that existed for some thousands of years. The need, the longing for the spiritual world, as we call it, that is, the longing for religion, does still exist today. In those most true to their nature this longing to have satisfaction has in fact continued to grow and grow. Such a person will say: 'As a child I still had real faith. But then things changed. I got to know science, as it is called, and its facts, and since this tells a very different story, for example as to how the world came into being, I am in profound doubt as to the things I believed in as a child.' A deep sadness then arose in life, with the soul as if torn apart, looking out into the world in desolation and not given any explanation for the inner conflict. Hence the feeling of being torn between religious longing and inner satisfaction, hence the tragic situation of today. Yet perhaps this is better than the other thing, which is that people no longer question things at all, have got entirely out of the habit of asking questions, grow superficial and just live their day-to-day existence, 'getting by'.

Is it due to the religions that we have come to this pass? No! It is perfectly evident that this is not the case. For every religion, and that even includes the ancient myths and legends, has the ways and means to guide the heart back again, to have every soul come alive again, if it wills it. Who would have thought that such tremendous impulses from the ancient myths, which seemed to have died away thousands of years ago, leading an almost hidden, unknown existence, could rise again the way they have in Richard Wagner's[1] dramatic work?

There is no need to found a new religion; the time for that has passed. Need has, however, arisen for people to take a new look at things, develop a new understanding. It is the human mind, the human soul which has changed and the human heart.

If we try and enter into the evolution of the human soul we will be able to understand, in the course of these lectures, that our souls have been on the physical plane many times before, that they only evolved gradually to the level where they are today. That may seem grotesque, but all our souls have heard the profound truths that are presented to us today in their earlier lives.

You will hear about the theory of reincarnation, for example; but just as you are listening to me today, so did your souls in the past listen to the Druids who were living and teaching particularly in this part of the world. Those ancient Druid teachers cultivated the theory of reincarnation among themselves, this most ancient wisdom concerning the mysteries of life. They went out to the people who felt the need for deeper insight in their souls. But if those ancient teachers had said things then the way I put them today, your souls would have been quite unable to take them in, for the mind had not yet developed by then to be ready for this. In those times the human mind knew nothing of logic. But what it did have was the possibility of understanding things in images. And those teachers did therefore express themselves in images, and those images are the legends and myths you know today. If our souls had not heard these things in the past, we would not be able to understand the truths which are now taught in a new form.

The soul has made tremendous progress through thousands of years, assuming new forms, and because of this the truth, too, must be presented to it in ever new forms. Let me give you a second example.

Let us go back in human evolution to the ancient Egyptians, Chaldeans, Babylonians. When their civilization was at its height they did not consider sun and stars to be purely physical bodies. When a materialistic astronomer of today looks at the heavenly bodies he sees only physical bodies and nothing else. To him the earth, too, is just such a physical body in the cosmos, with human beings scurrying about on it like midges on one's hand.

It was very different with the ancient Egyptian astronomers. When the Egyptian astronomer of old looked at a star he would not think of a purely physical body. The star meant something very different to him than it does for people today. Voicing the name of Mercury, for instance, he was not in the least thinking of addressing the physical body in the heavens, just as you would not think of addressing a body made of papier mâché. Everything the eye saw was for the people of that time merely an outward expression of something spiritual. For the ancient astronomers the physical Mercury star reflected the spirit of Mercury. You must understand this not with the intellect but with your heart, otherwise you'll have no idea of what lived in the soul of such an astronomer. Nothing existed that did not reflect something spiritual for him. He would say: 'Everything is spirit, and being a spirit myself I am part of this spirit.'

This is something you must keep in mind. The wise people of earlier times, we have to understand them, understand what they knew about events in the spiritual sphere. And if you enter more fully into this sentience which they had you will know that their view was infinitely superior to the materialistic view we take today. We must come to understand the sages of those times, fathom what they knew about events in the spiritual sphere; and it is only then that we realize the vast difference, and the infinite significance of the wisdom taught of old. It may seem ridiculous to someone who thinks in the materialistic way of our time, where we know only the purely physical view taken in astronomy, but that is how it is.

Why is it that people have today lost all feeling for the spiritual life that is behind the whole of physical life? And why did this have to happen?

Let us turn our attention to our immediate surroundings. If you were able to compare the world people had around them in the past with the world we have around us today, you would find that in those days people had only the most necessary, barely adequate means of surviving on this earth. But they did have more of a feeling for the things of the spirit. This feeling for the spiritual world had to recede so that human beings would be in a position to gain their present dominance on earth. All the advances made in technology and industry have only been possible because of a view of the world that had grown materialistic, with the spirit, the supersensible world, fading into the background. The price to be paid for gaining control of the physical world over recent centuries was therefore that we had to lose our spiritual vision. It is an eternal law for humanity that abilities can only be gained in one field if abilities regress in another field. Thus humanity could never have created the transport facilities we have today if other faculties had not regressed. To gain all the things we have around us today we had to lose our feeling for the spiritual. To conquer the physical world, the things that had once filled the mind of man had to recede.

We thus see how around the sixteenth century people lost their eye for the spiritual world, and how a materialistic way of thinking took over. Anyone who thinks that he himself is not fully caught up in materialism is deceiving himself.

Spiritual science does not exist to negate things or be critical, saying how bad the world is today. No, it shows that it was necessary for humanity to descend into the material world. The wide horizon of man's spiritual life had to recede in the meantime, and it is also in connection with this that the old way of understanding things of the spirit has been lost. The truths were there in the past, in different forms. Spiritual science serves to show them to people today in a way they will understand. This is what matters. Theosophy is therefore nothing but an instrument for making the most profound truths accessible to the modern mind, so that they may be understood in all their depth.

Today we have to draw attention to the spirit again. We cannot go on saying, 'See how much wiser we have grown today.'[2] The truth is open to us at all times and may be grasped in different ways.

Let us look back on ancient India, on Egypt, Greece, on the time when Christianity was established. The same old truths have always come up in different forms. There have always been leaders who made sure that the truths which had faded away as civilizations went into decline were told to humanity in new ways. The founders of the great religions were among them.

Before it came to more recent times, before Copernicus and before the sixteenth century, care was taken also in Europe that the foundations were laid for a new way of proclaiming the truth. Around the sixteenth century there were a few individuals who knew how to interpret the signs of the times. As early as 1459 an individual who had attained a higher level of spirituality, commonly known as Christian Rosenkreutz,[3] gathered just a few people around him as he established an occult school for the cultivation of wisdom. As I said, it is nothing new; it is the most ancient wisdom but in the form in which present-day humanity needs it.

How does this Rosicrucian wisdom relate to Christianity? There is no difference whatsoever between genuine Christian teaching and the teaching of the Rosicrucians. If we understand the core of Christianity, we have the theosophy of the Rosicrucians. There is no need to found a new religion; instead we must take Christianity the way it was under-

stood by the early Christians. However, hardly anyone still knows
something of the secrets of early Christian development. Even official
theology no longer gives any clue. There we find Paul himself as one
with the most profound knowledge of the Christian secrets, teaching
those tremendous truths that were to guide humanity through millennia. Paul had established a school in Athens, with Dionysius the
Areopagite[4] at its head. This Dionysius was a genuine disciple of Paul.

The teachings of Dionysius were always full of life; they were especially also taught to the people who were to take the Christ's living word
out into all the world. No new form would have been needed if
humanity had remained at the standpoint of Dionysius. But new times
came and with them the necessity to teach in such a way that Christianity would be rock solid and no science would be able to raise
objections to it. Because of this, Rosicrucian theosophy is the form of
religion that is right for us today.

You will only have an idea of the eternal life to be found in Christianity if you gain the right understanding.

If we were put in a position today where we would hear from all
around what Rosicrucian theosophy has to say about true Christianity,
the scientific facts would not contradict the description of what goes on
there. The point is that religion might be found not to be in conflict
with the scientific facts, and that these scientific facts are brought into
harmony with it.

What does this Rosicrucian theosophy bring us? Insight into higher
worlds, that is, into worlds to which humanity will still belong when
this physical body of ours has perished; insight into life, insight into the
nature of death and of human evolution. This is how it will reaffirm the
religious truths and religious life for the human race.

No one should say, 'I am firmly based on the old teachings and that is
enough for me. The doubts of others do not concern me!' Nothing is
more egotistical and less Christian than this. For something that may
perhaps still be possible today, that a number of people are still held
back on the basis of the old religions, will no longer be possible in the
none too distant future. Anyone able to see into the element which now
seeks to make great waves in the social sphere will not share that
opinion. They will see that the wisdom proclaimed in theosophy is not

something you fight over. What matters is merely the result you achieve. And it is exactly the same with spiritual science. Human beings need spirituality to bring healing, and it is only when this healing principle is coming in that humanity can gain health again. It is a factor in evolution and the giver of life in our civilization.

External arrangements will not serve the purpose; they are without exception directed towards the physical, the body. Theosophy aims to give health to the soul and the spirit. There is nothing arbitrary about spiritual science; it is demanded by our age and its problems. Everything it has to say is the teaching of all who have done investigations in this field.

Spiritual science takes us into higher worlds which the physical eye is unable to see into, but that is where the causes for the effects in this physical world are to be found. It will enable us to perceive the eternal in human nature, the very core of every individual's being, the spiritual worlds and their hierarchies. And when we come to know these we will get to know the reason for human existence. The true nature of man— that will be our subject. We'll get to know worlds that exist but cannot be grasped with our purely physical senses. Some people may say, 'It is all well and good what you are telling us, but we cannot have direct knowledge of it.' The answer is one which Fichte[5] has given. Imagine you are the only person who is able to see in a world of people born blind, and you speak to them of colours. They will also say, 'It is rubbish what you are telling us; there is no such thing.' If, however, it were possible to restore the blind people's sight, then they would indeed learn about this world of colour and of light.

The same holds true for the above objection. Anyone raising such an objection is of the same ilk as someone who was born blind. Yet no one should say, 'There is no such thing.' For no one has the right to speak of 'limits to our insight' as du Bois-Reymond has done.[6] There are as many worlds as we have organs to perceive these infinitely many worlds. We just are not able to perceive them today because we do not yet have the organs for this. The world is infinite not only in terms of space but also intensively infinite;[7] every sense has its own world. At present we cannot fathom them, but they are there; they are in the place where we ourselves are. All it needs is to open our eyes, for they are right in the midst of us.

The words spoken by the Christ 'The kingdom of God is among you'[8] must be taken literally. In spiritual science one speaks of the spiritual worlds in just that sense. And there have always been initiates who knew the ways and means of entering into those kingdoms of heaven. Reference is made to them in all religions. Spiritual science is merely the means by which this fundamental truth of all religions may be found again. Everything we see and perceive here around us is an outcome and effect of what is happening in the spiritual world. Everything that makes itself known on earth is but a development of something which is alive and active in the spiritual worlds.

In official Christianity people have long since lost the ability to understand the real depths of the religious documents. It therefore became necessary to have spiritual science provide the key to the forgotten treasures of knowledge, offering the means of redemption to a humanity that found itself at the crossroads. There is no fanaticism to this; it is merely that the information is given, the nature of the human being is made clear, showing what human destiny will be after death, showing how the soul develops when out of the physical body. Spiritual science tells us what happens in the higher worlds, speaks of the earth's and other planets' stages of evolution and casts light on human life in past, present and future.

One objection that may be raised is that surely all this is only for the 'seer' who is able to look into the spiritual worlds. What good is it to us? Those worlds are not accessible to us.

The answer would be as follows. There are methods of inner training which are suitable for the spiritual investigator and it may therefore seem justifiable to raise that objection. But Rosicrucian training takes a different course. To penetrate into the spiritual worlds does need a seer's eye and an initiate's ear. Ordinary logic is all that is needed for understanding. Everything said by the spiritual investigator is open to logical comprehension; all it needs to understand these things is sound, ordinary common sense. If you cannot do this you simply lack the logic. It does need the eye of a spiritual investigator to discover the spiritual secrets. Ordinary logic is enough to understand the things told in Rosicrucianism.

If you cannot see this you must not ascribe your failure to the training. Failure to understand is not due to the fact that you are not a seer, but you have not got sound powers of understanding and logical thinking. Logic is, however, something which is unknown to many. A musician of our time has said, for instance, that thinking about things is a difficult matter. Even academics think only a short way ahead. But when people use their powers of reason properly they will get to the point where they can grasp even the more sublime wisdom and truth and let them come alive in them. And if you go on to ask, 'What good is it to us?', the answer is: nothing can be given to us that is of greater significance than the insights gained in spiritual science; these alone make us into true human beings, able to have a heart that is content, a soul that finds harmony in itself.

Phrases won't get us far here; we have to set to work in all seriousness as we struggle for insight, entering fully into the needs and problems of life. We must unceasingly seek to penetrate from one realm of spiritual life to another. Then insight into the whole reality of world and human evolution will well forth from this. And the awesome magnitude of this will take hold not only of our heart but it will awaken new faculties in us, making us able to tackle everyday life. An immediate power wells forth from spiritual science, something which will be a positive element that will never be lost, something to make us into creative human beings.

You have to get to know the spiritual world if you are to understand the material world. Spiritual science is not something for oddbods but exactly for the most practical among practitioners.

All existence is spirit. Just as ice is water, so matter is also spirit. Mineral, vegetable, animal or human—all are a condensed form of spirit.

This is how Rosicrucian theosophy guides us to insight into the spiritual foundations of the world. It does not make us into eccentrics, outsiders, but into friends of existence, for it does not look down on everyday life, alienating us from our mission on earth; it brings us close to them. It spurs us on to be active in our work, knowing that everything we do reflects the spirit as much as everything in existence does.

LECTURE 2

YESTERDAY we had a kind of introduction, speaking about the aims and nature of the spiritual-scientific movement. Today we'll go straight into the essential nature of this science. There is the disadvantage that people who are not familiar with these things may suffer something of a shock, but one has to be patient and be clear in one's mind that many things that to begin with seem quite nonsensical will prove to be something that will turn out to be consistent in itself and comprehensible as time goes on.

As to the subject we have been given, we'll first of all have to consider the essential nature of the human being.

Let us consider this human being, meaning ourselves. Human beings are highly complex entities, the most complex we may meet with in the world which is familiar to us. This is why people who are able to see more deeply have always called the human being a microcosm compared to the macrocosm which is the universe. Paracelsus[9] found a good image for the nature of man. Consider the natural world around you and imagine every plant, animal and stone to be a letter in an alphabet. Make a word of these letters and you have the human being. We also see the truth of Goethe's words that you have to understand the whole of nature if you are to find the human being.

To begin with, the things I am going to say today will be just an outline of man's nature. They will relate to the things we will be considering in the next few days concerning the nature of man the way a charcoal sketch does to the finished painting.

Using our senses to study the human being here on earth, as we see him with our eyes, feel him using the sense of touch, this is the human being in his entirety seen from the materialistic point of view.

For a spiritual view of the world, which goes deeper, this is, however, only a small part of the human being whom we are able to perceive with our physical senses; it is the part which anatomists dissect in their endeavour to understand, reducing it to individual cells that can only be seen under the microscope and so trying to get a picture of the structure and functions of individual organs.

All this is taken to be the physical body by scientists. But people are very often getting the wrong idea about this physical body, for they believe that the human being one has before one in life is nothing but this physical body. That is not at all the case, for the higher aspects of human existence are closely bound up with it. They use the physical body as their instrument and it is only thanks to them that the individual appears the way he does to us, sharing our world. This physical body would look very different if we were able to separate it from the higher aspects of human nature. Human beings share their physical body with the whole mineral world. All the substances and forces that play between the individual minerals, iron, arsenic, carbon and so on, are also at play in the substances in the physical bodies of human beings, animals and plants.

We are immediately aware of the higher aspects of human nature when we consider the tremendous difference between this physical body and the other forms of matter that exist in the world around us. You all know that this admirable composition which we know as the physical body has an inner life, as we call it—conscious awareness, pleasure and pain, joy, love and hate, and that this physical body contains not only the mineral substances but also thoughts and ideas. You clearly see the red cheeks and the hair colour, but you do not see the pleasure and pain, joy and suffering, and so on. We do not see these but they do all run their course within the integument of skin. This in itself is the clearest and incontrovertible proof that there has to be something else, apart from this body, and not only physical matter.

When you see a tear arise, this tear is a purely physical expression of the sadness that is felt within. Consider the mineral world. Silence. No joy, no pain, nothing of all that is perceptible. A stone has no feelings, nor any of the conscious awareness we have. For the spiritual scientist, this stone is like the nails on our fingers or our teeth. Look at a nail. It, too, has no feeling, no sentience; and yet it is part of us. We must have something in us which causes nails and teeth to develop; in the same way there is something in the world which produces the minerals. Nails have no conscious awareness themselves, but they are part of something which does have conscious awareness. If a small insect crawls across the nail, the nail may perhaps be a mineral to it. That is how it is when we crawl across the ground and do not realize that there is a conscious mind behind this mineral soil, just as there is a conscious awareness behind the nail. We shall see that there is a world and a conscious awareness behind the mineral world. This I consciousness of the mineral world is a long way above us, more or less the way in which our conscious awareness which is behind the nail is a long way above that of the insect crawling across the nail.

In Rosicrucian philosophy this conscious awareness in the mineral world is ascribed to a world called the 'world of reason'. There the conscious awareness of minerals is to be found, and it is also the source and origin of human powers of reasoning which allow us to develop thoughts. But the thoughts that live in us are most deceptive; the human thought world relates to the spirits of this rationality more or less the way our shadow on the wall relates to us. The shadow on the wall is not me but merely my shadow. In the same way human thoughts are but shadow images of the spiritual world. The reason why a thought develops here is that there truly is a creative spirit in the world of reason which produces the thought. It is a world where our thoughts are real entities which you meet there just as here you meet another person. To initiates this is known as the upper devachan world, the arupa devachan of the Indians or also the higher mental world, that is, the Rosicrucians' world of reason. When an initiate goes through this physical world, life speaks to him on every patch of ground, and he feels the other world manifesting itself in everything. In our physical bodies we are mere pieces of this physical world and we therefore also have a subordinate physical awareness which goes as far as the upper world of reason, the world where the mineral world has its conscious awareness.

Our physical body is mineral as far as its substance is concerned, and the conscious awareness of this physical body is also in the place where we find the conscious awareness of the mineral world.

What is the difference, then, between this physical body and a mineral such as a rock crystal? If we compare our body with a crystal we will immediately see that compared to this it is highly complex. Just consider the difference between a mineral and a living entity. There is no difference as far as substance is concerned, for a living entity contains the same materials as a mineral, except that the composition is much more complex.

When you have a mineral before you it has its particular form, and left to itself it will stay the same. It is not like this with a life form, with plant, animal and human being. For as soon as matter becomes so complex that left to itself it can no longer stay as it is, be what it is, but would have to disintegrate, there is something present in this matter which prevents its disintegration, and we then have a life form before us. In spiritual science we therefore say that left to itself a life form would disintegrate into the individual components of its substance unless the preventer of such disintegration were also present in it. This preventer is something we call the ether or life body, though it is entirely different by nature from the physical matter that makes up the physical body. It is able to create and maintain the most complex organic matter in every life form and prevent its disintegration. We call something which thus shows itself quite outwardly in an organism 'life'. This ether or life body, or body of creative powers, cannot be perceived with physical eyes but certainly can be perceived if one has the first degree of clairvoyant vision. The seer must go through such inner development that he will be able to see this ether body just as we see the physical body with the physical eye. Modern scientists are no doubt also looking for this ether body, but speculation is used to get an idea of it, and people will speak of 'power of life' or 'vital energy' for instance.

How does this ether body present itself to the clairvoyant eye, the clairvoyant individual?

If you look with the seer's eye at something from the mineral world, say a rock crystal, leaving the physical matter aside by letting your focus shift, as it were, you will see nothing at all in the space occupied by the physical crystal. The space is empty. If you look at some life form—plant, animal or human being—in this way, the space occupied by the physical body will not be empty but filled with a kind of light form, and that is the ether body which we mentioned before. This ether body is not the same for all life forms but actually most variable, also with regard to its form and size relative to the physical body of the life form in question, depending entirely on the developmental stage that the life form has reached. In plants, the ether body has quite a different form from the plant itself; in animals it shows greater similarity to the outer form of the animal, and in human beings the ether body presents as a light form that has almost the same shape as the physical body. If you look at a horse from this point of view, you will for instance see the ether body as a light form that projects quite a bit beyond the head, anterior to the forehead, though it is approximately adapted to the form of the horse's head. In the average person today you will see the ether body project only a little above and on either side of the head.

As to the substance of the ether body, people usually have the wrong idea of the materiality of it. In the Theosophical Society, too, people say and write much that is erroneous concerning the ether body, but those are the teething troubles of the Society which have to be overcome. To get the right idea of the ether body's substantiality, please follow me in making a comparison.

Imagine you have a hundred marks and are spending more and more of it. Your funds will be less and less and finally there'll be nothing left. That would be the most reduced state of your finances. But there is one that is even more attenuated, for you reduce the zero funds even further by going into the red, i.e. entering into debt. It is thus possible to reduce your funds even further, for if you have a debt of, say, ten marks, you have less than nothing.

Or imagine the same concept applied to something else. Imagine a battle—the din is tremendous. Go further and further away from it and the din will be less and less; it will be quieter and quieter until you don't hear any more of it. Reduce this nothing you hear and it will be quieter than quiet, more soundless than soundless—such stillness does indeed exist. And it will be beatific to the highest degree though people will not find it easy to imagine this in the general run of things.

Now consider these examples applied to the density of matter. Initially you will have the familiar states of aggregation—solid, fluid, gaseous or airy. But we must not stop there, just as we did not stop in the case of our finances. We are able to attenuate our funds until they are negative. In this case, too, matter is attenuated more and more, beyond the gaseous state. Imagine a form of matter that would be the opposite of physical matter and you will have an approximate idea of what ether consists of.

With negative funds, the conditions are the opposite of positive— being in the black makes you rich, being in the red makes you poor. The more money I have the more can I buy; the less money I have the less can I buy. And the cosmic ether—the ether body of every life form being part of this—also has the reverse properties of physical matter. Where solid matter seeks to fall apart, the ether body seeks to draw everything together and prevent the physical body which it inhabits from disintegrating. This disintegration into the individual basic sub- stances begins as soon as the ether body of a life form departs from it or, in other words, when the life form enters into physical death. We have now followed matter into a world where its action is the opposite of the way in which physical matter acts.

When I say that in human beings the ether body is similar in form to the physical body, this takes us to a fact which we must know, a fact I am going to mention here because important conclusions for the later lectures arise from it. The words I have spoken require a most important limitation, for in reality the ether body is very different from the phy- sical body, really resembling it only in its upper part, the head region. It is very different from the physical body in that it is of the opposite gender. The ether body of a man is female, and conversely that of a woman is male. Every individual is bisexual; the physical gender is but an outward reflection and has its opposite in the ether body. A magnet has a north and a south pole and there is no magnet that has a north pole only. And here, too, we have pole and counter-pole.

This ether or life body, also known as creative powers body, is therefore the second principle of the essential human being. From birth to death it is closely bound up with the physical body, and death ensues when this life body separates from the physical body.

The physical body is created by the ether body which is the architect, as it were, of the physical body. To get an idea of this, think of water and ice. When water cools down it assumes a different form and turns into ice. Just as water turns to ice in a process of condensation, so is the physical body differentiated out from the ether body.

Ice, water; physical body, ether body—it means that the powers of the ether body have become tangible, physically perceptible in the physical body. Just as water actually contains the powers that then come to expression in solid ice, so does the ether body contain the powers that will build up the physical body. The ether body has the inherent power from which the heart, the stomach, the brain and so on differentiate out. The *idea* of every organ in our physical body exists already in the ether body—not in material form but as energy currents. Human beings have an ether body in common with all plants and all animals, that is, with all physical entities that have life.

Now the question may be raised if plants have a form of conscious awareness in the sense in which we have found the mineral world to have conscious awareness. As we have seen, the conscious awareness of minerals may be found in the upper world of reason using the means of spiritual science, which is also where our thoughts have their source and origin.

Our fingers do not have an independent conscious awareness, their awareness being part of the whole human being's conscious awareness. In the same way the conscious awareness of plants is part of a greater one and this is to be found in the lower world of reason, the world of stars, of heaven, of rupa devachan. When the spiritual investigator enters into this world he meets there the souls of the plants. These souls are entities there just as we are here, and these entities relate to the plants in roughly the way in which a human being relates to his fingers.

The conscious awareness of plants is thus anchored in this lower devachan world. There one finds the roots of all powers that are behind growth and all organic development. The powers that build up our own physical body also have their roots there, which means the powers of our ether body, which we have earlier called the architect of the physical body. This conscious awareness of the plant world is much more sublime and full of wisdom than the conscious awareness of human beings.

You will understand this as soon as you consider the wisdom that lies in the structure not only of the human physical body but of all life forms endowed with ether bodies. Think of the infinite wisdom needed to build the simplest physical body of some life form, let alone the most elaborate composition among all life forms on earth—the human body!

Consider the upper part of the human thigh bone, for example. The individual trabeculae [bars or columns of bone tissue] are most marvellously put together according to all the rules of architecture. The thigh bone is much more complex here than it appears when seen from outside. It is made up of a scaffolding of bars where the angles between them are arranged with such wisdom that the smallest amount of matter is needed to support the whole body. Truly a greater work of art than the most complicated bridge structure, and all the art of engineering in the world cannot match it. Or consider the structure of the heart; it is built with such wisdom that human beings with all their wisdom are mere children compared to the wisdom revealed in this. Amazing what the heart manages to cope with in spite of human stupidity, with people doing their best to ruin it almost every day, for instance by consuming stimulants such as coffee, alcohol and nicotine.

The powers needed to produce such a marvellous structure as the physical body extend all the way up to the astral world, and only the spirits of this astral world are sufficiently intelligent, to use a commonplace term, to build such a physical body.

This brings us to the third principle of the essential human being. Plants have a physical body and an ether body, but they do not have something which animals and human beings have—they do not have suffering, pleasure, pain or any kind of sentience. In this they differ from animals and human beings. The difference is due to the fact that internal processes take place in animals and human beings. In more recent times scientists have wanted to ascribe sentience also to plants because of processes observed in them. It is pitiful to see the nonsensical way in which terms are used, for here we do not see the kind of inner processes that occur wherever sentience is found. This 'sentience' might equally well be ascribed to litmus paper. But that is what happens when people look for sentience here in the physical world. In the physical world you do not find that the kind of phenomena observed in some plants involve sentience; you have to go to the heavenly worlds for that. Let me add at this point, so as to avoid misunderstanding, that in plants that are said to show reactions, mimosa, for instance, this stimulant process evokes sentience not in the physical world but only in the lower world of reason, which is where plants have their conscious awareness. Down here in the physical world only human beings and animals know desire and passions, pleasure and pain. Why? Because they have an astral body as well as a physical body and ether body, and that is the third principle in essential human nature.

The way the astral body presents itself to the seer is as an egg-shaped cloud that envelops the whole human being. This cloud reflects all sentience, every drive, every passion. It is therefore the vehicle for pleasure and pain, joy and suffering. The situation is different with this third principle from the way it is with the physical body and ether body. For when human beings sleep, only the physical and ether body remains in the bed; the astral body and the I have risen from it. When astral body and ether body depart from the physical body death ensues, and with it the disintegration of the physical body.

Why is this principle known as the astral body? No other term is more apt. Why? Because this principle has an important function, and we must be clear about this function. The astral body is far from idle during the night, for it is evident to the seer that it works on the physical and ether body during the night. During the day you wear your physical and ether body down, for everything you do wears down the physical body, and this is evident from the fact that it grows tired. During the night the astral body repairs the wear and tear caused during the day. It is a fact that in sleep the astral body takes away the tiredness. This shows the importance of and necessity for sleep. The seer is able to make those repairs deliberately. The refreshing nature of sleep is due to the fact that the astral body has really been working on the physical and ether body. Yet when the astral body has to return to the physical and ether body, the refreshing effect of sleep only shows itself gradually, about an hour after we wake up.

Another important thing is connected with the departure of the astral body during sleep. When it connects with the outside world during the day, when we are awake, the astral body must live together with the physical and ether body; but when it separates from the body in sleep it is freed from the fetters of physical and ether body. And then something quite wonderful happens—the powers of the astral body extend all the way to the world of stars, where the souls of plants are, and it gains its strength from that world. The astral body rests in the world in which the stars are embedded. That is the world of Pythagoras' harmony of the spheres. It is absolutely real and not fantasy. Living consciously in that world one hears the harmonies of the spheres; you hear the powers and relationships of the stars resounding. Goethe was an initiate in this sense, and it was in this spirit that he wrote the beginning of his Prologue in Heaven in *Faust*:

> The sun proclaims its old devotion
> In rival song with brother spheres,
> And still completes in thunderous motion
> The circuits of its destined years.
> Angelic powers, uncomprehending,
> Are strengthened as they gaze their fill;
> Thy works, unfathomed and unending,
> Retain the first day's splendour still.

Goethe is not well known today and people usually don't know that he was an initiate, simply saying that a poet uses such images. But Goethe knew that the sun is in a round dance and as sun spirit does resound. He stayed with the image, therefore, also saying:

> Hear the tempest of the Hours!
> For to spirit-ears like ours
> Day makes music at its birth.
> Hear it! Gates of rock are sundering,
> And the sun-god's wheels are thundering:
> See, with noise light shakes the earth!
> Hear it blare, its trumpets calling,
> Dazzling eyes and ears appalling,
> Speechless sound unheard for dread![10]

This is the world of stars where the astral body is during the night. During the day it enters into a kind of disharmony with worldly things, but at night, in sleep, it is secure in the bosom of the world of stars. And it then returns in the morning with the powers gained in that world. You return from the astral world with the harmony of the spheres as you awaken from sleep. The world of stars, the astral world, is the astral body's true home, which is how it got its name—astral body.

We have now made the acquaintance of three principles in essential human nature—physical body, ether body, astral body.

We'll get to know the fourth principle, the I, the next time. The I is the principle which makes man the pinnacle of creation, raising human beings above the animal level.

Animals do not yet have the conscious awareness which human beings have. They do have an awareness, just as we have seen in the case of plants and minerals, but this conscious awareness of animals is in the astral world. The fourth principle in human nature, this I, comes together with the other three in the sacred fourfold nature of man of which all the old schools would speak.

Human beings thus have their physical body in common with the minerals, their ether body with the plants and their astral body with the animals. The I is theirs alone and this raises them above all else. We find in human beings an essence, as it were, of everything that we see spread out around us. Truly a microcosm! If we want to know the human being we must first get to know the world around us.

We have to think of the three principles of human nature, these three bodies, as enveloping forms woven from very different regions. And we dwell in these bodies, that is, the I does, with the higher principles of essential human nature, the part of us that is immortal.

LECTURE 3

KASSEL, 18 JUNE 1907

ONE of the most sacred things human beings have is the principle known as self-awareness. People who understand this rightly will immediately realize that the term 'self-awareness' really gives us the meaning of human existence. Self-awareness is the ability to know oneself to be an I.

The best way of getting an idea of this is to consider that within the whole compass of the German language there is one word that differs fundamentally from all others, and that is the word 'I' [*ich* in German]. Anyone can call a table a table, but everyone can only use the word 'I' to refer to himself or herself. The word can never reach my ear from outside if it is to refer to me myself. This has been the feeling in spiritual science through the ages. In the Hebrew religion, for instance, when one would speak of this true nature of the inner human being, one would refer to the name of God that cannot be spoken. People would say: 'When the word I is to be spoken it must sound forth from the centre of the entity itself. No other entity can say that name.' It was therefore as if a shudder went through the whole congregation when the priest uttered the word Yahweh, 'I am the I am'. There the god in man begins to speak. That is the pure, original meaning of the Hebrew name of God. You will come to know other names as well, but all have a particular connection with this one name. We use this word 'I' to refer to the fourth principle of the essential human being. It is from this I that the human being works on the other principles—the astral body, the ether body and also the physical body. However far we go back in the history of human evolution, those four principles have always been there in the human being, and it is in this that human beings differ from the animals.

To get an idea as to how someone who is developed relates to someone who is undeveloped, compare one of the wildest human beings, one who still eats other human beings, with a highly developed individual such as Goethe, Schiller or Francis of Assisi. The cannibal lives directly by his drives and passions the way they are in his astral body. He does have an I, but it is still completely in the power of the astral body. The average person of today does know the difference between good and not good. This is because he has done some work on his astral body. He has worked on it and actually transformed some drives into 'ideals', as they are called. The more the individual has become transformed in his astral body, the higher his development. The average European of today has changed a great deal. Someone like Schiller or Goethe had transformed by far the greater part of his astral body. And someone like Francis of Assisi, who had subjugated all his passions to his will, did have an astral body that had been completely transformed by the I; there was nothing in it that was not mastered by the I. We call the part of the astral body that an individual has thus transformed his Manas or Spirit Self; that is the fifth principle in his essential nature. So we are able to say that the I holds the seed for transforming the astral body into Manas, Spirit Self.

It is also possible for human beings to transform not only the astral body but also the ether body, letting the I be master of the ether body. You have to understand, however, that this is much more difficult and proceeds much more slowly. The difference between transforming the astral body and the ether body is this. Consider how much you knew when you were eight, and how much more you have made your own since your young days! The astral body sustains all these transformations; it thus changes quite considerably day by day because of the many impressions you gain of the outside world. It is different with the ether body. To get an idea of this, imagine the following. If you were a hot-tempered child at the age of eight, you will probably still be hot-tempered now and then today. Very few people manage to change themselves to such a degree that they also transform their habits, their inclinations, their temperament, their character. This does not in any way contradict what I have been saying before. The astral body does have to do with pleasure and pain and our passions, but if these passions have become habit, character traits, they will be anchored in the ether body. And if we want to change such habits, the ether body has to change, seeing that it is the vehicle for all habits and character traits.

I have on several occasions compared the changes in astral body and ether body with the movement of the minute and hour hands of a clock.

Later on we will be speaking of the development of more advanced pupils. These are not pupils in the sense of merely learning things. Yes, such a pupil must also learn a great deal, but infinitely more important than learning is that they work on their ether bodies, managing to change a hot temper into a sweet one. Occult science gives directions for exactly this.

Someone who is able to transform a habit, that is, a quality of the ether body, from one day to the next has reached a high level of development. Such a transformation of the ether body must go hand in hand with all the other things a pupil learns of occult science. However, people will also change their ether bodies of their own accord even if they have never heard of such inner development. This will be slowly and gradually, through many incarnations. The parts of the ether body which have been thus transformed are called Buddhi or Life Spirit; this is the sixth principle in essential human nature.

Then there is the level which is much, much higher, where human beings also learn to work into their physical body and transform it. The parts of the physical body which have been transformed are called Atman or Spiritual Human Being, and this is the seventh principle. Atman relates to the German word for 'to breathe' [atmen], for this transformation comes from the breathing process. You can get an idea what it means to have your I master your physical body, doing so consciously, if you consider how little we really know of our physical body. This knowledge has nothing to do with present-day anatomical knowledge of the physical body. Long before modern anatomy existed, there were ancient teachings, which were not, however, part of public knowledge, where you would find knowledge of the internal human being. It enabled the sages of old to follow the way in which life and blood flowed, for instance. This enabled them to look at themselves internally, observing the physical body in all its organs. When we have developed as far as that it will be possible for not one particle in our body to be moving unless we will it. That is the transformation into Atman, Spiritual Human Being.

Someone might say: Surely the physical body is the lowest principle in our essential nature, so how and why is it possible to transform it into the highest principle? It is exactly because the physical body is the lowest principle that it needs the human being's greatest effort to gain control of it. Hand in hand with the reworking of this physical body goes the gaining of mastery over powers that flood the whole cosmos. And mastery of these cosmic powers is magic, as we call it.

In their true inner nature human beings thus have seven parts, but these parts merge completely into one another. We will only get the right idea of how the seven parts interpenetrate if we compare them with the seven colours of the rainbow, for all of them are also contained in sunlight. Just as light is made up of these seven colours, so man is made up of these seven principles.

Let us now consider the significance which this differentiation has for the whole course of human life. Yesterday we heard of the nature of sleep. The physical body and the ether body are lying in bed; breathing and blood circulation continue, reflecting the life of this ether body, but everything belonging to the astral body is together with the I lifted out of physical body and ether body.

In death, on the other hand, the situation is different. For the whole time from birth to death the physical and the ether body form a single whole. At death not only the astral body separates from the physical body, as in sleep, but also the ether body. This physical body is so complex however—you'll remember what was said yesterday—that left to itself it must disintegrate. Let us look with the clairvoyant eye at the human being immediately after death. All we have before us is the physical body, with astral body and ether body floating above it. Now, immediately after death, a strange phenomenon occurs in the sentience of the individual who has died, for at the moment of death the whole of his past life appears in the field of human memory, like a vast scene spread before him. Every, even the least, thing that happened passes before him in images. This happens quite naturally, for apart from preventing decomposition of the human body the ether body is also the vehicle for memory. At the very moment when this ether body is relieved of its first function it enters with great intensity into this second function. In life, every event involved pleasure and pain, joy and suffering, because the astral body was present throughout. Now, when the astral body has also departed, the individual goes through these memory images—the whole of his past existence—without sentience, without feeling, like a vast panorama.

For as long as this ether body is connected with the physical body, the instrument which it has to use, the brain, is something which ensures that our memories will never be complete, only retaining fragments of impressions gained in life. This is because this physical brain had defects. But the moment the ether body is free of the physical body it does remember everything. We have an analogy to this in ordinary life, and that is when we suffer a shock, when drowning, for instance, or falling off a cliff, and so on. This is due to the fact that the ether body is forcibly cast loose from the physical body at such a moment, something which also happens in a milder form when a limb goes to sleep, for example, or in hypnosis, in which case the clairvoyant sees the ether body hang out on both sides of the head. In materialistic physiology the objection is raised that it is a case of material changes in the blood, but that is just because the effect is taken for the cause.

The first thing that happens to someone after death is therefore this review of the past life, which varies in length, taking about three and a half days on average. Then comes a kind of second death, with the etheric also separating completely from the astral body, leaving behind a kind of ether corpse. This ether corpse soon dissolves in the general cosmic ether, at a different rate in individual cases, but not completely so. A kind of essence of the past life remains and is taken along by the I. This is imperishable and remains ours through all further incarnations. A new page is added to the existing ones, as it were, with every new incarnation. In theosophy this is called the causal body, and the quality of this causal body determines the form taken by later incarnations.

The astral body is now on its own. How does this condition differ from sleep, when it has also departed from the other principles—the physical and ether body—and was therefore also on its own? The powers it had to use in sleep to develop and repair the physical body have come free when this physical body is ultimately laid aside. The astral body now uses them for itself and becomes aware of this. In this state of awareness of itself the astral body now goes through a period which is best explained as follows.

Think of enjoying a lovely dish; someone is eating it and takes pleasure in it. This pleasure is not in the physical but in the astral body. But the astral body needs a tool if it is to have that pleasure—a tongue, a palate. The physical body thus provides the tool—a tongue, a palate—for the astral body to have that enjoyment. What is the situation after death, when this physical body has been cast off? The instrument, the mediator of that pleasure, is no longer there, but the astral body has not lost its longing, its desire for that pleasure. Envisage this in the liveliest possible way. It is a condition like that experienced by someone suffering thirst in a desert. The astral body will still have the desire for the pleasure after death, and this to the degree to which it has been accustomed to having it in the past life. Because of that, this time after death is a period of unfulfilled longing for all human beings. This condition is known as the kamaloka. Kama means 'desire', locus 'place'. The condition is the same as the one we find in many myths, such as the torment of Tantalus, or purgatory. This condition is not only a torment, of course; it is torment only until the astral body has got out of the habit of wanting pleasures. The more needs the astral body has had here in physical life, the longer will this condition continue. You may conclude from this that depending on the quality of the needs a person has had in the past life, the astral body may meet with not only torment but depending on circumstances also with something that is very good and pleasant in kamaloka. It will, for instance, live through the joy it took so many times in the beauties of nature. To take pleasure in the beauties of nature we do, of course, have to have eyes to see, but beauty is something which goes beyond the physical, and because of that this condition is a source of real pleasure also in kamaloka life. Things like this are the source of great joy and wonderful experiences also in the kamaloka period. People can therefore make this period an even better one if they refrain from sticking to physical pleasures. If you think of this you will understand many things in life, for instance with regard to everything we call art. The more ideal the art, the more the ideal element shines through, the stronger and more elevating will be the influence of the work of art also beyond this life. The spiritual is its element. It is merely that materialistic short-sightedness has led to naturalism in art.

Having lived through kamaloka we have reached the point where the human being no longer desires material pleasures. This point in time signals going through a completely new situation. There the soul also lays aside everything in the astral body that has not been worked on by the individual, by his I. And this laid-aside astral body is the third corpse which a human being leaves behind him.

Having come to be at one with everything gained from the other bodies, that is, the essence of the ether body we spoke of and now also that of the astral body, the I moves on into spirit land. And then the soul lives through the time that passes until it is born again.

We will consider this tomorrow. Today I would merely want to stress once more that all these spiritual worlds are around us all the time and not somewhere outside the space we live in. They are evident to the seer's eye at all times. Someone who is able to look into these spiritual worlds can also see these shadows or phantoms which are those corpses. It is these corpses which very frequently push their way into spiritualist séances. But when people attending the séances believe the astral corpse to be the actual individual concerned, that is just as silly as if you were to consider a dead body to be the actual person. This astral corpse—being exactly something for which the I has no use—often seems most ridiculous therefore in those spiritualistic séances.

LECTURE 4

KASSEL, 19 JUNE 1907

OUR task today is to go on following the destinies of human beings through the spiritual world. It will be good, therefore, to form an idea first as to what we actually call a 'world' in spiritual-scientific terms.

Sentience of the world around us depends on our own abilities and organs of perception. If we had different organs, the world, too, would be completely different for us. If people did not have eyes, for instance, to see the light but an organ with which they could perceive, say, electricity, you would not see this hall filled with light, but you would see the electricity flowing through the wires in the hall. You would see it flash, spark and flow everywhere. The world we call ours is therefore dependent on our sense organs.

The astral world, too, is nothing but a sum of phenomena which human beings experience around them when it has separated from the physical and ether body, and when they use its powers inwardly to see things we are otherwise not able to see. That is indeed the case when we have cast off the physical body and ether body. The organs for perceiving the astral world are those of the astral body, analogous to the sense organs for the physical body. Let us take a look at the astral world.

Seers can perceive this astral world whilst still here in their physical body by using a method which we'll consider later. This astral world differs quite considerably from the physical world. You can get a first idea of what is around you in the astral world if you call up the last remnant people still have of the clairvoyance of earlier times, and that is their dream life. All of you know this dream life from personal experience, know it as a world of chaotic images. So why is it that people do dream? We know that during this dream life the physical and ether body lies in the bed, with the astral body floating above it. The astral body is fully outside the ether body in full, deep, dreamless sleep. In dreaming sleep astral body tendrils remain in the ether body, and because of this the individual then perceives the more or less chaotic images of the astral world. The astral world is as porous as dream images are; it is as if woven from dreams. But these dreams differ from ordinary dreams in that the images are something real, as real as the physical world. The way we perceive them is very much like the way we perceive dreams, for it is also symbolic. Anything of the outside world which has been taken up into sleep is symbolized in the dream. Let me give you some typical examples of dreams and you will immediately see how the dream becomes symbol based on a simple impression from outside.

You may see yourself catching a frog in your dream. You really feel the slithery frog as you wake up. On waking you find that you have a cold bit of the bed sheet in your hand. Or you may dream you were in a dim cellar full of cobwebs. You wake up and have a headache. Or you see snakes in your dream and when you wake up find you have a pain in your gut. Or an academic dreams a long saga of a duel, starting from being jostled and all the way to the challenge to pistols—a shot, and he wakes up to find that the chair has fallen over. You will also see from the whole way this last dream image went that the relationship to time is very different. It is not only that time is made to go back, as it were, but also that in the dream experience the whole notion of time loses significance. In the fraction of a second you dream a whole life, just as the whole of our life passes before the mind's eye the moment before we fall off a cliff or drown. The most important point with all these dream images is, however, that they present images relating to whatever triggered the dream. That is how it generally is in the astral world. And we have cause to interpret these images. The same astral experience will always present as the same image; this shows utter regularity and harmony. The usual kind of dream images on the other hand are chaotic. Ultimately one can find one's way about in the astral world just as one does in the world perceived through the senses.

The astral world is a tissue of nothing but such images, but the images reflect soul entities. After their death, human beings are themselves enveloped in such images, some of them very rich in colour and shape. And when people go to sleep, their astral bodies present in flowing, changing shapes and colours. All astral spirits appear in colours. Someone with astral vision perceives these astral spirits in a flowing sea of colours.

The astral world has one feature that may seem strange to someone who hears of it for the first time. Everything in the astral world is like a mirror image, and as a pupil you will gradually have to get used to seeing things in the right way. You will for example see the figure 365, and that means 563. It is like this with everything you perceive in the astral world. Everything coming from me, for example, appears to be coming towards me. It is of extraordinary importance to take this into account. For when such astral images arise, perhaps because of morbid conditions, one has to know how to rate them. Images of this kind frequently arise in delirium, and the people involved may see all kinds of distorted faces and forms coming towards them, for in pathological states of this kind the astral world is open to them. These images do, of course, look as if things were rushing towards people, though the truth is that they go out from them. Future physicians will need to know this, for with religious longing suppressed they will be more and more common in future. The theme of the well-known painting *The Temptation of St Anthony* is based on such an experience of astral images. If you think it all through, right to the end, it will no longer seem quaint to you that time, too, is inverted in the astral world. You get a sense of it from things learned in dreams. Remember the example of the duel just now. There everything went in reverse, including time. In astral experience you may, for instance, have the fruit on a tree first, then the blossom and all the way back to the seed.

After death and the time of freeing yourself from habits, the whole astral world goes in reverse and you then go through your whole life once more in reverse order, concluding with the first impressions gained in childhood. It takes much less time than it did here in the physical world, about a third the length of your life on earth. You will also experience some other things when going through your life in reverse.

Let us assume you died at 80 years of age and are now going back through life to your fortieth year. At that time you slapped someone's face, let us say, so that the other person suffered pain caused by you at that time. In the astral world this sensation of pain will also be in a kind of mirror image, which means that you are now feeling the pain which the other person suffered at that time because of the slap. The same does, of course, also hold true for all joyful occasions.

It is only when human beings have gone through their whole life that they will enter into the heavenly world. Religious documents are always truths to be taken literally. Considering what I have just been saying you will immediately see that human beings can truly only enter into the spiritual world—meaning the 'kingdom of heaven' of the Bible—when they have lived through the whole of their life in reverse, back to their childhood. This truly is what is behind the words of the Christ: 'Unless you become as little children you shall not enter into the kingdom of heaven.'[11] For when human beings have gone back again to their childhood stage they take off their astral body and enter into the spiritual world.

I must now tell you of the spiritual world in a narrative way. This realm of the heavens differs even more from the physical world than the astral world does. One is, of course, only able to describe everything using the terms that belong to this physical world, and it holds true even more than it did with the astral world, that all these descriptions must be taken as mere analogies.

The realm of the heavens is also tripartite, as is life on earth. Here we have the three states of aggregation—solid, liquid and aeriform, accordingly distinguishing continents, oceans and the atmosphere. In spiritland we may also distinguish three such spheres, though only as analogues, except that the sphere of the continents is made up of something other than our rocks and stones. The solid ground in spiritland consists in the archetypes of all things physical. Everything physical has its archetype, including the human being. To the seer these archetypes look like a kind of negative, that is, you see the space as a kind of shadow figure, with radiant light all around it. This shadow, corresponding to blood and nerves, for instance, is not uniform, how-ever. A stone or a mineral makes a uniformly empty space appear in the archetype, also with light rays around it. Whereas you walk on solid rock when on earth, you are there walking on the archetypes of physical things. The land of this spiritual world is made up like this. When human beings first enter it they always see one particular thing—it is the moment when they see the archetype of their own physical body. They clearly see their own body lying there. For they are spirit themselves. If the life on earth had taken a normal course, this will be about 30 years after death. The basic sentience is: 'That is you.' Knowing this, *tat tvam asi*—this you are—became a fundamental statement in Vedanta philosophy. All such terms have come from deep down sources of spiritual insight.

The second sphere in the spiritual land are the oceans. Everything which is life here in the physical world, that is, everything which has an ether body, is like a flowing element in spirit land. Flowing life streams through spirit land. It also collects, like in an oceanic basin, like the water in the sea or, better, like the blood that flows through the veins and collects in the heart.

Thirdly we have the atmospheric part of spiritland, made up of all passions, drives, feelings and so on. All this is outwardly perceptible there, like the atmospheric phenomena here on earth. All this roars through the atmosphere of devachan. As a seer you can therefore perceive in spiritland the suffering that takes place here on earth and the joys that we know here. Every passion, all hatred and the like is like a gale in spiritland. A battle, for instance, produces the effect that the seer experiences a thunderstorm in the devachan world. The whole spiritual realm is full both of wonderful joys moving along and of dreadful passions. We may therefore also speak of spiritual ears. When you have advanced so far that you have gained insight into this devachan world, these moving, billowing phenomena can be seen and heard, and what you hear is the harmony of the spheres.

We have now characterized the spiritual sphere up to this level. But there is still another, a fourth, sphere in devachan. So far we have seen:

the archetypes of all physical forms	=	continent	⎱
all life	=	ocean	⎰ of devachan
all inner life, feelings and so on	=	atmosphere	

Now there is one thing in human life that cannot have its basis in the outside world. Its spiritual content makes up the fourth sphere of devachan. Every original idea is part of this, all the way to the creative impulses of genius. Anything original, that is, everything human beings create in this world, to enrich it, all these archetypes make up the fourth sphere of devachan. This brings our description of the lower parts of devachan to a conclusion.

Beyond this are three more regions but during their life here human beings need higher initiation to reach these. After death, too, they are only perceptible to more highly developed individuals. When such an advanced initiate is able to enter into the next higher sphere of devachan—what does he find there? Initially something which in occult science is called the Akashic Record. Everything that happens and has ever happened in the world leaves its imprint in a subtle form of matter that is imperishable. Let me give you an example to help make this clearer. I am now speaking to you, but you would not hear me if my voice were not able to create waves in the air. These movement forms will, of course, pass away; but when we come to that higher world, everything leaves an impression in that subtle spiritual form of matter and remains there for ever. Every word, every thought, everything that has ever happened in humanity can be read in this Akashic Record. It needs either initiation or that moment when human beings enter devachan after death, that is, when they have developed so far that after death they are able to perceive this region of devachan which certainly is most elevated. They are then able to look into the past. This Akashic Record is a place where everything is kept that has ever happened. It is not a written record in the physical sense but takes the form of images. You see Caesar in every situation in his life, for example, not the things he actually did but the inner impulses that guided his actions. These Akashic images have great vitality, and if one does not know how to interpret them they can make one fall into serious error. They are therefore the source of many spiritualist aberrations—that is when an Akashic image appears in the séances. If you quote Goethe, for instance, and the answer is given to a question, that answer is given the way Goethe would have given it if he had been asked that question on 25 November 1797. You have to know the spiritual world really well to see if this is something real in such a case or a phantom. Descriptions like this give you an idea as to what these higher regions of the spiritual world are like.

The first thing is therefore that one perceives one's own body; all other things have their origin in this. The individual then feels great relief at being free of the bodily shells, for this is the joyful moment when they have laid aside the last of the corpses, which is the astral corpse. A plant held in the confinement of a narrow rock cleft would feel liberated to be freed from it, and that is the basic sentience, the joy felt by human beings at that point. This happiness penetrates and trans-figures all feelings which earlier had been more earthly, those of friendship, for instance, which may have gone through certain changes here on earth and are deepened and purified in yonder world. A mother's love for her child also goes through this purification, and conversely the originally animal feeling of being connected, which became a moral feeling here, unfolds to even greater moral power in devachan. All bonds formed here on earth are deepened in the spiritual region, interpenetrating one another. Through love, human beings rise whilst still on earth from the narrowness of self-seeking to the all-encompassing world experience. Yonder, however, nothing is shut off, separated, from anything else; one works for the other, for there, too, work is the element that sustains and helps souls, bringing them together, with love the inexhaustible source spring of all life.

LECTURE 5

KASSEL, 20 JUNE 1907

Today we'll to some extent characterize the human being in deva-chan between death and reincarnation. The first thing we must do is to get an idea of what human beings actually gain from the things which they are initially doing for themselves during the time when they pass through this spiritual world. It will be easiest to get an idea if we bring to mind the relationship between two things—how the things we live through relate to what becomes of the experiences, to begin with during the time between birth and death. Consider all the things you have to go through when learning to write, for instance. You would find it difficult to keep in mind all the skills you had to acquire until you had learned this noble art of writing. Consider all the admonishments and perhaps also the anger of your teachers. All this will then have been your inner experience. And what has remained? The ability to write. Everything else has become blurred, and what remains is the skill of writing. That is how it is altogether in life, and not only in our life between birth and death, but in the whole universal life going through the physical and supersensible world.

We can get an idea of how what I have just said also applies in the supersensible worlds. Take Mozart, for example. He was just a little boy when he heard a long piece of music played in St Peter's in Rome. Tradition had it that this must never be written down, and he wrote it down wholly from memory afterwards. That needed enormous powers of memory. And he was only a young boy! What does a materialist have to say about this? He would absolutely refuse to believe that an ox grows from a patch of soil, that such a thing as an ox could develop in a way that does not follow the ways of nature. He would say there is no such thing as a miracle, and he would be absolutely right. But he gets terribly superstitious and believes in miracles when it comes to things of the spirit. A fact like the one just described speaking of Mozart is simply accepted by materialists, who do not go into it more deeply but put it down to heredity. And yet it would be a miracle just as much as an ox coming from a piece of ground if we were not able to explain it through spiritual science. For it is possible, when people turn their mind to a particular thing over and over again that they will gradually train outstanding powers of memory. Just as perfection has gradually developed from imperfection, so memory develops, but it would have been a miracle if the kind of memory Mozart showed were supposed to have sprung forth from nothing. The answer in spiritual science is that in this case, too, memory quite naturally developed gradually. Materialists cannot dodge the issue when giving their explanation. They must either believe in miracles or they must admit that faculties of this kind prove that they had existed in an earlier life and were following the natural course of development. Reincarnation is but the logical conclusion when such a line of thought is pursued. People who take the materialistic point of view and assume that a memory as perfect as that of young Mozart can appear out of the blue should also accept the consequences of that point of view and assume that frogs, for instance, simply develop from mud, as naturalists had assumed before Francesco Redi.[12]

Anyone concerned with logic in spiritual science will say: Just as an oak grows from seed, gradually developing from it, so our mental faculties develop bit by bit, and when someone enters into a life with such highly developed faculties as Mozart did, for example, this is absolute logical proof that the individual gained those faculties bit by bit in earlier lives on earth. This gives us a handle for grasping human destiny in the spiritual world.

The point is, therefore, that things met with in one life become faculties for the next life. All potential we have in this life we have brought with us as the fruits of experiences we had in earlier lives on earth. We must therefore look at the road taken through devachan if we

want to understand fully how events in one life develop into faculties for
the next life.

Going through life here on earth we come up against a great many
things every day, and all these experiences come before the eye of the
soul in the great panorama perceived immediately after death. The
faculties we have gained from all these experiences stay with us as an
essence, and we take this essence, which will be ours for all time, with us
into the spiritual world.

When human beings enter into devachan, they perceive the regions
we spoke of yesterday—the continental element which consists of the
archetypes of all earthly forms, the oceanic element which consists of all
life, and the airy element which consists of all soul qualities (pleasure,
pain, joy, sadness and so on). The first thing human beings perceive of
the continental element is the archetype of their own physical body, and
the first thing they perceive of the airy element will also be the pleasure,
pain, joy, sadness and passions that passed through their soul in the past
life. This means that they perceive all the experiences of the past life but
in a very different way than described for the period in kamaloka. There
it was an inner experience to make them cast off habits. Now all these
experiences spread before the soul as outside world, doing so for a long,
long time. There they get to know the particular nature of their bodily
life in the flow region of devachan, and all their inner experiences as if in
the atmosphere of the heavenly world.

Again it is of great interest to understand how everything we have
experienced in the course of a life—sentience concerning the world,
pleasure, pain and so on—will be the outside world surrounding us in
the spiritual world. It is not a sad thing to have pain spread out around
us. It is not at all sad, for all suffering is around us there the way
thunderstorms are here in the physical world, and all joyful experiences
are like marvellous cloud phenomena. And there the things we have
experienced inwardly are not inside us, as they are here, but in our
surroundings in that outward form, like a picture of nature. It surrounds
us as if it were around us in images, sounds or atmospheric phenomena;
it is made objective as a heavenly form. As I said, it is not sad to have
pain shine out towards us, for example, just as here in life it is not really
sad when thunder and lightning surround us. Someone who under-

stands the situation will know what we owe particularly to pain. Those who have known pain and suffering will always say that whilst they are happy to accept joys and pleasures they would not want to do without the pain and suffering. We owe all our wisdom to the pain and suffering in past lives on earth. A countenance which reflects wisdom in this life does so because it has been sentient in earlier lives of the pain that is cosmic cohesion.

As I said, everything we have known here in life on earth surrounds us in images and so on in devachan. What is the significance of this? It will be easier to understand this if you are clear in your mind about the effect which our surroundings here have on us. You all know Goethe's words: 'The eye is created in light for the light.'[13] What does this mean? We must have eyes if we are to see the light. The world would be in darkness if we did not have them. But where does this organ come from? Light itself has developed it, just as the absence of light makes the eye degenerate again. This has been directly observed in creatures that had migrated to the caves in Kentucky,[14] for instance. Light is the cause of our powers of vision. Long ago human beings were not endowed with eyes because they lived under very different conditions; in those earlier times of earth evolution the sun was not yet visible to an eye's sense of sight. Think of the stories of Niflheim [world of mist]. The more human beings lived in the light of the sun the more did this sunlight gradually develop the eye. All other sense organs have also developed in such a way, with sounds creating the ear, heat the sense of warmth. If there were no hard objects there would also be no sense of touch. The outside world is the creator and shaper of our whole body. This is most important in practical life, and theosophy is always meant for practical life. It is also tremendously important in education, for the only right way of education depends on the teacher's ability to look deeply into human nature. The physical body develops up to the time of second dentition, the ether body up to about the age of 13 or 14, the astral body up to the age of 20. You have to know all this if you want to be effective in education in a practical way rather than with fantasies. So when it is above all a matter of laying the foundations for the physical body up to the seventh year, profound and thorough attention must be paid to these physical impressions in teaching, that is to everything children perceive with their sense organs. Anything not laid down by way of forms and potential in the children's bodies up to the seventh year will be lost forever.

Understanding this will give medicine in particular tremendously many guidelines for appropriate treatment, among other things of rickets, for instance. Why does this disease develop at this particular age? Exactly because children are forming their body at this time, and the symptoms will take the form of bent bones, poor teeth, wrong shape of the skull, and so on. But up to the time of second dentition children still have the ability to restore these wrong forms to normal. We see that with appropriate treatment even the most bent legs can be straight again, and that even if the milk teeth are poor the second teeth may be perfectly sound. Bent legs that are not corrected by the seventh year will remain for life.

The brain is also developing its three-dimensional forms up to the seventh year, and any development, configuration of these subtle forms that has not been achieved by then will be lost forever. As the physical brain is the instrument through which mind and spirit come to expression, it is of enormous importance that this instrument is worked out and in the first seven years laid down in the best possible way. Even the greatest mind cannot do anything with a poorly developed brain, just as the greatest pianist cannot play well on a piano that is out of tune. It is also particularly with regard to the development of the brain that spiritual science provides important guidelines for both education and medicine. It is here that one frequently comes across a complete failure to establish the facts in modern medicine. Rickets is evident in malformation and abnormal development of bones but just as frequently also involves malformation in the glandular system and mucous membranes. This means that children with rickets very often show phenomena such as glandular swellings, adenoids and so on. And the third sign of the disease is that these children will often be mentally retarded, lagging behind at school, with poor levels of attention and do indeed show some degree of mental deficiency. Truth is that the same deficit shows itself in physical brain development, especially the grey matter, as it is called. Its most subtle organization has to be developed in those early years, and like the rest of the phenomena the problem is due to defects in development. In modern medicine today, physicians with all their scientific training and attitude are too much inclined to do the same as in natural science, completely disregarding the deeper spiritual causes and simply lining up the external signs and symptoms as direct cause and effect, like a string of pearls. What is the consequence? The facts are bones affected by rickets, adenoids, and poor attention and ability to learn. The immediate conclusion drawn is that children with adenoids are mentally weak, and the adenoids must therefore be removed. This is done. If the conclusion were correct, every child treated in that way would have to show a reduction in and disappearance of the hindrances coming from the brain. Yet what does one see in the vast majority of cases where this method of treatment was used? That the intervention resulted in a very short-lived apparent success, with further proliferations developing in a short time. If the disease is tackled properly, at its root—and that is perfectly possible, but it would take us too far away from our subject just now—both the bent shape of bones and the proliferation of mucous membranes and glands would disappear as would the sluggishness of the brain.

After this digression let us return to our subject. The right physical forms thus catch fire and are configured through contact with the outside world. Up to their seventh year children are really all sense organ. Everything taken in through the senses is worked through, above all everything children see and hear in their most immediate surroundings. Up to second dentition children are thus imitators, and this also enters into their physical organization. It is really perfectly natural. Children take in the whole of their surroundings through their sense organs. They also practise using their limbs. They see how their father, mother and so on does one thing or another and will immediately copy this. This goes as far as every movement of the hands and legs. If the father or mother is fidgety, for example, the child will in a great number of cases also be fidgety; if the mother is calm, the child will of course also be calm. We must try therefore to bring about the right counter-effect by creating the right surroundings.

To give the child exactly the right guidelines in developing the brain it will be absolutely necessary to stimulate the imagination as well as providing sensory impressions. It is therefore absolutely essential to give young children the simplest possible toys. A natural child may have a truly 'beautiful' doll but will again and again reach for the old doll simply made of a rag. Why is that so? Children must exercise their powers of imagination and in their imagination transform the item so that it comes to resemble a human figure. That is a really healthy exercise for the brain. Just as physical exercise strengthens one's arm, so does this exercise develop the brain.

Colours in the environment are also important. Their effect is very different for young children compared to adults. People often think that green has a soothing effect on a child. This is completely wrong. A fidgety child should have red surroundings, and a calm child needs green or bluish green. The effect on the child is this: if you look at a bright red and then quickly at a sheet of white paper, you will see the complementary colour, which is green; this is the tendency to produce the opposite colour. Children also attempt to do this;[15] they try and develop the inner activity that will evoke the opposite colour.

This has been an example of how the environment acts. The whole environment has a hand—in addition to many, many other things which we'll be considering later, elsewhere—to an extraordinary degree in developing the child's physical body from birth to second dentition, the ether body from the seventh to the fourteenth year, the astral body from the fourteenth to the twenty-first year, and so on. Yes, the environment has a definite influence on individual human beings for the whole of their life. There's a saying 'Tell me what you are involved in and I'll tell you who you are'. It is based on this insight, for 'what I am involved in' means, of course, 'what is going on around me'. This environment has a powerful influence on me. This applies particularly during the time when the astral body develops, from our fourteenth to our twenty-first year. And it is an almost everyday experience that a young person is astrally ruined by his environment during these years.

And it is exactly the same with life in devachan as it is with our physical life here. For instance in devachan people are always under the influence of the elements just as they are here. This takes us back to our starting point—talking about Mozart. Here on earth people are all the time under the influence of the external atmosphere. It is the same in devachan. The atmosphere there consists in all the inner life of ourselves and the people we know. All this inner life is a constant influence and because of this it is exactly there that talents develop. They attract the astral powers in the world around them that are in harmony with their soul and allow them to influence them. Mozart was born with that vast memory for music because once in his earlier life he had gathered experiences which went in that direction and had allowed them to influence him for a long time in devachan. In devachan, our inner nature develops more highly thanks to our environment, and indirectly therefore everything we have lived through in our earlier life. All our faculties are therefore the fruits of earlier lives, and they have been further developed in devachan. We hatched out the things we are now capable of doing when we were in devachan, and the feelings human beings have in that intermediate life are in accord with this. We are completely in harmony with the world in everything that is brought forth there.

Here we often feel pain, but in devachan even pain makes us feel in harmony, for there we are aware that it is through pain that we gain wisdom. A materialistic academic has actually discovered this. In a treatise on facial expression of thinking[16] he says: 'Every wise face reflects crystallized pain.' Human beings do indeed have experiences in devachan where they create talents and wisdom for their next life on earth. And the feeling that goes with producing them is one of infinite harmony.

You can see a pale reflection of this here when a hen is sitting on her eggs. Transposed into the spiritual this gives you the feeling of continuous, infinite harmony in the time between kamaloka and rebirth, for that is where human beings develop all their potential and faculties for the next life. There everything turns into a wellspring for existing in utter harmony.

We have seen now that one source of being in harmony in devachan is that all bonds entered into here in life are lived with again yonder in devachan, and that the spiritual aspects of all these relationships are lived through in a tremendously enhanced way. The other source of being in harmony is the producing of potential for the next life.

When the spiritual investigator turns his eye to this actual activity in devachan, he realizes that this activity of producing potential is important not only for the individual human being, for his future organization, but that human beings are actively involved and work on the progress of all further earth evolution. It is wrong to think that we are only concerned with ourselves in devachan. As one of the blessed in the realm of the spirits, what do we have to achieve there?

The activities of the dead contribute to the evolution of this earth. One might easily ask: Why be born over and over again when we have already gone through the experiences of a life on earth? Surely that is pointless?

But that is not how it is. Human beings are never pointlessly reborn. Our individual lives on earth are so far apart that we are always learning and having to go through new things. Centuries pass between two incarnations, and the earth has really changed when we return. Let us assume we have been on earth in the second century AD and have now reincarnated. What did the earth look like at that earlier time? Even descriptions of regions produced at a much later time, of the River Elbe, for instance, or the River Weser, would have been completely different; primeval forests then grew in that part of Hessen-Nassau.

When people are born again the situation is that their lives will be completely different from the last time. We go with the earth's evolution in our incarnations, exactly because we incarnate again and again. Added to this are the changes due to the prevailing civilization. What was a Roman boy child able to do, and how different is a boy's education today. All these life experiences are tremendously important, as we have seen. So there definitely is a point to human beings having to come back over and over again.

We now ask ourselves: Who is changing the face of the earth? The dead actually do, who live in spiritland, and with the powers they have there they work to reshape the earth. Here human beings work to shape the outer face of the earth; there the dead work on the spiritual archetype of this physical earth. It is they who send their powers into this physical world and have a part in reshaping it. There are leaders there and higher spirits that assume control. And in this realm, which is right here amongst us, the dead are working to reshape the face of our earth.

Why was I born at this time and in this place? Because I have made my bed here, as it were, the bed into which I have been born. The powers that wreak change in the oceans as well as the surface of the earth, are those of our dead. We know that the Atlantic Ocean of today was a vast tract of land in the past, and again the dead have done their part in bringing about the change. These powers act in a natural way; there is nothing remarkable in this.

Insight into these things makes us aware, in a wholly logical way, of how important and necessary the work is which we do in spiritland. Here people breathe in the air; they cannot breathe unless they have air. It is similar with the dead, except that there light does what air is doing here. The initiate sees the spirits of the dead in the spreading light. Plants, for instance, are to him surrounded by the spirits of the dead, and as the light changes the plants, making them grow, it is the spirits of the dead which bring this about. In the spiritual world we will all be floating above the earth and will work on the plants.

The world gains in greatness and significance when we thus consider it in connection with the spirits. We ourselves are literally reshaping the earth.

In conclusion, here are a few things that may help us to understand some more subtle aspects of civilization. The seer is occasionally in a position where his own observations substantiate certain phenomena in the history of ancient peoples that have until now been a puzzle to him. It is a known fact that primitive peoples initially are clairvoyant and sometimes see things we know nothing about. These primitive peoples often see something in the shadow that has to do with the soul. The clairvoyant comes back to this again when making his observations. For when you look into the shadow cast by yourself, for instance, you first see your spiritual emanations. If you hold back the physical light you will see the spiritual in the shadow space. This has survived in spiritual science, and some have made use of it though they did not know what they were doing, like Chamisso,[17] for instance, in his *Peter Schlemihl*. That is a man who has lost his shadow and is most unhappy about this. It is a spiritual fact that the soul becomes visible in the shadow, and because of this the man without a shadow is a man without a soul. There are hundreds of such examples. We truly only come to understand the world fully when we come to know its spiritual basis. Because of this, spiritual science is not for the broody but exactly for people who really want to be practical. Not because we want to withdraw from the visible sphere but exactly because we want to gain better understanding of the visible world.

The more sublime facts relate to the visible world as magnetism does to iron. We only get to know iron fully when we also learn about magnetism. Some examples will show that the things we get to know in the spiritual world bear fruit specifically in practical life.

LECTURE 6

WHEN human beings have got so far in the spiritual region which we discussed yesterday that they have transformed, as it were, everything by way of abilities and talents which they had gained in their life on earth, the time comes where they get ready for a new incarnation. We must understand that there are two things we see when we meet individual human beings—elements they have inherited and others which they have brought with them into this world from earlier lives.

We will be considering the human being's descent into this world. Please do not let the term 'descent' upset you, for it is not a descent in spatial terms but rather a gradual emergence from the world that surrounds us. We saw yesterday that this spiritual world must not be sought in some yonder region but that it also exists right here all around us. It is just that people have no possibility today of perceiving this spiritual world. A new incarnation or embodiment develops out of that world. We have seen that human beings have retained an essence of both the ether and the astral body from their earlier lives, an overview of what they lived through, and also as much of their astral body as they had refined—they had taken all this with them into the spiritual world. Only elements that had not been ennobled and refined had dropped away.

We will get a better idea of reincarnation if we understand a few things about the life after death. We have seen that immediately after their physical death human beings continue to live in their ether body for about three and a half days, and that their past life rises up before them in a kind of tableau during those three and a half days. After this the ether body dissolves and they enter into kamaloka, a period of purification, removing all astrality that needs to be purified and cleansed.

At this point I must speak of another experience. Human beings go through a significant experience at the very moment when this memory tableau comes up immediately after death. They feel as if they are suddenly getting bigger, as if they were rapidly breaking through their surface and growing out into space. This feeling stays with them until they are born again. They feel themselves to be as large as the world to which they belong, as big as the whole of cosmic space. This will also give you an idea of how it is possible for human beings to see and be sentient of their bodies as if they were something alien. It is a strange feeling, being thus spread out through cosmic space.

Then there is something else, which is even more difficult to understand. During the whole of the kamaloka time human beings feel as if divided up in space. You'll understand this better like this. When someone lives his life back to childhood in kamaloka, as I have told you, he feels everything he had experienced in life as if it were a mirror image. He will really feel the slap in the face he gave someone; he literally feels himself to be in part of the space the other individual had occupied. So if you died here in Kassel, let us say, and the other person, whose face you did slap in the past, is living in Paris, you will feel as if a piece of you were there. You feel yourself altogether as if divided up in the cosmos; you feel as if pieces of you were in all the places where you have to deal with things, as it were. You have to understand that it is such that you feel nothing in the space between Paris and Kassel. So if you consider all events in your life in this respect you literally feel cut up in pieces during this whole period after death.

The following may serve as an analogy. A wasp is in two parts, an anterior part and a posterior part which is connected with the other one by a very fine thread. Think of this posterior part cut off completely, though the wasp is still lugging it along. That is more or less how you may imagine this. You feel that you are in separate pieces and there is no connection between the pieces. However, when human beings enter into devachan, they will feel again the way they did immediately after death, as if they filled the whole of cosmic space.

When human beings have transformed all their potential for talents and abilities in devachan the I will feel itself drawn to the physical earth again, seeking to descend to earth again for physical embodiment. First the I will surround itself with an astral body. It does so by drawing everything astral to itself—it all comes together like iron filings coming together when a magnet is used and creates a particular configuration. The I has received impressions of everything it has gone through in traversing the soul- and spirit-land, and all this creates the basic powers involved in building the new astral body. The new astral body thus takes with it everything which the individual has gone through in earlier lives and in kamaloka. All impressions gained now play a role in the way in which the individual becomes integrated in a new astral body.

The human being now has his astral body; but he must also have the other levels of existence. The astral body has been created merely by using powers of attraction. Prior to conception the individual is garbed in this astral body only. The seer therefore always sees these astral seeds of human beings as they wait for their conception and birth. He sees them fly about at tremendous speed—bell-shaped forms moving through space at enormous speed. Distances are nothing to them; they move so fast that distances do not matter at all.

Now comes the assumption of an ether body. In this case the human being cannot garb himself using only his own powers. His inherent powers cannot provide for the ether body on their own. Here human beings need the assistance of certain spirits which have to give a hand. You will gain an idea of these spirits if you consider that you sometimes use words that do not really mean anything to you, for instance the terms 'soul of a nation' or 'spirit of a nation'. Using these terms today people have no real idea of what they mean, or think of something completely abstract. The seer has a different idea of this. There truly are—just as truly as we ourselves truly exist—spirits of a higher kind. These do not become incarnate and are nothing but the souls of nations or tribes. There is nothing vague in speaking of the spirit of a nation; the soul of a nation is a distinct spiritual entity,[18] though it does not have a physical body, the ether body being its lowest one. The spirit of the nation also has an astral body, I, Manas, Buddhi, Atman, and one even higher principle, which human beings do not attain to, which in Christian esotericism is called the Holy Spirit, whilst theosophists call it the Logos.

The seer is thus able to speak to the spirit of a nation just as he speaks to another person. People have no real idea of these things today and think the term merely refers to the combined characteristics of an individual nation, which is not true, however, for they are genuine spiritual entities. Understanding for such things had to be lost because of materialistic thinking, but it will be regained. Today people tend to let the meaning of such terms vanish into thin air. But that is something which had to be. And it also had to be that a book was written and much admired—*Die Kritik der Sprache* (critique of language) by Fritz Mauthner.[19] Fritz Mauthner is someone who dissolves everything that cannot be perceived with the senses. One has to be a radical thinker devoid of all common sense to write such a book, someone with the courage to break with all that is spirit and real. In future centuries people will have to read this very book if they want to know what the thinking was at the turn of this century.

The soul of a nation is absolutely real. It spreads like a vapour cloud, and all the ether bodies of individual members of the tribe or nation are embedded in it. Its powers flow into the ether bodies of individual people.

Spirits that hold exactly this rank of soul of a nation take part in putting together the ether body of a new soul. This kind of spirit causes the human being to be directed towards a particular nation, one that is the most suitable for her or him. Now this ether body does not always fit in completely, and all the disharmonies you find in life are often due to the fact that the individual could not create his or her ether body using their own powers. Full accord will only come at a much later stage of earth evolution.

The process of garbing with an ether body happens at great speed, something you cannot visualize knowing only earthly conditions. And then even higher spirits will guide the individual to the parents who will be able to provide the right material for a physical body.

A modern materialist will find it hard to believe that when a son looks like his parents there is still something else connected with the body he has inherited from his parents. Yes, we do look like our ancestors physically, but this does not contradict what I have been saying. Let us consider a special case—the Bach family. Over a period of 250 years more than 29 more or less important musicians came from that family. A materialist will say that this shows that it is all due to heredity. In the same way the Bernoulli family produced eight mathematicians. How can this be? We will find it easiest to understand if we take a good look at heredity. As this is easier to understand in the case of a musician, let us look at the Bach family. Let us assume a young Bach had been in Rome, let us say, in an earlier incarnation, had worked through his potential gifts and wanted to incarnate again. Supposing he had brought the greatest musical gifts with him as the fruit of earlier incarnations, he would not be able to do anything with all his gifts unless he found a well-developed ear. Without a well-developed ear he would be as helpless as a virtuoso without an instrument. It was absolutely necessary for this individual to enter into a body that had a good organ for the gifts which he was bringing with him. The outer form of our internal and external organs is inherited, and to be a musician, this individual had to have a well-developed organ of hearing in that new life. Where would this be most easily found? In a family of musicians. He was therefore guided to where he would find the best organ for the further development of the gifts he had, and that was with the parents of Johann Sebastian Bach.

How was it with the Bernoulli brothers? Mathematical thinking is not based on the nature of the brain, for the logic of mathematics does not differ from any other logic. No, the talent for mathematics depends on the particularly accurate organization of the three semicircular canals. This organ, not much bigger than a pea, lies embedded in the petrous part of the temporal bone and consists in three semicircular canals that correspond exactly to three-dimensional space. So if one canal is exactly vertical, the second goes from left to right and the third from front to back. They are all at right angles to one another at exactly 90 degrees. This is the important point. The closer the canal is to a right angle, the better does the organ function. If it is injured in some way, vertigo develops and you lose your bearings in space. A talent for mathematics depends on these canals being particularly well developed, which provides the opportunity to use one's talent in mathematics. This organ is inherited, just as a good ear for music is.

The brain reflects on space just as it does on philosophy, for example; but to have a feeling for shapes in space—that depends on these three semicircular canals. An individual with great mathematical gifts will incarnate in a family where this organ is really well developed, and that was the case with the Bernoulli family.

It also needs the right instrument to be truly moral. Someone with great morality will therefore look for parents likely to provide him with the best instrument for this. People may light-heartedly say that you can't be careful enough in choosing your parents, but it is true in the deepest, most serious sense, for a child may indeed be said to choose his parents. Some people may object and say: 'What about mother-love then? For that surely arises because a mother feels the child to be a piece of herself.' Seen in the right light, mother-love is not negatively affected in any way by this; quite the contrary, we gain an even deeper understanding of it. Why is the child born of that particular mother? Because the child's spiritual qualities guide it to a mother of the same spiritual quality, and the child loves its mother even before it is conceived. Mother-love is the counterpart, as it were, to that primary attachment. An insight like this will give even deeper meaning to the term.

It will essentially depend on the qualities of the father and the mother what opportunity they provide for incarnation. And this is where father and mother are different. When a human being comes down to be born again, the I, having more powers of will, is attracted more to the father, and the part which has more astral powers to the mother. The father thus has a greater influence on the I, on will and character, the mother more on the astral body, that is the power to envisage things. In the ideal case both parents are just right for the individual wanting to incarnate.

The powers with which the human being is imbued in the ascent also have an effect in the descent. All this creates powers of attraction, and the individual will be drawn into the sphere that has always borne a relationship to him. He is thus guided towards the people with whom he has already been involved to a degree in the past. Let me give you an example based on a real situation. Four or five judges in a Vehmic court[20] condemned a man to death and he was executed. A spiritual-scientific investigation of these six people showed that all these men had been together on earth in their previous life, with the condemned man the chieftain, and that the others had been executed by him. That last execution was therefore a kind of balancing out. This particular case provides a good demonstration of the law of karma. The different powers which someone has drawn to him in his previous life thus act in concert; on reincarnation they determine the bodily constitution, the place where the individual will be born and his further destiny. Dissonances are often more evident in the physical body than they are in the ether body.

All this shows us how human beings are garbed in three bodies on reincarnation. With every incarnation the I works on the astral body, ether body and physical body. We will hear later how they rise to this high level of perfection. But the astral body and ether body is transformed more and more, and the refined astral body turns more and more into Manas, the refined ether body into Buddhi, the refined physical body into Atman. That is how we may think of the progressive perfection from incarnation to incarnation.

It is most beautifully put in words in the Lord's Prayer,[21] though we will only understand it rightly if we take it in the truly Christian sense, as it was taken in St Paul's occult school. In this school the true Christian meaning of the Lord's Prayer was explained. The pupils were told something like 'Think of the higher levels of human existence which develop as human beings progressively refine their three lowest levels.' The early Christians saw these three higher levels—Manas, Buddhi, Atman—as the human being's divine nature. In progressively developing these higher levels, human beings came closer and closer to the Godhead. Taking this point of view, the early esoteric Christians called the three highest levels 'divine nature' and called the highest level 'Atman', the Father. This is the most profound divinity in human beings—the Father in the heavens. This Father is the goal of all human development; it is the focal point in the world's creation. The best way of looking at creation in Christian terms is to have real understanding of sacrifice, offering. Think your mirror image and assume you can be so selfless as to offer your life to the mirror image. We have to see selfless creation as a process in which one gives oneself up wholly to one's creation. Imagine the Father spirit at the centre of a hollow sphere that is mirroring itself, so that the image of God presents itself a thousand times. The early esoteric Christian would thus say: 'Consider the world. What are all creatures but images of God!' And in their esoteric teachings they called this mirrored Godhead 'the kingdom', meaning 'God in his mirror image everywhere'. Now let your feeling develop further. If you see God in everything you will have dissolved the Godhead into countless separate details, and to tell them apart you must give every one of them a name. This name must be hallowed, for every single creature is, after all, an image of the Godhead.

Developing into these three, human beings come closer to God. You must not, however, think that the human being then is God. Take a drop from the ocean—it is the same by nature as the ocean but it is not the ocean. In the same way the drop of divinity in us is of the same nature as the Godhead, but it is not the Godhead. In progressively developing the three highest levels of existence, human beings come to be more and more at one with the kingdom, for the spiritual world is coming down to them. There you have the first three petitions in the Lord's Prayer, first in calling upon the Father, secondly in the plea that the kingdom come to us, thirdly in the hallowing of the name. We will then always endeavour to do nothing that is not in harmony with the Father spirit from which we have sprung forth and towards which we develop as we develop the three highest levels of existence in us. Esoteric Christianity then considers the four lower levels of human existence to be in contrast to the three higher levels, and that these must also grow more and more perfect.

The physical body consists of the same material as the natural world around us, substances that are also all the time entering into this physical body and leaving it again. They have to enter and leave if the physical body is to continue in good health.

The ether body has powers which are in a reciprocal relationship to the whole soul of the nation, just as the physical body has a reciprocal relationship with the whole of the natural world around us. If the physical body is to be in good order, physical substances must enter and leave day by day. If the ether body is to be in good order, it must not develop in isolation but be in harmony with the whole soul of the nation and all higher spirits.

The term 'debt' has to do with 'debts'. Debts are something which really shows that you are not on your own but in a social context, that you owe something to the others around you. The astral body can fall into disorder, and in original Christian esotericism this was considered to be something to do with its tendencies and passions, drives and desires. Everything that may cause such disorder is expressed in the term 'temptation'. Debt therefore is something through which people relate to the community, temptation something to which every human being can be subject as an individual.

If physical substances were not entering and leaving our physical body, this physical body would soon be out of order: 'Give us today the bread we need every day.' If the ether body were not in harmonious interaction with the soul-of-the-nation qualities, that is, if it were not to fit in harmoniously with the whole social system, it would also fall into disorder—'Forgive us our debts'. If human beings were to fall into error and give way to every temptation that came to them, their astral principle would fall into disorder: 'Lead us not into temptation' [or 'Do not bring us to the test'].[22]

The I can be subject to the errors which are referred to as 'evil'. These errors of the I—which is our self—include everything which changes a normal, sound self-awareness into evil, that is, into self-seeking. This involves all transgressions of egotism: 'Deliver us from evil.'

The physical body can develop in a sound way if we let it have its daily bread in the right way. The ether body can develop in a sound way if we find the right harmony with the social body in which we live. The astral body can develop in a sound way, that is, be brought to purification and cleansing, if we overcome all temptations. The I can develop in a sound way if we make the effort to transform all egotism into altruism, all self-seeking into selflessness.

The Lord's Prayer is thus a prayer which encompasses the further development of the whole human being.

Someone may object—and you will come across this objection quite often—that the Lord's Prayer is a prayer which Christ Jesus gave as a prayer for everyone. So what is the point of such an interpretation which is beyond the knowledge of most people?

Naive people need not know any of this. Look at a rose. The greatest wisdom has led to its development and yet it is there for all to enjoy. It is not necessary to know of this wisdom. And that is also how it is with the Lord's Prayer. It affects the human heart and soul even if naive people know nothing about this. But it would never have that power if it had not arisen from that most profound wisdom. All the great forms of prayer have arisen, like this, the greatest of them all, from that profound wisdom. And the power of these forms of prayer is based on this alone. You may think that it is something thought up, but that is not so. The spirit who gave us the Lord's Prayer has given it that profound power.

You see, therefore, that it needs the help of spiritual science to understand something which we practise daily, and the power of which has been with humanity for two millennia.

Now, however, the time has come in human evolution where we cannot go on unless we gain deeper insight. In the past, meaning before this, humanity was able to feel the spiritual power of this very prayer without being aware of its deeper meaning. Now, however, humanity has advanced so far in its evolution that people must ask, and so they must now be given the answer.

The Christian religion will not lose in value with this but rather gain in depth. The greatest wisdom will lead to the religious content being gained afresh. One example of this is the esoteric elucidation of the Lord's Prayer.

It shows us the direction that human beings have to take through their many incarnations. If they proceed in the spirit of the four lower petitions, these will help them to do the work that leads to the con-figuring of the higher levels of human existence as they are presented in the first three petitions.

LECTURE 7

TODAY we have to talk about the law of karma, as it is called, the law of cause and effect in the spiritual world. To begin with we must recall the earlier lectures which showed us how the whole course of life consists in a number of incarnations, so that all of you have been on earth many times and will also return many times more. Later we shall hear that it is not right to assume that these incarnations are repeated, forward and back, for all eternity. Instead we shall see that they did once begin and that there will be a time when they will cease again, when human beings will have different ways of further development.

To begin with we'll therefore consider the period of time when reincarnations of that kind take place, and we have to be clear in our minds that everything we call destiny when it comes to character and inner qualities and also to outward destiny and our situation in life is due to our earlier incarnations, and that the things we do in this life will in turn have an influence on later lives. The great law of cause and effect governs all our incarnations.

Let us consider how this law takes effect in the whole world, not only in the spiritual but also in the physical world.

Assume you have two jugs of water; take an iron ball which you have made red hot and drop it into the first jug of water. What will happen? The water hisses and the ball cools down. Next take the ball out and put it into the second jug. The water will not hiss and the ball will not cool down much more. The ball thus behaves quite differently in the two cases. It would not have done what it did in the second case if it had not been put into the first jug before. The behaviour in the second case is therefore the effect of what happened to it in the first jug. This is what we call karma. It is the ball's karma that it no longer hisses and does not cool down in the second jug.

Now an example from the animal world which will show you that later conditions depend on what has happened in the previous life. Take the creatures which have migrated to the caves in Kentucky.[23] In the total absence of sunlight the eyes did slowly regress. The material which was otherwise used for the eyes migrated to other organs, and the eyes wasted away. The animals gradually grew blind. It is the destiny of all their descendants to be born blind. If the parents had not migrated to the dark caves, it would not be the destiny of the descendants to be blind. This state of blindness has thus been the consequence of an earlier activity—migration to the dark caves.

According to occult science, everything that happens in the world is due to karma. Karma is the general cosmic law. The Bible also speaks of this karma right at the beginning. It says: 'In the beginning God created the world.' If a superficial view is taken of this, which is common today, you will not realize that this is in the terms of karmic law. You will realize it immediately, however, if you take the original of this ancient document, where we hear of this activity, or one of the earliest translations into Latin, the *Septuagint* for example[24]—the standard translation of the Old Testament used in the whole Roman Catholic Church to this day, especially Genesis.

In this kind of introductory lecture course, intended to show you the tremendous depths of the spiritual-scientific view of the world, it is, I think, reasonable to take a step outside our actual subject.

People today really have no relationship any more to the living word. Speech and language have on the one hand become a conventional means of communication and on the other the language of business.

This was very different when the word was created in ancient times. Then human beings still had a living relationship to the word. Indeed, in earliest times every single letter used to make up a word had profound meaning. People today have no idea as to what went through the mind of a Hebrew sage in those times when he spoke the word *bara*, which comes in the first sentence in Genesis and was later translated into Latin as *creare*, 'to create'. What meaning lies deep down in *bara*? We still have the same stem in our language today in the word 'bear' [give birth].

The root 'kr' in 'karma' also belongs to *creare*, so that when you say *creare* in Latin this means nothing more or less than 'something arises due to the influence of earlier conditions', meaning that something arises which karmically is due to something that went before.

We can only speak of karma in the present-day sense since Lucifer has come on the scene, that is, from the moment when man was first at fault. Because of this anything connected with the word 'karma' also always has something of the concept 'fault' to it. *Creare* therefore means to give rise to something because of a karmic debt. The stem *bar* does not yet have any of this fault or debt connotation. How has this come about? Doubtless because the ancient Hebrews were still much more closely connected with the spiritual world and perfectly clear in their mind that at the time when the Elohim were creatively thinking up the world there could as yet be no thought of karma. In the Latin stage of human evolution human beings had already been completely separated from the spiritual world, as we shall see on another occasion. They were therefore quite unable to think of the Elohim's creative thinking in anything but a karmic context.

Both *bara* and *creare* never mean that God created the world from nothing; the meaning behind both these words is that God let earlier states flow across into new ones. In the same way a mother does not bear a child from nothing. To 'bear' or 'give birth' means that the infant emerges and becomes visible in the world when before it was hidden in the mother's womb.

You see how much the meaning of the Bible can be distorted. First of all, theologians said that God had created the world from nothing. This was because they no longer knew about the periods of cosmic evolution that had preceded the earth state. Whole libraries of books have been written about this. But all those theologians were like Don Quixote fighting windmills. It is always necessary to know whom or what you are fighting, and we must always establish the original meaning of those ancient documents.

When we see the law of karma the way it truly must be seen, as the connection between cause and effect not only in physical life on earth between birth and death but also in the life in the spiritual world after death, this law of karma will cast light on our own life. Insight into it means profound satisfaction not only for the rational mind but in the deepest sense also for heart and mind, providing real insight into our relationship to the world. You will see its great significance more and more clearly, realizing that it needs real insight into this law of karma if we are to make life with the world around us harmonious. It will explain not only the riddles of the world that one must first dream up, but also those we truly meet with at every step in life. Surely it is a riddle to see how one individual is guiltlessly born in the most miserable conditions, and how in the case of another the greatest potential gifts have to come to nothing because of the social situation into which the individual is born. We often ask ourselves why one individual is born into such poor conditions, through no fault of his own, and another, without having done anything to deserve it specially, is born into a well-to-do family who give her or him all love and attention? These are questions to be ignored only by people today who do not care about things.

The deeper our insight into the law of karma the more shall we see that all the harshness disappears which seems to prevail when one takes only a superficial look at it. We'll then see more and more clearly how it has come about that one individual has to live under one kind of conditions, and another under different ones. One or another person's life will only seem harsh if we look only at the one life. If we know that this one life is the absolute effect of earlier actions, this harshness goes away completely and we realize that human beings prepare their lives for themselves.

Someone might say, 'Yes, but that is a terrible thing if one has to think that people are themselves responsible for the strokes of destiny in their life.' Here we have to understand that the law of karma is not for sentimental, brooding people. It is a law for action, making us strong, giving us courage and hope. For although we have ourselves created the life we live, with all its difficulties, we also know that it is a law the main significance of which lies not in the past but in the future. However much we are at the present time oppressed by the consequences of past deeds, insight into the law of karma will bear fruit in later lives.

Depending on what we do, the fruits of these actions will be there in future lives, for no action is taken in vain. Think how much more theosophical it is to see the law of karma as a law for doing! For whatever we do, we cannot escape the fruits of our actions. The worse things are for us in our present life, the better we are at accepting it, the better will things be for us in future lives. The law of karma solves the riddles we meet with at every step in life.

How does the previous life relate to the later one? We have to understand that all the inner effects of outside experiences have an effect in the coming life, being pleasure or pain.

As you know, all pleasure and pain, joy or unhappiness that live in us are in our astral body. Everything our astral body lives through in this life, especially if events repeat themselves, will in the next life be evident as a quality of the ether body. The joy you awaken again and again in your soul with regard to an object in your life will mean that you will have a deep regard and preference for this object in your next life. Regard and preference are character traits, however, which are present in the ether body, so that anything which the astral body brought about in the previous life will be qualities of the ether body in the next life. Things you experience repeatedly in this life will be your basic character in the next life. A melancholic temperament develops if the individual has had many sad experiences in the previous life that put him again and again in a sad mood. It has given the next ether body the tendency to be melancholic. Conversely people who are able to look always on the positive side and so generate pleasure and joy, happy high-mindedness in their astral body will in their next life have a lasting character trait in the ether body that gives them a cheerful temperament. When someone who has to face difficult things in life overcomes them with energy, his ether body will be born with a choleric temperament in the next life. Knowing all this we can actually prepare ourselves an ether body for the next life.

The qualities which the ether body has in one life will in the next life appear in the physical body. So if someone has bad habits and character traits and does nothing to overcome them, this will appear as a disposition of the physical body in the next life, literally a disposition to disease. It may sound strange to you, but the disposition for particular diseases, and especially infectious diseases, does indeed come from bad habits in the previous life. With this insight it is therefore also up to us to prepare health or sickness for our next life. If we get out of a bad habit we make ourselves physically sound and resistant to infection in our next life. It is therefore possible to take care of our health in the next life if we endeavour to cultivate only good and noble qualities.

Now to a third thing that is extraordinarily important for seeing the law of karma in the right light. We have to put the right value on our actions even in this life. So far we have only spoken of things that occur within the human being; but the things we do in this life, that is, the way we act towards the world around us, will in the next life have their effect in this very world around us.

I have not really done anything if I just have a bad habit, but if it makes me act then this action will change the outside world. And everything which had such an effect on the physical world outside will come to us as external destiny in our next life in the outside world. The actions of the physical body in this life will be our destiny in the next life. We learn of this as we find ourselves in one situation or another. Whether a person is happy or unhappy in one situation in life or another will depend on actions performed in the previous life. The Vehmic murder again serves as an apt, instructive example which shows how an outward action in one life comes back to the individual concerned as destiny in the next life.

So these are the karmic situations of individuals in brief outline. We must, however, speak not only of the karma of individuals; that would be absolutely wrong, as wrong as when an individual finger on our hand wanted to see itself as an individual entity. Someone who would rise above the earth for a few miles would get exactly as far as the finger would get if it were to separate from the organism. Concerning ourselves with the science of the spirit we would literally be forced to realize from the insight we have thus gained that we must not deceive ourselves and insist that we are individual entities. It is like this in the physical and very much more so in the spiritual world. We are part of the whole world and also have our destiny as part of the whole. Karma affects not only individuals but also the life of whole nations. An example. You all know that leprosy was a disease of medieval times. It did not disappear from Europe until the sixteenth century. There was a quite particular reason why it appeared in medieval times, and this was a non-physical reason. Materialists are, of course, inclined to ascribe such an infectious disease to bacilli, but it is not just the physical cause which plays a role in such a disease. This is just as if someone were given a thorough thrashing and one was asked to investigate why he had been thrashed. A reasonable person will easily see that the cause of the thrashing was that there are some rough characters in the village. But it would be downright silly in this case to conclude—like a materialist—that when someone comes and tells us that the man's back is black and blue that this is wholly and entirely because sticks struck his back so and so many times. The sticks are undoubtedly the materialistic cause of the back being black and blue, but it is the rough people who are the deeper cause. Thus leprosy has bacilli for its materialistic cause but there is also a cause in mind and spirit.

Crying provides a perfect analogy to this. The mental cause is sorrow, the material one the secretion from the tear glands. It is hard to believe that a quite significant academic of the present time has managed to come to the same foolish conclusion as the one just given, for he made the downright mind-blowing statement that human beings do not cry because they feel sorry; they feel sorry because they cry.[25]

Back to leprosy now. In this case, if you want to explain the deeper cause of this disease, the one that is not physical, you must look back on a significant historical event, the time when great hordes invaded Europe from the East, causing fear and terror. Those Asian hordes were peoples who had remained at the ancient Atlantean stage and were therefore in decline. They were peoples, therefore, who had a powerful kind of decline or decay element in their astral body. Nothing would have happened if their rush on Europe had not caused shock or terror. As it was, those hordes caused fear and terror and shock; whole nations experienced these states of fear and shock. The decaying astrality of the Huns then got mixed into the astral bodies harrowed by fear and terror of the invaded nations. The degenerated astral bodies of Asian tribes offloaded their bad astral matter onto the astral bodies of the Europeans, and this decaying matter was the cause of the physical effects of the disease at a later time. That is in truth the deep spiritual cause of leprosy in medieval times. Something which happened in the minds of people did later on appear in the physical body. Only those who know this law of karma and are able to see through it have the right to intervene actively in the course of history.

I am now going to tell you about something which contributed to the establishment of the theosophical philosophy of life. It is this. Karma has its effects on individuals and also on nations and indeed humanity as a whole. Any student of the history of European civilization will know that materialism came up about four hundred years ago. It is essentially harmless in science, for there faults will always be spotted and made up for. It is much more harmful in practical life, for there everything is done from the point of view of material interests. Materialism would never have entered into practical life if people had not felt attracted by it. And there would not have been a Buechner[26] and so on if people had not already been so much attached to material things. Materialism is, however, most harmful in religious life, that is, in the church; the church has for centuries been steering towards materialism. How? If you go back to the times of early Christianity you would never have heard of anyone thinking that the seven days of creation actually were seven days, which is still widely assumed to be the case today, and that one would imagine the 'seventh day' to be one when someone who has done heavy physical work sits down and takes a rest. Our materialistic age no longer knows anything about the reality of these seven days of creation. It will be the privilege of theosophy to enlighten people again about this ancient document called Genesis.[27]

These materialistic views in religion have eaten their way most deeply into the life of nations. And this materialism will prevail more and more, especially in the field of religion, and it is exactly there where there will be less and less insight, people not understanding that it is the mind and spirit which matters and not things physical and material. You will of course agree that material thinking, feeling and doing has entered more and more into the whole of people's view of life, and ultimately this will have an effect on the state of health of later generations.

An age when people have a sound view of life will create a strong inner focus for human beings, making them self-contained and their descendants strong and robust. An age where people believe only in material things will generate descendants in whose bodies everything goes its own way; there is no focus, and this does give rise to the signs of neurasthenia and nervousness. This would get worse and worse if materialism continued to be the future philosophy of life. The seer can tell you exactly what would happen if materialism were not counter-balanced by a firm spiritual orientation. Mental diseases would then be epidemic, children would be nervous and suffer with tremors even at birth, and the further consequence of attachment to material things would be a human breed lacking in inner focus, something we do see even today. About 30 years ago[28] it was this thought and this prospect for humanity if spiritual means were not used to counter this effect of materialism which led to the inauguration of the theosophical move-ment. There may be much that can be said for or against this kind of remedy, but all the objections won't carry much weight; the main thing is that it will help. That is how it is with the healing powers of theo-sophy. It is intended to prevent something which would inevitably come if humanity continued with materialism as before.

You see, therefore, how in thinking about the law of karma in its deeper sense we cannot consider the human being to be a separate entity but must see him as being subject to the law of karma also within the community. The law of karma is not for people who want to believe in a destiny that is completely blind. You would be wholly in error if you were to take the law of karma in that sense. Yet one keeps coming across people who have fallen into this error. One person will say, 'I know, it is not my fault that something or other happens to me. It's just my karma, and I have to live through it.' Someone else will say, 'I see someone who is in trouble but I must not help him, for it is his own fault; it is his karma and he must go through it.' All this is completely nonsensical.

To get an idea of karmic law that is easily understood, you might compare it to the business law of debit and credit. A merchant is subject to this law in everything he does, and it is the same when it comes to living with karma. All the good and bad things you have done in your last life are your balance-sheet entries. All good qualities on the debit and all bad ones on the credit side of your karma.[29]

You should not, however, say, 'I must not interfere.' That would be as foolish as if a merchant, having drawn the balance, were to say, 'Now

I must not do any more deals, for that would change my balance.' Just as a merchant improves his balance with every good deal, so I too improve my karma with every good thing I do. Just as the merchant is free to make an entry on the debit or credit side at any time, so people are free to do this in the ledger of life. People are always free in this action, not in spite of the law of karma but exactly by taking it into account. If we know that everything we do, acting in full freedom, will have an effect in this ledger of life, we cannot agree with someone who will not help someone in need. That is just as if a merchant were about to go bankrupt and asked us to lend him twenty thousand marks. Surely you would lend him the money if you knew that he was a good businessman and would use the loan to get into a sound position again. And that is also how it is with those in need. You help them to mend their karma so that their destiny may take a turn for the good, and you are at the same time improving your own karma, having done a good deed. The law of karma is indeed a law for active intervention in daily life. It is particularly important to gain the right understanding of the law of karma exactly from this point of view when we look at the way it relates to Christianity. Serious misunderstandings exist today among theologians. Modern theologians are saying, 'We are teaching that with the death on the cross all sins are forgiven; you teach the law of karma and that contradicts our teaching.' The contradiction is only apparent, however, for the law of karma has not been understood. Conversely there are theosophists who say that they cannot accept that the death on the cross means forgiveness of sins. They do in fact also fail to understand the law of karma.

Let us assume you help someone and intervene in his destiny so that it will be positive. Now if you were able to help two people this would also in no way go against the law of karma. Next assume that you are an individual who is called upon to rid the world of an evil by doing a particular thing. Does that go against the law of karma? The Christ spirit has done exactly the same thing—on a large scale—as a human being who helped not only hundreds or thousands of people but the whole of humanity in performing his deed. The death for redemption, of atonement for others, was therefore wholly in accord with the law of karma and can in fact only be understood in connection with this law.

Only those who do not understand will think there is contradiction. It is just as little in contradiction to the law of karma as is the help which I give to a single individual in need.

With regard to the law of karma you have to think of the future, for we make an entry in our accounts ledger with everything we do and this will bear fruit. Contradiction between Christianity and karma could only be seen by those who are still caught up in the childhood diseases of theosophy.

Insight into this law of karma will explain many things. In the first place we can exactly demonstrate the connection between bodily development at this time and our previous lives. A life full of love prepares for a development in the next life that will keep the person young for a long time. Premature ageing, on the other hand, is due to much antipathy in the previous life. Secondly, a particularly selfish desire for gain creates dispositions for infectious diseases in the next life. Thirdly, it is particularly interesting that the consequence of pain and, above all, certain diseases one goes through will mean a handsome body in the next life. Such an insight makes it easier for us to bear with some diseases.

In reference to and with insight into such destiny connections, one of the greatest Bible scholars, Fabre d'Olivet,[30] used a beautiful image to show how things are interrelated in life. He wrote: 'Consider the pearl in the shell. The creature had to suffer, and this suffering has given rise to the beautiful pearl.' And that is indeed how illness in this life is often connected with something that will add something positive to the next life.

Tomorrow then about how this may be developed further in a number of different directions.

LECTURE 8

KASSEL, 23 JUNE 1907

TODAY I want to add a few things concerning reincarnation and karma. I would then move on to discuss the evolution of our planet earth, for this alone will give us accurate understanding of the true nature of man as it presents itself in relation to the cosmos. I then want to end this course of lectures by considering, together with you, how human beings develop when their endeavours are directed towards gaining a view of the higher worlds. If we are to enter into those worlds we will need to consider 1) pre-Christian inner development, 2) Christian inner development, and 3) Rosicrucian inner development.

What remains to be said about reincarnation should be reserved for a separate chapter, for it is the most difficult for beginners to understand. We will have to consider things that initially relate to the time between two incarnations, and that in itself is an issue which comes as a shock to the materialistic mind of our time.

The one source of knowledge available to the spiritual investigator cannot be checked by people who do not yet have spiritual vision. It is living experience. However, anyone who goes through the inner training which we still need to discuss will be well able to establish when the majority of people living at the present time were last incarnated here on earth. I will also have to speak of the means used in Chaldean, Pythagorean and all other mystery centres of pre-Christian times to make it possible for people to enter into the spiritual world.

All those able to look into conditions in the spiritual worlds and therefore to trace the previous incarnations of human beings will discover the majority of people now living to have been incarnated in the early time after the birth of the Christ and until the eighth and ninth centuries. These are averages; the time between two incarnations may also be shorter or longer.

There is something else connected with the fact I have just been mentioning, something which has become particularly evident in our time. It is the fact that right now in our time unusually radical thinkers are demanding equality. This is nothing but the demand for equality that existed in early Christian centuries applied to the material world. The early Christian tenet was equality before God and equality before the worldly authorities.

Many of the people who thus claimed equality in the early Christian centuries went through the gate of death with their demand not met. They took their longing for equality before God and the worldly authorities with them in their souls into the spiritual world. They have reincarnated exactly at the present time, and as a matter of course have brought their attitude to these demands with them—though not in a metamorphosed form that would be in accord with today's materialistic view of the world. Having now incarnated they fail to see the wholly materialistic quality given to this demand in our time. It is incorrect to think or indeed maintain that today's sense of freedom comes from Christianity.

Metamorphosed into today's demand for equality in all earthly situations, this demand for equality before God and the worldly authorities can only be given the right direction if we understand the true situation, something which the theosophical view of the world makes possible. However, if you know the true situation and at the same time look at the materialistic view that governs people today, you will immediately realize that in the form in which it is presented by today's radical thinkers this demand is something which had to come in the natural course of events. It is equally true, however, that from now on people have to rise above materialism and come to spirituality. This is the only way in which social conditions can be given a sound basis again. There is no other remedy but the science of the spirit itself.

The subject is discussed in more detail in an issue of the journal *Lucifer-Gnosis*.[31] There it is shown how all other means put forward for solving the social problem, however elevated their source, suffer from dilettantism, for people today simply do not know anything about the higher worlds. If the social thinkers of today were to let themselves be inspired just a little by theosophy, they would find the truly effective means for tackling this issue.

It is true that humanity had to descend from a spiritual past into materialism. It is equally true that they must rise again to the spiritual. It needs this spiritual view of the world to come to the principle that gives harmony, peace and love. Here, too, theosophy will therefore be practical in the most eminent sense.

I will now have to show how the view of human evolution gained with the help of clairvoyant observation takes us back to the events that occur between death and rebirth.

I said that it is not for nothing that human beings appear on this physical earth again and again. We found that the reason for this is that they meet completely new circumstances on earth every time they incarnate, and that every new physical life yields new fruit for the future, for the earth will have changed every time where both civilization and the purely external natural world are concerned. The face of the earth will be completely different every time the individual comes to it in a new incarnation.

The Chaldeans considered the change in the earth to be due to the relationship which the sun had to the other heavenly bodies. You will find details of this in various lectures.[32] I can only refer to it briefly here.

If you were to pay attention to the heavens when the sun rises at the beginning of spring, if you were to observe the place where it rises, and what the world of the stars looks like at that time, you would see that the relationship of the sun to the other heavenly bodies is a different one every spring. The spring equinox moves on year by year and it will be about 26,000—25,920—years before it will reach the place again where it was 26,000 years earlier (a cycle). But the sun is only seemingly moving in a circle; it is in fact a spiral. The spring equinox was determined according to the constellation it was in. The sun thus moves in a circle through the heavens, a circle of the twelve constellations. It moves a little bit further year by year, passing through all twelve constellations in 26,000 years.

About 800 years before Christ the sun first rose in the Ram; since it needs 26,000 years to pass through all twelve constellations, it needs the twelfth part of that time, 2,200 years, to pass through one constellation. The changes in the face of our earth are truly connected with the progression of the spring equinox. After about 2,200 years the face of the earth has changed so much that conditions are completely different; this is therefore the time when human beings are on average reincarnating again. Observations made in spiritual science confirm this. The ancients always had a definite feeling when the sun rose in the Ram at the spring equinox which may be described as follows. The sun is for the first time again sending the rays that magic the plants from the soil from the Ram. It felt to them as if the Ram brought the rays, and they venerated this constellation. Sacred feelings are connected with the names given to these constellations. The Ram sends the powers of the spring sun; the peoples of those times therefore saw the lamb as a symbol for the powers that revived nature and the human soul. Many legends are connected with this, for instance that of Jason who brought back the Golden Fleece, and this was something that was most precious to human beings. The veneration of the Ram, or the lamb, prevailed through many centuries and was adopted in Christianity. Originally a lamb would therefore appear on the cross instead of the Christ. And this is why the Christ was called 'the Lamb of God'.

Thus we see how the ancients connected important images and ideas with the passage of the sun through the individual constellations. This is also connected with the reincarnation of human beings after a particular period of time, when about 2,200 years had passed. It makes a big difference, however, if an individual incarnates as a man or a woman at a particular period, and this makes it a bit more complicated to calculate individual incarnations. The experiences which human beings have as man or woman are so different that they must incarnate twice within that length of time, once as a man and once as a woman. There are therefore two incarnations within approximately two thousand years, and in reality therefore only 1,100 or 1,200 years between individual incarnations. And on average it is correct to say that a male and a female incarnation alternate. In exceptional cases, several incarnations may be in the same gender; the greatest number observed being seven. After that, however, the gender changed. These are exceptions; as a rule genders change from one incarnation to the next.

This is what may be said about the time between two incarnations. It does, however, also depend on other things and not on the human being only. It may be the case, for example, that a particular individual is exactly right for conditions on earth at a particular time, when a particular thing needs to be done. In that case the individual may well be drawn to incarnation by the higher powers before the whole period of time has passed. The individual is brought down because he or she has the exact disposition needed to achieve a particular mission. This applies above all to the great leaders of humanity. It will be balanced out in the whole sequence of lives and the individual will later spend a suitably longer period in devachan.

One more thing to be said is that there is a kind of counterpart to the experience of which I said it came immediately after death, when the human being looks back on the past life as if in a great tableau. This counterpart is a kind of preview of the next life on earth.

Let us bring to mind again how the review of life arises at the moment of death. As you know, the ether body has two main functions: the first is to stimulate all vital functions in the physical body, that is, to protect the substance of the physical body all the time from decay and regulate its anabolism; secondly the ether body is where memory lies. So when the ether body leaves the physical body at the moment of death, it is relieved of that first main task, and that is also the moment when the second function comes strongly to the fore, remembering everything the human being experienced in the past life. And that is the tableau of life. So at this moment the human being essentially consists only of ether body, astral body and I.

For a new incarnation, the I descends from the spiritual world with all the immortal extracts so far gained of both the etheric and the astral. It initially draws together all astral qualities to be its new astral body, qualities that reflect development up to that point. Only then does it draw together all the etheric qualities. All this happens in the first days after conception, and it is only from the eighteenth to the twentieth day onwards that the new ether body is working independently to develop the physical germ of the human being. Before that the maternal ether body did the things which the ether body would have to do later on. It is only on this eighteenth to twentieth day after conception that the individual who is about to incarnate and who has until then garbed its I in a new astral body and ether body, takes possession of the physical body which has so far been developed by the mother.

The moment before possession is thus taken the human being has exactly the same levels of existence as at the moment of death. In the latter case it had just cast off the physical body, in the former it has not yet taken up the physical body. You will therefore find it easy to understand that at the moment when human beings enter into a new physical body, something happens which is analogous to the moment when they laid it aside. At this moment they have a kind of preview of the life to come, just as at the moment of death they had a review of the past life. They will, however, forget this preview, for the constitution of the physical body is not yet such that the preview can be retained as a memory.

It is at that moment that human beings are able to see: Such are the conditions in the family, country, place and destiny situations into which I am being born. And it then happens at times that the individual, having had the preview at this moment, seeing that things will go hard for her or him, gets a shock, takes fright at the life that lies ahead, and that the ether body does then not connect properly with the physical body, does not want to enter into it. The consequences of that fright—of the ether body not being willing—then show themselves in the form of idiocy. The seer can see the ether body project beyond the physical head in such individuals. And with the ether body not integrated the brain lags behind in its development, because the ether body is not working on it the way it should. Many cases of idiocy are due to that cause.

It is easy to see why cases of this kind appear so easily in this day and age if we consider that the majority of people reincarnated today had their last incarnation in the ninth to eleventh centuries AD. It is possible to influence the ether body to such effect with a form of physical treatment that it gradually pushes its way into the physical body, and one can improve the situation in this way. This will only be possible, however, for those who are able to see through the whole and know its spiritual background, which would enable them to take the right kind of action.

We now know from what has gone before that human beings are made up of the physical body, the ether body, the astral body and the I. All these are not merely sitting one within the other but interpenetrate and influence one another. Thus they all act on the physical body, taking part in working on it so that it can develop in the way it is meant to develop. Unless you have developed your higher organs of perception you will see only the physical body of someone before you. But this physical body only appears to you the way it does because ether body, astral body and I are integrated in it and because they have each in their own way had a part in developing that physical body. The physical organs in this human body have not been developed in a chaotic way by the three higher bodies, however, but we can distinguish very clearly how these three higher bodies are involved in developing the physical body. Let us try and get an idea of this.

To begin with we therefore have something in this physical body which in a certain respect are purely physical organs. These are the ones which are based on purely physical laws—eyes, ears, larynx and so on. The eye is certainly a live organ that is given its life by the ether body which fills it and feeds it; yet seen purely in terms of physics it is a physical apparatus where the same forces apply as in inorganic nature, in a crystal, for instance. We can therefore consider the functions of the eye wholly in terms of physics. These sensory apparatuses must first of all work their way out of the physical body. They are the organs which we realize are in the narrower sense constructed by physical forces according to physical laws. We then have a second group of organs—those serving nutrition, growth and reproduction, and these are predominantly glandular. The ether body plays the key role in developing them. Then the nervous system represents a third group, and this is developed essentially by the astral body. In fourth place we have above all the red blood of higher animals and human beings. The warm red blood is developed by the I.

So we have 1) the actually physical parts, the sense organs, and later also the purely mineral skeletal system which the physical body itself develops, 2) the glandular system, reproductive organs and so on, developed by the ether body, 3) the nervous system, developed by the astral body, and 4) the blood system developed by the I. We'll understand this much more clearly if we also take a closer look at the evolution of our earth.

We cannot trace the re-embodiments of our earth forward and back ad infinitum. Even the best of clairvoyants cannot see further than to a particular embodiment, for limits are set also to their powers of insight. Clairvoyants can look back as far as three embodiments of our earth, and also the next three ahead. Together with the present state of the earth they are therefore able to see a total of seven embodiments.

Some people hearing this for the first time may feel that it sounds a bit superstitious that the seer puts the earth exactly in the centre of this evolution; one might say that this was rather odd. But one would only say so if taking a superficial look, for it is no more odd than that out in the open I see the same distance in all directions and find myself at the centre of the horizon. In the sevenfold order of the human being that has been presented the I is also at the centre—physical body, ether body, astral body, *I*, Spirit Self, Life Spirit, Spirit Human Being. This is due to taking the same point of view.

People may also be surprised at the things I have to say about the evolution of our planet earth, finding it strange.

The earth has evolved from an earlier planet. The planet from which our earth has evolved is no longer there in the heavens. But the present moon is still a piece of what did once exist; it is a piece of our earth's predecessor. So if you were to mix together our present earth and the present moon and all the spiritual entities living on them, this would give you an approximate picture of the previous embodiment of the earth, called 'Moon' by occultists. Now you must remember that a hypothesis of this kind is established merely to make the process more easily understandable for you, but that, like all hypotheses, it is of course not entirely correct. If one were to mix the present earth and the present moon together the way one mixes two substances in a retort in one's laboratory, let us say, nothing like the Moon of that earlier time would result. For you have to consider that from the moment when they separated earth and moon developed further, each in its own way. Solid matter, the mineral world, only developed in this planet earth from the beginning of the present stage of earth evolution. Mineral in the present sense did not exist before our present earth evolved.

We would therefore have to remove in our minds everything that has since developed as we stir together earth and moon. The old Moon mass had nothing in it as yet by way of mineral matter. It had only reached a fluid, mushy consistency. As I said, such a hypothesis is established to help people who have never heard of the planetary evolution of our earth and the whole of our cosmos understand it at least to some extent. It needs infinitely much more to gain deeper insight into this evolution, but we cannot go into this in an introductory course like this. The evolution will be considered again and again as time goes on, looking at it from new points of view to throw more light on it.

Before going through that old Moon state the earth went through one which occultists call 'Sun'. There our earth went through conditions similar to those still existing on the sun today. And if we wanted to make the same assumption it would get a bit more complicated. For to visualize that condition you'd have to mix up earth, moon and sun to get a single heavenly body, the Sun state of old, but with the same proviso as before. The old Sun had in the course of its evolution separated out all the parts, the powers and substances of today's earth and today's moon, casting them off, and thus changed from a planet to a fixed star. Our earth will also be a sun one day, when it will have made all entities on it into light entities.

Our earth was therefore Moon in the past, and the Moon had previously been Sun. We are able to look back on an even earlier stage of evolution which occultists call 'Saturn'. We thus distinguish the following evolutional stages of our earth—Saturn, Sun, Moon and earth, with Jupiter, Venus and Vulcan to follow.

Someone might come and say: 'You are telling us that the earth was once Saturn, but Saturn is up there in the heavens right now!' But the Saturn which our earth has once been has nothing to do with the heavenly body called Saturn today. This is not to say that the entities which exist on earth today have in the past been on the Saturn we see in the heavens today. Today's Saturn only has as much to do with that earlier Saturn state as the present moon has with the Moon state. Anything we see in the present-day Saturn has itself gone through further evolution after that long-ago time, and old Saturn relates to today's Saturn more or less as a baby does to a very old man. Today's Saturn has at one time been in the same state as old Saturn, just as the old man has once been an infant. It is the same with the sun and the other heavenly bodies. And when the spiritual investigator looks at Jupiter today he finds there conditions and spirits of the kind which earth will have once it has itself become Jupiter.

This is what the earliest initiates taught, and initiates have dinned this into their pupils through the ages.

The parts of our language that can be traced back to earliest times were created by initiates. I cannot go into detail about this in an introductory course, for it would take us well away from our subject. But in the old days, when initiates were still determining language development, language was something quite different. Today people may well be looking for a name that has not so far been given to something else, but it will not have any kind of deeper meaning. In the past, the giving of names had a deep meaning arising from inner connections. The aim was to set up a kind of memorial for the progress of earth evolution through all those periods of time and planetary states. A timetable was created, as it were, so that human beings would always remember those stages in time. There is something else we must know if we want to understand this timetable.

From what has been said so far you'll realize that before it was earth, our earth went through a Saturn, a Sun and a Moon existence. But before it became the present earth, that is, in the transition from Moon existence to today's earth existence, this earth was under the powerful influence of another heavenly body, the planet Mars. At the very beginning of our earth evolution came this most important Mars influence, of tremendous significance for the further evolution of the earth. By the way, the earth received iron from Mars on this occasion, something which had not been part of its substance before. In its first stage of evolution the earth thus stood under the influence of Mars, and in the second half, which is now, it came under the more powerful influence of Mercury. This is why the term 'earth' is dropped in occultism, and the earth's conditions are divided in two—the first half, the Mars half, and the second, the Mercury half. The system previously presented is therefore differentiated into Saturn state, Sun state, Moon state, Mars-Mercury state, Jupiter state, Venus state and Vulcan state.

This would make the Vulcan state the eighth, and it has the same role in evolution as the octave has in music. The octave is a repetition of the first note but at a higher level. The Vulcan state is a repetition of the Saturn state, but at a higher level of development. The whole cosmos has evolved from the realm of the spirit and with the Vulcan stage everything will have developed in the direction of the spirit again, but at a higher and more rich and varied level. One spirituality has turned into infinitely many spirit human beings, just as the seed which the farmer puts in the ground has by autumn become the ear of corn, with many seed grains. 'All that must disappear is but a parable.'[33]

The early initiates made these seven names part of the great memorial which I mentioned and which we have in the names given to the seven days of the week:

Saturn day	Saturday, Samstag
Sun day	
Moon day	
Mars day	Mardi, Mars, Ziu, Dius, Dienstag, Tuesday
Mercury day	Mercredi, Mercury, Wodan, Wednesday
Jupiter day	Giovedi, Donar, Donnerstag, Thursday
Venus day	Vendredi, Venus, Freia, Freitag, Friday

The names of the weekdays truly are a monument for the seven stages of Earth evolution. Something which seems to be everyday thus points to profound spiritual realities.

Now you have to consider that the whole of human evolution is most closely connected with this planetary evolution. The whole of human evolution can indeed only be understood against the background of these planetary stages of Earth evolution, for during each of these stages the basis was created for one of the bodies that make up the human being. The potential for the physical body was created in Saturn time, that for the ether body in Sun time, the astral body in the Moon stage, and the I only became part of essential human nature in earth time. This is why the physical body is so far the most perfectly developed principle, whereas the ether body is only in the third stage of its evolution, the potential for it having been established on the old Sun; the astral body is in its second stage, potentially established on old Moon, and the I is the infant among human levels of existence, being only in the early stages of its evolution in the present earth state.

We get a direct pointer towards what has just been said if we consider the evolution of the four bodies, or levels of existence, for the human being.

In the early years of the Theosophical Society people would widely use the terms 'higher' and 'lower' levels, with the physical body considered the lowest of the four. And values would often attach to those terms, with people only too often tending to consider the physical body as less valuable and even despising it. But that is entirely wrong.

Take a careful look at this marvellous structure which is the physical body. You will immediately see that it has reached a tremendously high level of perfection, something which is definitely not the case with the ether body, for instance. If you look at the physical body with eyes of wisdom, you will see that every organ is something to marvel at—the heart, the bones, and so on. Just consider the structure of the heart, full of wisdom, and think of the work which this relatively small organ does day by day and hour by hour. Compare this with the development of the astral body, still relatively inadequate today—how passions stir in it every day that have not yet been refined, how people among other things still long to enjoy things every day that seriously maltreat the heart, which is such a marvellous structure, and yet the heart is able to set all this astral damage at nought and does not break down, indeed not even getting damaged in many cases. The astral body thus is not as far developed today as is the physical body, which has reached the greatest perfection. In the future the astral body will have developed so far that it outstrips the physical body. The ether body is less far developed than the physical body today, and the astral body comes only in third place. The youngest of the bodies that make up the essential human being is the I; it will therefore be the last to achieve perfection.

Everything you have as part of your physical body, the actual physical principle, is the oldest part of you. Our physical body had gone through development before an ether body was integrated into it. And this development, which the physical body went through purely as physical body, was the Saturn stage. There this first beginning of the physical body was nothing but physical apparatus. It continued to develop and it was only on the Sun that the ether body integrated itself into this physical body. This ether body filled the whole of that physical body, as it were, transforming it in some respect. During the Moon stage the astral body came in, and the I only came in at the beginning of our present earth state. Today, human beings are made up of four principles. On the old Moon they were made up of physical, ether and astral body, on old Sun of physical and ether body, and on old Saturn of physical body only. The physical body has therefore four stages of development, the ether body three, the astral body two, and the I only its first stage. Because of this the physical body is the most perfect, having had most work done on it.

You see, therefore, how the individual levels of human existence are connected with the evolution of the whole planetary system. In old occult books you will therefore also find the following terms:

for the physical body	Saturn body
for the ether body	Sun body
for the astral body	Moon body
for the I	earthly body, the actual earth part of human beings.

Tomorrow we'll study the configuration and the whole life of Saturn, then go on to Sun and Moon. We shall see how human beings came to be more and more perfect up to their present condition.

LECTURE 9

KASSEL, 24 JUNE 1907

To DAY we will take the outline of planetary evolution that was given yesterday further. It was said that our earth has previously gone through a Saturn, Sun and Moon state. Today I would like to describe these consecutive states for you in the way that is customary in occultism. When we then come to speak of inner development by following the road of insight, we shall see what is really meant by many things presented as hypothesis today. As we now go straight to consideration of the Saturn state, which existed millions and millions of years before our time, it looks very different from what people assume on the basis of present-day conditions. We must above all be clear in our minds that the most perfect entity we know, the human being, has followed the longest line of evolution. You will therefore hear a history of evolution that may be said to differ greatly from that of Haeckel and Darwin. You will find the advantages of this purely materialistic theory presented in my book.[34]

In the first place we have to understand that the most perfect entity has gone through the longest period of development. And that is the human being, to begin with the human physical body—it needed the longest time for its evolution. Looking back with the spiritual eye we therefore find its first beginnings even in Saturn existence. The whole of cosmic space with all spirits and objects in it exerted an influence on the first stage of Earth evolution. You still have all the organs in you that were developed as the most perfect part of our physical body at that time; these were the sense organs, the apparatuses that can be understood in purely physical terms. The potential for them was established at that time. Do not imagine that the eye did then exist the way it does today. But the first beginnings of the eye, the ear, all the sense organs and all otherwise purely physical apparatuses in the human being came into being on Saturn. The only activities on Saturn were those which still produce the mineral world today. Human beings existed then in the first beginnings of their physical body, everything else—blood, tissue and so on—did not exist. The first beginnings of the human body were physical apparatuses by nature. Emeralds, mica and so on are the outcome of physical laws, developing as cubes, hexahedra, and so on. On Saturn apparatus-like configurations developed that were as crystals are in the earth today. And the mode of action on Saturn's surface was essentially a kind of reflecting or mirroring into cosmic space. The spirits which surrounded Saturn, scattered through cosmic space, cast their activities down to it. Another thing which was strongly developed at that time was the 'cosmic aroma'. You can only get a feeling for some of the things that existed on old Saturn when you hear an echo in the natural world outside; the sound of the echo would be something which on Saturn was made to flow out of the impressions that had influenced Saturn. The apparatuses which threw back those images into cosmic space were the first beginnings of what later developed into the eye, for instance. We might trace every detail like this. The things you have in your body today were a physical world on old Saturn which reflected the whole image of the cosmos back to it in space.

Myths and legends have retained the phenomenon much more clearly than we would think. The Greek myth taken from the Eleusinian Mysteries still has something of it in the image of Kronus and Rhea, except that the facts underwent one great shift because of the way in which the cosmos was seen in those early times. We are told that Kronus cast down his ray and it returned to him in many different ways; hence the image of Kronus devouring his children.

You should not think, however, that the mass of Saturn was as solid as physical bodies are today; even water or air would not give you an idea of the ground substance of Saturn. Speaking of bodies, occultists refer to solid, watery and airlike bodies. The elements of old were what chemists call states of aggregation today. You should not think that the ancients meant the same when speaking of elements as we do. But there is another, higher, state of aggregation which was called 'fire' by the occultists of old. 'Heat' or 'warmth' would be more appropriate. Physicists will be forced to admit that the 'heat' they speak of can truly be compared to a kind of fourth state of aggregation, a form of matter that is different from air and water. The Saturn mass had not even condensed to the consistency of air; it was purified heat. Its action was similar to the warmth in your blood today, and it was connected with inner life processes, for these physical processes were genuine life processes. Saturn consisted of heat matter, a tremendously subtle mass which with regard to our kinds of matter might be said to be neutral.

If we now consider the spirits that inhabited Saturn, we must in the first place be clear in our minds that the entity which goes about on earth today only had the first beginnings there of its physical body; I or astral body were not in it. But other spirits, which today are much higher than human beings, populated Saturn. They did not move around there in physical bodies but were embodied in heat matter, presenting as a current of heat moving along. Such heat currents were the activities of the spirits living on Saturn. As you shape a table today, so did these spirits do their work by causing heat currents. Apart from this they were not in evidence. They would meet and greet, as it were, on Saturn in the way in which two currents of heat would move hither and thither. The spirits that went through their human stage on Saturn did not have a physical body as their lowest principle; they did not descend into matter to a depth where they would have had need of a physical body. Their lowest principle was the I, just as you have the physical body as your lowest principle. Then came their Spirit Self or Manas, their Life Spirit or Buddhi, the Spiritual Human Being or Atman. And they had also developed an eighth, ninth and tenth principle which we must include in their case.

In theosophical literature these principles which human beings have not yet developed are called the 'three Logoi'; the Christian terms are the Holy Spirit, the Son or the Word, and the Father. We may say, therefore, that just as human beings consist of physical body, ether body, astral body and I, Spirit Self, Life Spirit and Spiritual Human Being so did the spirits dwelling on Saturn whom we may compare to today's human beings as they relate to the earth consist of I, Spirit Self, Life Spirit, Spiritual Human Being, the Holy Spirit, the Word or the Son, and the Father. In theosophy they are called Asuras. It is they which implanted independence, self-awareness and sense of self in that physical beginning of a human body. You would not be able at all to use your eye to serve the I if your beginnings at that time had not been prepared in such a way that you could make them serve the I.

The spirits of the I—also called the spirits of egoity—thus prepared these principles. They have given us something that is the wisest thing if properly developed. But all things most sublime are turned into their opposite, do the most damage and cause perdition if not properly developed. Human beings would never be able to reach the level which we call independent human dignity if those spirits had not implanted the sense of self in them. There have also always been spirits that took the evil route. We therefore have to say that the spirits which implanted selfhood, spirits which today are far above human beings, spirits we look up to as the most sublime there can be, have made selfhood serve self-denial, sacrifice; the others have continued to pursue selfhood in a self-seeking way.

We bear in us the influences of the spirits of the I which took the good route, in seeking freedom and human dignity; we also bear in us the seed of evil, for the spirits that had fallen away at that time continue to have an influence. People have always been sentient of this duality. In Christianity itself distinction is made between the Father God, seen as the spirit of Saturn which has risen highest, and his adversary, the spirit of all evil Is and all that is radically immoral, a spirit which fell away on old Saturn. Those are the two representatives of Saturn.

Just as you will meet other forms of existence after death, so does such a cosmic body enter into a kind of intermediate state before it enters into a new state. It is a kind of sleep state, a pralaya, the opposite of a manvantara,[35] so that a kind of rest, latent state, of the planet comes between the Saturn and the Sun state. Then the whole planet emerges in a new form from that sleep state—which is a spiritual condition, however, and not a resting state. Saturn thus emerged again, now as Sun. Then came a considerable change. An ether body entered into a great number of the potentials which had developed on Saturn and are today growing and developing within us. Something happens during such a planetary transition which we may compare with taking the fruit of a plant and putting it in the soil; it will rot away, but the potential for a new plant develops. Everything which had developed on Saturn came up as new potential on the Sun and took in an ether body. Not everything—some of it stayed behind so that the former potential for a human body split into two realms. Some rose to a kind of vegetable human being. Where plants today have their ether body and physical body so did the Sun human beings have a physical and ether body. And others remained at the mineral and physical level; we can compare them with today's mineral world. This the Sun included within itself as a subordinate natural world. It had elevated another to a vegetable-cum-human level. You will have the right idea of the Sun's air if you imagine a chemically dense gas no longer being just a mirroring body but now taking into itself everything that rayed towards it, only casting it back again after changing it within itself, which is the way it is with the colour of plants today. The plant produces its green pigment and other colours and then gives what it has developed to the world.

We cannot compare whatever lived in the Sun's body with an echo or mirror image as in the case of Saturn. A peculiar phenomenon arose for the spirits that were embodied on the Sun, something which can only be compared with a kind of mirage, mirrorings in the air in colourful images. Phenomena of this kind, today seen only in specific regions on the earth's surface, would be able to give you a sense of how the bodies of plants became visible at that time. You have to imagine that your own bodies had mirage-like precursors which a present-day body can simply pass through. They were as subtle as mirages but not only light effects but at the same time also sound and smell effects whizzing through the Sun's gaseous sphere. All entities on the Sun were luminous, like everything that exists as a fixed star is today. The old Saturn realm of the entities that had remained behind looked like a dark inclusion, dark patches compared to the light, like dim caves within the Sun's body, upsetting its harmony. It was particularly with regard to the world aroma that sensations got mixed in that came from the retarded spirits, spreading all kinds of bad odours. Mythology has held on to this, saying that the devil stinks and leaves behind an evil smell. As the Sun developed further a dark inclusion would indeed remain behind and today's sun spots are stragglers from old Saturn on the sun. This is also why they can be hypothetically explained with accuracy, the way it is done today; it all holds true.

We have now had a brief outline of the earth's Sun existence in its material aspects. Let us now see what spirits had reached the human level at that time. We would have to describe them by saying: Their lowest principle is the astral body, then came their I, Spirit Self, Life Spirit, their Spirit Human Being or Atman, then in Christian terms the Holy Spirit, and the Son or the Word. The Father was something they did not have, something which had developed only in Saturn time. These spirits have since risen higher and are far beyond human beings today. The leader of the Sun spirits, in so far as he had the greatest influence on the earth, the representative of these spirits which has the Son or the Word as the highest principle, is the Christ in the esoteric sense of Christianity, the true regent of the earth in so far as the earth has had Sun existence before. This was the teaching in early Christianity, and the very difference between true Christianity and exoteric Christianity which is based on many misconceptions is that the early Christians sought to use all thinking and all views in order to understand the real nature of the sublime spirit which had at that time assumed human form in Jesus of Nazareth. The early Christians wanted to have an idea of what was really behind this, and so no wisdom was too sublime and too difficult to handle, and they thus pictured the Christ in Jesus of Nazareth. Much that is said in John's Gospel will only be comprehensible to you if you consider it from this point of view. We need to point to just one thing. If you take the words 'I am the light of the world'[36] literally, they indicate that the Christ is the great Sun hero, that the light of the Sun is his true nature. We call the whole army of spirits who are led by the Christ 'fire spirits', and we say: At the time of Saturn the Asuras or I spirits were at the human level; at the time of Sun existence the fire spirits or Logoi, the most sublime representative of which has been called the Logos or Word. Thus the Christ himself is called the 'Word' which was there in the prime origin; 'prime origin' being the biblical term for a specific starting point in cosmic evolution.

There followed another in-between state, a kind of sleep state for the whole cosmic body, after which it shone out as old Moon. You have to consider that initially the present-day earth and the present-day moon were one with the sun. It was only when the Sun first shone out that some of the spirits and part of their environment separated off, resulting in two cosmic bodies. One of them, the sun, was beginning to change into a fixed star, with the part that had separated off orbiting it. The old Sun thus divided in two; substance which had been taken to a higher level remained on the Sun, and the less perfect parts were eliminated. Before this, things went one way, there being only one heavenly body. Now there were two ways—the Sun way and the Moon way. The Sun way developed on the Sun body; the Moon then developed its own world. You would have the old Moon if you were to combine the present-day earth with the moon; this will give you some idea of the consistency of the Moon. The present-day moon is far below the earth physically and non-physically where its qualities are concerned, and that is actually the reason why the earth separated from the Moon; it needed better conditions for the entities on it. The earth has since developed further, beyond its former Moon state. The best things had, of course, remained on the Sun.

What were things like on the Moon? The spirits that had prepared themselves on Saturn by laying the physical foundations for the sense organs had refashioned them on the Sun in that an ether body was incorporated; the sense organ had thus been centralized and the first beginnings for all organs of growth, including the glands, had developed under the influence of the ether body on the old Sun. This was one of the last products of the Sun state.

On the Moon, the astral body was similarly incorporated. Everything astral did, of course, first exist in the environment. The fire spirits had the astral body as their lowest principle; they were therefore a kind of plant, having a fixed habitat, for instance. The whole body of the Sun was gaseous, but you have to think of denser layers of air and these were bodies for the plant-human entities. Incorporation of the astral body led to the beginnings of a nervous system developing. The realm which had gone through the plant stage in its development on the Sun changed into something with animal nature. The physical ancestors of man therefore had three bodies—physical body, ether body and astral body—but were more than a degree higher than the most highly developed apes of today. They were animal and human, and nothing in biology today can prove to you that such an intermediate realm existed that was between human and animal. Today's vegetable, animal and mineral worlds altogether developed later. But just as there were human-animal entities, so we have to assume that a realm existed that was intermediate between plant and animal—plants with half capacity for sentience that would actually squeak if touched. These plant-animals could never have grown in the kind of mineral soil we have on earth today; but that actually did not yet exist then. The Moon mass did not consist of today's mineral matter, not even something like agricultural soil. The ground on Moon consisted, to use an analogy, of something like if one were to cook lettuce or spinach to a pulp. A kind of mineral-plant existed in it, and so the whole Moon mass was a vegetable entity. If you think of a peat bog of today, it resembles what at that time was a realm between our plant and mineral worlds. There were no rocks either; anyone walking on that ground would have been walking about on that kind of peat bog or vegetable soil, and instead of rocks you have to think of woody elements. The plant-animals grew from that ground, and the human-animal entities would move across them in the peripheral part of the Moon which is called 'fire air'. Think of all the air filled with saltpetre, carbonic and sulphuric acid vapours. The Moon's human beings lived in the fiery air which this would give you. Occultists have always known this fire air; and under the early earth conditions it was actually possible to produce such fire air chemically, something which can today only be done among a very few people. Knowledge of it has been preserved in genuine alchemy. So if we read in Goethe's *Faust I*, 'A bit of fire air, which I'll prepare,' we have an echo there of the very depths of occultism. Fire air surrounded the Moon, and was its atmosphere.

We may perhaps understand this Moon existence even better if we mention something else as well. We had a realm of plant-minerals, of animal-plants growing from the vegetable-mineral soil, and then the animal-human beings moving around. But there were also entities at every level that lagged behind, like children who have to repeat a year in school. They appear in very strange situations in the later stages of evolution. We have the laggard of the animal-plant realm in parasites, for instance in mistletoe. This plant is unable to grow in mineral soil because it was accustomed to grow in vegetable-mineral soil. It bears witness of something like a pupil lagging behind, though the entities which lagged behind in world evolution were much, much worse off than that. This, too, is reflected in the mythology especially of northern regions. You will know the story of Balder and how Loki brought about his death in Norse mythology.

The gods were enjoying disporting themselves in Asenheim, playfully throwing all kinds of objects around. But Balder had had dreams showing that his end was near. The gods were anxious, not wanting to lose him. Frigg had therefore made all creation swear that none would ever harm Balder; for the sport the gods were enjoying was to throw all kinds of things at Balder. Loki, the enemy of the gods, had learned that one entity, considered harmless, had not been asked to swear, and that was mistletoe, hidden somewhere far away. He got hold of mistletoe and gave it to the blind god who threw it at Balder. The mistletoe wounded Balder, for it had not been asked to give the oath, and thus Balder died.

The myth was intended to show that something invulnerable on earth can only be harmed by something which has belonged to an earlier time and was now bad. It was felt that there was something in mistletoe which had come into the present time from an earlier kind of existence. All the entities on our present earth have a relationship with Balder. It had been different on the Moon. An entity that had remained behind from Moon was therefore capable of causing Balder's death. Various customs and rituals connected with mistletoe have also developed from this.

We must now consider this Moon existence from yet another side, the spiritual side. The entities which were at the human level on the Moon have to be described as entities which had the ether body as their lowest principle, secondly the astral body, then the I, Spirit Self, Life Spirit, Spiritual Human Being or Atman, and then also the Holy Spirit. They no longer had the ninth principle that had only belonged to the fire spirits of the Sun. The highest of these spirits on the Moon, which had the human level at that time, are in Christian esotericism called the

Holy Spirit. In original Christianity the threefold divinity was therefore inwardly connected with earth evolution, with the Holy Spirit, the spirit which is above man and able to inspire human beings directly.

You see, therefore, that the spirits of the Moon are today above the human level. They are also called 'lunar Pitris', Moon Fathers, and spirits of twilight. The whole host, however, belonging to the Holy Spirit is in Christian esotericism called the host of angels. The angels are nothing but the spirits that are immediately above human beings and had the human level of existence on the Moon.

The life of animal-human beings and plant-animals on the Moon was different from the life of the entities on earth which developed from them. The movement of the Moon, which had already separated from the Sun, was very different from the movement of today's earth around the Sun. That Moon orbited the Sun by always facing it with the same side of itself, just as the present-day moon faces the earth, and therefore only went through one full rotation as it orbited the Sun. This meant that all entities depended on the Sun's existence in a totally different way than they do on earth today. During the whole period of the Moon's orbit around the Sun it was always day on one side of it, and a kind of night on the other. The entities which were able to change location at that time moved around the Moon in a kind of circle, which meant that they were under the influence of the Moon for a time. The time when they were under the influence of the Sun was the time when they reproduced themselves. A form of reproduction did already exist then. The Moon human beings did not yet have a possibility of expressing their pain or their pleasure in sound; what they did express was of more cosmic significance. The Sun period was a time of sexual ardour, being on heat, but when it was lived through it was connected with horrendous roars made by the entities, something which still survives in the animal world today.

Various other things have also remained. You know that the migration of birds is being investigated today. They, too, orbit the globe in a way. Many of the things that are mysteriously hidden today can be understood if we consider the whole evolution of our existence on earth. There was a time when life forms would only get ready to procreate as they were moving towards the Sun; we might call that the period of sexual life. Generally events in lunar life came to expression in sounds that came up at certain seasons of the year; silence reigned on the Moon at other seasons.

You have now got to know the earth's progress through three earlier states—Saturn, Sun and Moon.

LECTURE 10

KASSEL, 25 JUNE 1907

TODAY we'll consider how the old Moon changed into our earth. But before that we must refer to an important phenomenon in Moon evolution itself. When the things I spoke of yesterday had happened, the old Moon reunited with the Sun itself. It dropped back again into the Sun, as it were, so that there was a single body again. This then entered into a kind of sleep state of planetary existence, and the fourth metamorphosis finally emerged. It was not immediately the earth as we know it, for the earth state only came about after a long period of preparation. Looking at earth evolution we have a good example of a cosmic law which is that later states must in some respect recapitulate what had gone before. Before our earth could truly be our earth after waking up it had to recapitulate briefly the Saturn, Sun and Moon states. This evolution was, however, slightly different from that of the three planets themselves.

We learned that the first beginnings of the sensory apparatuses which we have existed on Saturn. At their first recapitulation these sensory formations had advanced so far that a kind of human form developed, though the automatic sensory apparatus did not as yet have an ether body. On recapitulation of the Sun state, the ether body came to be incorporated, and then the astral body at the third metamorphosis, the recapitulation of the Moon state. In the third stage, Sun and Moon were again floating separately in cosmic space. The entities had developed to a slightly higher level for they were more and more moving towards preparation for the things they would have to go through on earth. The three bodies which animal-human beings had on Moon were joined by a fourth principle, the I. This did not happen very quickly, however. When the earth went through its Saturn period, the whole human automatic sensory apparatus had to develop the form that made it possible for the I to be taken in. The ether body had metamorphosed during recapitulation on Sun so that it could be the vehicle for the I. The astral body had metamorphosed during Moon recapitulation so that it might take in the I. These principles were in a way waiting to take in an I at that time.

We have already had the separation of Sun and Moon. Then, when we are already coming closer to our own evolution, we have Moon and earth splitting apart. The old Moon turns into two bodies. One consisting of the worst forms of material, both entities and substances, was cast out into cosmic space; the other one is our present-day earth. The things that would have been an obstacle to further development for the entities had to be eliminated. It was only after this that the earth existed as an independent cosmic body. So we have tremendous cosmic events before us—the Sun separating out earth plus Moon, and then the earth itself separating out from the Moon. These two events were the preparation for our present evolution.

I have taken you to the point where our earth became an independent globe. Let me now take you to this point from another side, so that you will know exactly where this point comes for our earth.

Let us now go back from the immediate present into the past; starting out from the form of the earth, which you all know. Even in modern science reference is made to considerable differences between the earlier and the present appearance of the earth. It is all based on hypothesis, of course, but we can be glad that natural science and spiritual science are seeing a little bit eye to eye on this point. The regions where we live today were vast virgin forests and the climate was the way it is on the Equator today. Huge creatures would be encountered there. According to modern scientists the face of the earth was very different then. The tropical climate in today's temperate regions was followed by the Ice Age, and so on. You will find this in any book on geology today. I am telling you this so you are aware of how we must very much bring to mind that the face of the earth changes enormously through periods of time and then looks very different. Natural science, being limited to powers of deduction, its apparatuses and so on, can look back only on the earth's outward appearance for a number of millennia. When a seer looks back, he has to describe things in a somewhat different way, but harmony will one day be established between natural science and spiritual science. In natural science, attention is even today drawn to the fact which the seer has to insist on stating, which is that the face of the earth has changed not only with regard to plants and so on but that very different parts of the globe were land or sea in the past than they are today. Thus Huxley[37] has pointed out that a large part of Great Britain has been under water no less than four times. The face of our earth has therefore looked very different many times over.

In the journal *Kosmos*, No. 10,[38] you will for instance find an article on 'ancient Atlantis'. A learned gentleman, who bases himself wholly on natural science, discussed the configuration of the European flora and fauna to demonstrate that the area which is today the Atlantic Ocean must have been land in the past, and that large parts of Africa must have been not land but ocean at that time. Instead there was the land called Atlantis to the west of us, between Europe and America.

The author may only be able to speak of a flora and a fauna, but that is perfectly natural. Even if there were any remains to be found of those ancients, our ancestors, it should be possible to find them on the bottom of the Atlantic Ocean but it is not yet possible to explore the bottom of the Atlantic Ocean to that degree. A spiritual scientist looks back to the turning point of time and knows that the ancient Atlantis of which even Plato[39] still spoke did exist at that time. Essentially the whole area which is ocean today was ancient Atlantis, and the physical forebears of the human race of today did live there. They did, however, look very different from what people imagine in modern science. We simply must not compare them to present-day apes. Atlanteans differed greatly in soul and also body from present-day human beings, but they were not apes. Apes did not exist at that time; they only came later, and the way of it was that some human forms had then lagged behind at the level of development of that time and gone down to an even lower level. There is an error in Darwinism and it is easy to see what it is. If someone sees two people and is told they are related, one of them deficient in many things, the other, who has applied his abilities to good effect, an excellent person, he will not say: 'They are of the same blood, and the excellent person therefore is a descendant of the deficient one.' That, however, is the conclusion which is drawn in Darwinism. The excellent and the deficient person are, however, side by side; it is just that one has improved himself by using his abilities to good effect, and the other one has let them deteriorate and has grown decadent. This is also how apes—branched off from human beings—compare to human beings. An ape coming towards a human being looks to the latter like the caricature of a human being and not a human being as such. During the time of Atlantis, a very different human race existed which then developed to a higher level. Some entities remained behind. And because the earth changes, they too did not remain at that earlier level but deteriorated and became that caricature of human beings, the race of apes. Lower entities are therefore higher ones that have fallen into decadence.

Looking at the human beings on Atlantis we will best understand how they lived by considering their qualities of soul.

The things present-day human beings can do—think logically, do arithmetic and so on—have all come later. Logical powers of judgement, all this was still utterly unknown to the Atlanteans. But they had one inner quality which has grown much less today, and that is a sheer inconceivable power of memory. To do sums, having learned to follow the rule of two plus two makes four, and doing this again and again on the basis of personal judgement—that did not exist. But they were able to remember what happens when you put two and two together, and recall this again and again. This was connected with the fact that that ancient continent was very different by nature. If you want to imagine this continent in its physical nature, you will best get an idea of it if you think of a valley in the mountains filled with dense water vapours and billowing mists. Atlanteans never knew air that was not filled with water. Their air was always heavy with water. The ancient Atlanteans retained a memory of this when they came over to Europe and called the land where their ancestors had lived Niflheim, land of mists. It was only towards the end of the last third of Atlantean times that human beings began to realize that they are an I. The potential had been there for a long time and also a certain feel of it. But to say clearly and definitely 'I am an I'—that was something which they were able to do towards the end of the Atlantean age. This has to do with the relationship between ether body and physical body. Looking at these two bodies you see that they are more or less congruent, though the ether body projects a little beyond the physical body. There is a place between the eyebrows that is a focus for certain powers and currents in the ether body. A quite specific point in the physical brain belongs to this. The two must be congruent and that means the ability to be sentient of oneself as an I, also the ability to do sums, make deductions, and so on. The two points in the head are not congruent in idiots, for instance. Human powers of judgement are no longer present in the right way the moment the two go apart. Among Atlanteans it was normal for the two points to be apart. It is still like this with animals today; if you look at a horse's head you find the two points well apart. Atlanteans had a projecting ether head and the physical head had a receding forehead.

But Atlanteans had something else, though this was lost again when the physical body was integrated into the ether body. They had developed an ancient, dim clairvoyance, though they truly could not count to five. All judgement they had came from the power to remember back to an incredibly far distant past. And the old clairvoyance was an enhanced form of our present-day dream life. Think of this dream life enhanced to the highest degree and you would ascend to the powers of vision, to the old, dim, dreamlike clairvoyance of the Atlanteans. Walking along, they would indeed see human beings within their physical outline, roughly the way we see them today, but in some respect still nebulous, vague. But they would see something else as well. When you meet someone today you see nothing in particular of their inner nature, only as much as their faces show—if you get a darkling look you assume that there is a sadness and are able to guess a bit about the person's inner life. But when an Atlantean met someone who had evil intentions towards him a brownish red vision would appear; if the other loved him, he'd see a bluish-red vision. It was a kind of colour vision in tune with the other's state of mind; one still saw something of what was going on inside. When Atlanteans were walking along and a terribly reddish-brown mist would appear before them they would run away, knowing that a dangerous animal liable to devour them was clearly coming towards them, even if still miles away.

The ancient Atlantean clairvoyance even had a physical basis. Atlanteans would only consider their closest kin to belong to them, but to a much greater degree than was the case later on—only very small communities that would scarcely extend beyond the immediate family. It was of prime importance to marry only within this small blood-related group. Marriage within the narrow blood brotherhood produced such a blood mixture that the ether body could remain receptive to things spiritual. If the Atlanteans had attempted to marry outside the blood relationship the powers of clairvoyance would have been suppressed; astrally speaking they would have turned into idiots. To stay within the blood brotherhoods was ethical and moral. Before one got a real feeling for one's individual I one would altogether say 'This is I' with regard to the whole blood brotherhood. Individuals felt themselves to belong to the blood relationship, like an individual finger on a hand.

Something else also arose from this. Atlanteans would remember not only their own experiences but also those of their father, grandfather, great-grandfather and so forth through generations, all the way to the founder of the family. Everything coming from there and continuing on was felt to be a single whole. This will show you the enormous powers of memory which Atlanteans developed. It was all based on memory. We shall hear later how breaking through the system of marriage within the clan meant that that power of memory was lost.

A soul like that necessarily calls for a very different physical nature and also needs a different environment, like the Niflheim which the ancient Germans did remember. Legends and myths definitely are not folk tales or fantasies. You are now able to see where those legends came from. The Atlanteans still had an old, dim clairvoyance, and the things that were later told to others and have survived did actually happen there, though they have often lost much in the telling, in the legends and myths of different nations.

The eastward migration of Atlanteans has survived in a most wonderful way in a number of legends in Europe. On the ancient Atlantean continent human beings were not able to call themselves 'I'. They therefore also did not have the egotism which later became the basis of the social order. The Atlantean owned everything which all the blood relations possessed, and he would merely feel himself to be a part of this blood family. Then came the migration to the east. Awareness of being an I emerged more and more in individuals and with it also egotism. Before, people lived much more in the outside world than within themselves; nature also belonged to them. Now that they gained self-awareness everything narrowed down around them; they came to be more and more separate from the world, more and more of a stranger to it, with the I emerging more and more strongly. This was at the same time connected with a natural event. When ancient Atlanteans looked up to the heavens they could not see the sun the way we do; dense mists filled the air. They would see a mighty halo in rainbow colours when looking at the sun or moon. Then came the time when Atlanteans did see the sun and the moon as such. But one phenomenon which they did not yet know at all was the rainbow. There was no rainbow in that atmosphere heavy with water vapours. Now you will recall that the flood on ancient Atlantis left behind large stretches of dry land; this has been preserved in a magnificent way in legend and particularly in the Bible. Just think of the profound truth found in the Bible where it tells us how when the waters had abated Noah saw the rainbow.[40] It was only when the old Atlantean mists had been cleared away that the sun emerged in the distinct form which it also has for human beings today. This went parallel to the narrowing down, the tying up, of the human being to selfhood, I-nature.

There are deep reasons why in the wisdom of the spirit the light which fills space is called the etheric gold, and gold is seen as condensed sunlight. The ancient Atlanteans knew from their Atlantean teachers that sunlight and gold had something to do with one another, and this was the image they were given: 'Sunlight, the sun's gold, emerges. It puts the ring around you which frees the self, so that you will no longer feel yourselves to be selfless in the world of nature.' For the Atlanteans the self was still scattered in the clouds of mist; now it lay around the individual in a ring.

The mists of Atlantis cleared from the air, were pushed down and made their appearance as rivers in the west. The Rhine itself was nothing to the Atlantean descendants but the mists which have descended and now flow down. They would see the waters of the Rhine as still filled with sunlight; they would sense the sun's gold in the Rhine, sun's gold that had originally been selflessly active in ancient Atlantis. This was the treasure of the Nibelungs in the Rhine to them, and anyone who wanted to have the treasure of the Nibelungs for himself was the enemy.

Richard Wagner did not have full awareness of this tremendous, all-encompassing fact but was inspired to represent it in music. Remember the mighty pedal point in E flat major in the prelude to *Das Rheingold*—what is it but the point where the I entered into humanity? But just as a plant does not know the laws according to which it is growing, so the poet has no need to know. We have to see the creative artist as someone inspired by powers that are behind him. Here, a significant artist felt what has to be part of the human being again. We see therefore that provision is made that in art, too, the spirit flows into our culture which is also the basis of theosophy. It comes from two sides. This is how we must look at life as a whole.

We have so far been tracing the human being back as far as Atlantis. Let us also consider some details. People then did not build their houses the way we do today. Something they were able to make use of to a much greater degree, something which existed in the natural world, were rock masses, and these were shaped, also using the trees which existed there, and put together. People thus had houses for their homes that looked like part of nature. The further back we go the more do we find people endowed with clairvoyant powers, with conscious awareness in the form of images. They would see the feelings of entities around them rising before the inner eye in a visionary way. The will was also very different in the early part of the Atlantean age. Today your will can spread out your fingers; it is something which is connected with the present-day power to envisage things. In early Atlantean times the body was still a much softer mass. Atlanteans were able not only to stretch out their fingers but also to make them longer or shorter; they would have found it easy to make their hand grow. If they had a plant that was small they could make it grow by an effort of will. It was a kind of magic they had at their command. Their relationship to the animal world was also peculiar. They perceived something which later could no longer be perceived. Using their eye they were able to exert a power of fascination on an animal.

Going still further back we come to a time when Atlantis also did not exist and people lived on a continent which we call Lemuria. To the south of present-day Asia this continent extended as far as Africa and Australia. This is where our ancestors lived when they were still Lemurians. Their bodies were much softer than those of the Atlanteans, and their will was much more powerfully developed. On the other hand they lived on uncertain ground that was all the time thrown hither and thither in eruptions of fire, of volcanic forces. The ancient Lemuria was a kind of fire land. Going back to its beginnings we come to a time when the skeletal system was only just beginning to separate out from the boneless mass. Then we come to the time where the earth altogether had not yet produced the mineral world of today. Everything which exists as mountains today was then in a continuous motion and flow.

The further back we go in earth evolution, the higher are the temperatures we find. We then come to times when the configurations which are solid land today were flowing, as mercury or lead would do at a higher temperature today. Solidification only came for the Lemurians. The mists grew denser and denser. At that point there was not only a sea of mist but also a dense incandescent mass of water vapours with all kinds of substances dissolved in them, whirling to and fro. There were, however, some parts in this water vapour where the possibility existed for the human ancestor of that time to live. But life forms were very different then.[41] We are getting back to a time when human beings lived in a kind of prime ocean, in a warm, watery and fiery element. The earth's core was as if surrounded by a prime ocean which contained the seeds for everything that would evolve later. So that is how things were on earth immediately after the moon had left and grown independent.

We have got a glimpse of an evolution up to the point where the sun first separated from the earth and from the moon, then the moon from the earth, leaving the earth in the state I have just been describing.

Tomorrow we'll take another look at this process, which we have just now put together in two of its aspects, and also at the progress of humanity and the earth right up to our time.

LECTURE 11

Yesterday we reached the point in considering the evolution of the different states of our earth where we saw how the united three cosmic bodies—sun, moon and earth—separated off one after the other. On the one hand we started from there and stopped at the point where the moon separated from the earth; on the other hand we also sought to reach that point by starting from the present and going back through Atlantis to this same point. Let us be clear in our minds what the state of the earth itself was then. You have to think of long, long periods of time, millions of years, and then it will also not be so surprising how great the changes were in the universe and also on earth.

Let us now take a closer look at the separate earth. It was still enveloped in a mass of air, though this looked very different from our present-day atmosphere. You should not think that this air was something like the inside of a red-hot oven, although the temperature was much higher than today. Many substances that are solid today were then liquid in the earth. An air densely packed with the vapours of all kinds of substances enveloped the earth, something we might perhaps call fire air, a recapitulation of the former Moon state. When the earth had grown independent following the departure of the present moon, it was surrounded by a strange atmosphere which we might call fire air. Because the earth had become free of the atmosphere that had gone away with the moon the life forms were capable of gaining certain higher levels. Within this atmosphere the most advanced animal-humans had reached a higher level than the one they had had on the

Moon, but only those which later became human beings. A large number of these animal-human beings stayed at the Moon level. The result was that they did not just stay where they were but under the completely new conditions which pertained—animal-human beings could exist only on the Moon—went down by half a level and became animals which had not existed on the Moon. So we have two realms—human beings, and the world of animal-human beings which remained behind and gradually went down to animal level.

It was the same with the plant-animals. A number of them had developed further, into animals; others stayed put and became plants. And the plant-mineral world divided itself up so that some became heavy minerals and others developed into plants. Things did not develop according to one single standard; the animals we have today have partly evolved down from human-animals and partly up from plant-animals. In the same way the plant world consists of plant-minerals that have moved up to be plants and plant-animals that have moved down. The plants which today are mainly making up our aesthetic plant cover are plant-minerals from the Moon that have moved up, the violet, for example. But everything that strikes us as musty has evolved downwards, whereas our green herbaceous plants will move to higher levels in the future.

Our minerals have altogether evolved on earth. Nothing mineral as we know it today existed on the Moon. This is the plant-mineral world which has gone down, forming a solid crust in the earth. When the earth cast out the moon everything which remained to be mineral, solid metal and so on, later on was still altogether in the liquid state. Anything that had turned solid was flung out into cosmic space, for if the earth had retained these substances there would have been no further development. Then inclusions arose of the metals which were the earliest to grow solid. Some had strange forms. The granite, the gneiss in our mountains today did at that time still clearly show its origin in plant forms that developed down, turning to stone.

Essentially you may take it that on Sun and Moon the whole mineral world had still been plant world. The plant world did not evolve from the mineral world, but the minerals from the plant world! The anthracite you dig up today is but a sum of petrified plants, plants that perished, rotted down and turned to stone, so that they may today be dug up as plants turned to stone. If you were to go still further back, you would find that even the densest stones have once been plants, only coming into existence when plants developed down into the mineral world. For the seer, things are as follows. Looking at gneiss, mineralogists will say that it consists of felspar, hornblende and mica. That is as far as they can go. The seer says: 'The felspar in gneiss still shows itself to the spiritual eye to be the stem and green leaves that made up the plant which have grown solid, and the mica part has something to do with what does today still develop in the sepals and petals of plants.' So an occultist looking at a piece of gneiss will say: 'That is petrified plant, and where today the plants have leaves and flowers and so on, the mica part comes from the old sepals and petals.' We can tell how all minerals have developed from plants. For it was plants that came across from the Moon, and they only condensed in the fluid earth mass. It is like having a vessel filled with water today where the water begins to solidify, to form ice. More and more inclusions formed and gradually the solid earth crust evolved from the liquid earth. The further we go the higher and more pure will the life forms be; those that were unable to rise turned to stone. It was the same in the case of animals and human beings. Human beings got so far that they were able to refashion their body to a yet higher degree.

The Moon human beings moved by floating and swimming in the prime ocean; they were designed to swim around like this. This may sound most peculiar to present-day people, but it is true nevertheless. Let me say unreservedly: I don't even want to make any of this sound less grotesque. People will always laugh at truths when these first show themselves.

The human beings floating in the prime ocean did not have eyes that could see the way our eyes do today; the potential for eyes had been created on Saturn, but down there in the prime ocean human beings had no need to see; they had to get their bearings in other ways. The prime ocean also contained everything they consumed in order to keep alive. Some animals in the ocean were friends, others not so friendly towards them. The prime ocean was warm in places and cold elsewhere. Human beings were able to tolerate the former but not the latter. They still had an organ, the size of a cherry stone, which today is inside the head—the pineal gland, although it is not a gland in the usual sense. At one time this organ had been enormously developed. It was the organ they used to get their bearings in the ocean, and it projected from the head like a kind of lantern. Human beings moved around with the aid of this lantern-like structure. It was a subtly sentient organ, sensitive to temperatures, allowing them to perceive temperatures they were able to tolerate or not. This organ gave them their bearings but did not provide vision. It served them as they swam. Later it was no longer needed and therefore shrunk in size.

At that time one could not speak of even the potential for an I. Human beings depended on the guidance of higher spiritual powers in everything they did. We may roughly compare them to the animals of today. From the spiritual-scientific point of view, present-day animals are seen more or less as follows. Human beings differ from animals in that they have individual souls; every human being has an individual soul, an individual I or self. It is not like that in the case of animals. They have group souls. Thus all animals belonging to the lion family have a soul which lives in the astral world; all animals of the tiger family have one soul in common. All horses have one group soul; they belong together. Individual animals relate to their group soul as individual fingers relate to the hand. We therefore also cannot speak of individual responsibility. We only speak of a soul being good or evil once it is an individual soul. The human beings of that time still had a kind of group soul which was in the keeping of the Godhead.

It has to be clearly understood, therefore, that the principle which lives in us did exist at that time but it was not within the human body. Human beings have their origin in two streams. The animal-human being down below had come across from the Moon and developed further. But the individual soul which lives in you today was then up above, with the Godhead; only your body was down below, in the prime ocean. The two came together later on when the soul descended and inspirited your living body as an individual soul.

Think of a vessel filled with water; it contains many, many drops of water but one cannot tell them apart. If you now put in hundreds of tiny sponges, the droplets that were in the body of water will become individual. This is how you think of your spirituality hovering above the prime ocean. Compare the soul resting in the Godhead's keeping with the drop of water. The living bodies take in the souls just as the tiny sponges take up the drops of water. Souls became independent, just as the water has been individualized in the tiny sponges. Below the prime ocean with the floating, swimming bodies, and above the souls. There is no better way of describing this but to say: 'And the Spirit of God moved upon the face of the waters.'[42] It means that God developed the element which was below so that it became possible for the soul drops to be taken up.

The bodies themselves had to keep afloat and for this the entities needed an organ. At that time human beings did not yet have a lung, but they had a kind of air bladder that kept them afloat in the prime ocean. The fishes, which have stayed at this level, still have air bladders and no lungs today. The lungs developed slowly and gradually, as the air was cleared of water, and human beings were able to get above the waters and turn into air breathers. It was a long process, a process that took millions of years, with human beings gradually taking up air through lungs. This provided the physical structure which was able to take in the soul. You cannot put it better than 'And God breathed into his nostrils the breath of life, and man became an individual soul.'[43]

Human beings did at the same time gain the ability to develop something which they could not have developed earlier. They were now able to develop red blood. Earlier, all human beings had been made in such a way that their temperature was the same as that of their environment; with more warmth around them they would be adapted to that warmth. Red blood did not exist at all before that; the animals which are above the amphibians are human bodies that remained behind at a still later time. It was only after the time when human beings developed into creators of red blood that animals which had red blood also developed. No plant has ever evolved from a stone, but the stone developed from the plant. And in the same way animals developed from the human being. All lower creation has evolved from the higher; that is the principle of evolution. Human beings had to become red-blooded creatures before they could leave behind the animals. In the animals you literally see the stages spread out which we have left behind

us. Human beings more or less see a part of themselves in them which
they have left behind. Paracelsus put this beautifully: 'Looking around
us we see, as it were, the letters of an alphabet; it is only in man that
they come together in a word; because of this man is the meaning of
everything spread out about him.'[44]

There is one thing you must consider. A seemingly insignificant
process went on at that time which is however extraordinarily important
for the science of the spirit. Basically it had started when the earth first
appeared, still together with the moon. It was that Mars and earth
worked together, in a sense. During the whole first half of earth evolution, Mars powers flowed down on to the earth. Because of this that
first half is referred to as the earth's Mars state. Iron was connected with
this passage through Mars and from then on played a completely new
role in the earth process.

With plants, the role of iron is a much more external one. But you see
how things interrelate. Cosmically the earth passes through Mars and
Mars gives it iron. The iron was then stimulated to perform the functions which it now has. Iron appeared in the blood at that time. And
iron-containing blood means aggression for human beings, making
them warriors on earth. In Greek mythology Mars is therefore the god
of war.

The human body was then able to take in an I, for a body cannot be a
vehicle for an I unless it has warm, red blood. After this the processes
needed on earth developed, getting incorporated into the blood.
Human beings gradually evolved into a lung-breathing, red-blooded
life form and left the other creatures, the lower warm-blooded life
forms, behind.

In occult terms animals are differentiated not only in the usual way.
There is another characteristic. We differentiate them into creatures
that have inner sound, those able to give expression to pain and pleasure
in sounds, and those that do not produce sounds. If you move down to
lower animals you will also hear sounds but these are merely external,
produced by rubbing organs together or through external climatic
influences. The sounds are produced externally. Only the animals which
branched off at the time when human beings evolved into warm-
blooded creatures were of a kind that could utter pain and pleasure in

sounds coming from inside. It was at that time in the past when the human larynx was transformed into an organ that produces sounds. With the liquid earth outside changing into a crust, an inner process happened in human beings. Parallel to the solidification outside, the soft parts inside became a skeleton of bone and cartilage. Before that, bony creatures did not exist. The minerals in the outside world are the counter-image to the bones. The earth has preserved this period in its rock masses, human beings have done so in bone. Man was progressively changed from a creature that was horizontal as it moved to one who went around in an erect posture. He turned that way so that his fore-limbs became organs for work, and only the other limbs served loco-motion. The two things were connected. No creature can have I nature unless it has a larynx that produces sound and also walks erect.

The animals did have the potential for this but they regressed. They have therefore been unable to change into creatures endowed with speech, for that needs a vertical larynx. We can see this if we consider a perfectly commonplace fact. Some dogs are undoubtedly more easily taught things than parrots are; but a parrot does learn more because its larynx is vertical. Parrots and starlings learn to talk a little because they have a vertical larynx.

So you see how earth and man progressed through more and more stages of evolution. The atmosphere changed at the same time; the condition arose where the earth was merely surrounded by misty air. This was at the time when the Lemurians saw their continent scatter and migrated across to Atlantis. This made them Atlanteans. During this stage of evolution, when human beings acquired the first elements of speech—though these were mere sounds reflecting sensations they felt—the soul did also emerge more and more. Atlanteans had essen-tially retained a dim clairvoyance. Now the eyes had developed to the degree to which human beings, rising up from subterranean depths of the sea, received such sunlight as penetrated the mists. They were able to see and perceive more and more, but the old clairvoyance was all the time regressing. It was only in the last third of the Atlantean era that the most advanced race of Atlanteans had evolved at one point on the earth's surface. That was a most significant conclusion to that era.

The Atlanteans who had moved more to the west became inwardly neutral under the conditions then prevailing, cold, indifferent. They became the copper-coloured population of America. The others, who migrated more to the south, became the negro population, and those who turned more to the east later became the yellow, Malayan populations. These masses of people had concentrated in the most unfavourable places where one could not go any further. But in the place where Ireland is and to the west from there, where there is ocean today, human beings had been able to evolve most. There you had those mixtures of warm and cold that allowed the human body to progress most. Will power, still magical then, evolved into the first beginnings of an unspoken sense of I. It was at this very point that human beings learned to say 'I' to themselves for the first time. Then came the first steps in counting, reckoning, the beginnings of powers of judgement, making combinations. But there were always also advanced individuals among them, the guides of humanity, who related to people the way spirits from a higher realm do. They had become the teachers and guides and gave the impetus for migration to the east.

Nations had moved from that point in today's Ireland all the way across to the east and to Asia. Now the most advanced mass populations moved eastwards and established some kind of colony everywhere along the way. The most powerful, with the most highly developed civilization, was in the vicinity of today's Gobi desert. From there individual groups later went into all kinds of different regions in the world, some of them to present-day India; they found existing populations there, with yellowy-brown skins, and partly mingled with them.

It was after the flood on Atlantis that this colony went south and established the first civilization of the post-Atlantean era, the first civilization in our era. The most advanced teachers who went with them, the first teachers of ancient India, are known as the ancient Indian Rishis. Present-day Indians are descendants of that earlier population but to come upon the traces of their civilization we must go a long way back into times where darkness reigns for the study of history. The Vedas came later than this; for nothing was recorded in those times. The ancient Indian people were the first civilized group in post-Atlantean times, and they were still closest to the Atlanteans. The Atlantean was a kind of dreamer. His conscious awareness was dim, and he had no powers of judgement and self-awareness; he went about like a dreamer, half unconscious. The ancient Indians were the first to have overcome this state but were still half caught up in it. Because of this the ancient Indians still had that longing for experiences in the old land of spirits and for the vision that Atlanteans had had.

Ancient Indian yoga training still took people back, in a state of reduced consciousness, into the time when human beings still saw the spirits around them. The Indians would long to be back in the time when people had clairvoyance on Atlantis, and in their yoga training the Rishis would teach the methods which were then, however, given a different form. The Atlanteans had not yet developed powers of judgement; in India people did have those powers but they loved, as it were, something which had been overcome. They knew how to evoke it again, reducing consciousness and remembering the visions of earlier times. Indian civilization had still preserved this in its greatest representatives. Indians sought not to increase conscious awareness but reduce it to a dreamlike level—hence the inactivity which one sees in Indians. And it would be grossly detrimental for Indian life to take up our present-day civilization to any greater degree.

In the beginning, human beings had never seen minerals at all; Atlanteans would still see minerals in the vaguest possible way. The world of the spirits was there in their visions; it was this which lived in everything. They would see colours around a human being, nice colours if that individual was nice to them. That was the kind of world the Indians sought to conjure up again. But human progress means that people must develop more and more of a relationship to things in the material world. The Atlanteans had no need of tools; they took their orientation from their visionary powers—they did not consider tools important. The Indians were still trailing behind the Atlanteans; this is why the physical world was maya to them, an illusion in a way, a lie. They were not interested in the world perceived through the senses. They would say: Rise to the world of dreamlike spirituality.

Progress from that Indian civilization to a later age was that in the next civilization, the Persian, which was before Zarathustra, people came to appreciate the external reality around them. This was a second colony to have come from the Gobi. A far distant realm arose in Asia

Minor, and the realm of Zarathustra arose from this. The Persians came to realize that there was a world around them in which they must be active. The divine was something to them with which they must connect. Two godheads existed for them—Ormuzd and Ahriman. Matter still seemed to them to be something they must overcome, something to measure themselves against. They were still taking the powers they needed to do work in this world from the world of the spirit. The world was something dark to them that had to be transformed using the light of the good.

The Indians established a body of knowledge of the purely spiritual world, but this did not tell them anything about the real world they lived in. This world was something different to the Persians, something to be constantly transformed by their labours.

The third colony to come from the Gobi moved on to Asia Minor and established the Chaldean, Babylonian, Egyptian civilization. These peoples had the earlier science of the spirit and now also a body of knowledge relating to the earth world. The Egyptians developed an astrology, a geometry, by which they learned how to treat and cultivate the soil. Their knowledge extended to the sphere where the Indians still spoke of illusion. Now the world of illusion had become a world of astute reflection, reflections on things perceived through the senses. When an Indian contemplated the world of the stars it would reflect the spiritual for him. The Chaldean, however, loved the physical world; to him it was the part of the Godhead which you worked into, focused on. And working one's way from the divine to the sense-perceptible is something we also see in the Babylonian and Assyrian civilization.

We now come to the fourth civilization, the one we call Graeco-Roman. There the actual human being was the subject of careful study. The Egyptians had known that the world was not chaos but built in a meaningful way through countless aeons. The Sphinx and the pyramid reflected great cosmic truths. The ancient Egyptians would magically make their knowledge part of the picture; they created the Sphinx which stands before us like a riddle of evolution—the higher principle of human nature evolving from earlier animal-like states. That was the wisdom which the Egyptians would in their own way express to the world. And you find surveying skills there that have been taken from the heavens. The cities were arranged in such a way that a sacred order was reflected in the way in which they were built, an order that was prescribed. The Egyptians would seek to present a reflection of the order of the heavens. But it did not extend to individual human nature. This you find only in Greek art, where human beings were already grasping themselves in immediate reality, seeking to create their own image in three dimensions.

Human beings were growing more and more familiar with the world which the Indians would call maya. Man met himself. He created a world within the Indians' illusion, and was aware of the fact that he had to create this world without help from the gods. He connected more and more with the real world outside, using his own powers to create the divine in the real world outside. But when you study the Greek *polis* [city or city state] you find nothing there that had to do with rights and laws. This had to be established in the Roman world as the law of Rome, living with others as a private Roman citizen.

The fifth civilization is our own materialistic world. It is the time when man has descended deepest into the outside world. Compare our time with those that went before. We do know how to apply the powers of the spiritual world to the world around us; we take the spiritual world into everything. But from the point of view of spiritual science this offers a peculiar prospect. Remember the time when people still ground their flour between two stones. They used little mental power for this. But in ancient Egypt and Chaldea they would enter deeply into the wisdom of the heavens; there much was told of the spiritual meaning of the starry heavens and the earth itself. The Greeks created the idealized human form, making it part of this real world.

What is the picture today? Much mental power is used to develop our natural science using technical applications. But how great is the difference if you use primitive means or we use the telephone, machines and so on to bring foods over from America which merely serve to satisfy a need here which the animals also satisfy? Try to see how much of everything created serves the life of the spirit and how much mental power is used for material life. Think of the enormous mental powers humanity has to develop today to satisfy material needs! There is no great difference between an animal going to feed on grass and us using all kinds of means to bring foods over from America and Australia. But this is not disparaging criticism, for it has to be. Human beings have had to enter so deeply into this world.

The ancient Indians still saw the world as illusion; today we see this world as the only real one. We have gone down to the greatest depth and in doing so have made the greatest advances on the physical plane. But the descent must not be for nothing, also in the spiritual sense!

A new element has come up in our time, something literally implanted into the first third of the post-Atlantean age. It is the coming of Christianity, the most significant event altogether in earth evolution. For the occultist, everything that went before has been mere preparation for Christianity. Buddha, Hermes and so on have been prophetic pointers to Christianity which is to raise humanity from being most deeply caught up in matter. And it will do so. The ascent from matter is now beginning. And it is the task of spiritual science to help humanity to ascend to the world of the spirit.

The next period of post-Atlantean civilization will bring even more discoveries but human beings will increasingly see the outside world as just the letters. A genuine Christianity will speak of that world in the way in which we speak of condensed spirit, and the spirit will rise again for us from matter. We will not say that the outside world is illusion, we'll have the whole of it and lose nothing and yet rise to higher things in the spirit. And Christianity will make the greatest contribution to this development. In the sixth period the things which today are made known to only a few will be able to reach vast numbers of people and take them along with them, and with this humanity will gain insight into the spiritual world. The thought of today will be a power in the future. Many will have this power of thought in the sixth period of civilization; they will be creative, influencing even the human form.

The human body looked very different in the past from the way it looks today; you'd be surprised if I were to describe it to you. But the body was still soft then and so the I had a much greater influence on its configuration. Today only a sparse remnant remains of the influence which the soul's will once had on the body's configuration. You'll go pale if you get a shock because your state of soul affects even the blood; the colour of the body changes. Looking at other bodily states you will see, however, that human beings have little influence on their body. This will change again in the ascent; the body will grow softer and softer, and the human being will have an influence on it again by letting his thoughts grow stronger and stronger, thoughts that do not come up very much today. They will then refashion the body itself. Human beings will be able to create their own bodies again, though this will only be in a far distant future.

Gender nature was only imposed on humanity during the Lemurian age; before that they were hermaphrodite, both male and female. As the I came to be integrated, human beings fell apart into two genders. We shall know more about that moment when we take a closer look at the progress of human blood. We will then consider this problem of division into genders and also of the future disappearance of gender division.

We are thus looking towards a future when human beings will be able to influence their bodies again but in a very different way.

What is going on when someone goes red from embarrassment? What does this mean? A last remnant of the influence human beings had on their body in the past. They will be able to work into their bodies more and more, deliberately so. And then a time will come when human beings will be able to make their heart muscle into a voluntary muscle. In modern science the heart is presented as if it were a mere physical apparatus, a pump. But the blood does not just flow through the body because the heart pumps it through. Everything in the blood depends on the soul. The blood pulsates faster or more slowly under the different feelings, and it is the blood which produces the movement of the heart. But in future human beings will gain a deliberate influence on the heart, and the heart is therefore an organ which is only at the beginning of its evolution. It is a muscle of spiritual evolution, an organ in which human beings who have advanced to a higher level will express themselves and so act creatively on the whole rest of the body.

The heart is only in the beginnings of its evolution, and this makes it a problem for materialistic science. Scientists will tell you that all muscles you use to move around are cross-striated; in involuntary muscles, like those in the digestive system, the striations run lengthways. The heart is a unique organ for it turns it all upside down. It is an involuntary muscle, and its muscle fibres are cross-striated, for it is on the road to higher development and therefore has cross-striated fibres even today.

Tomorrow I am going to show you how some things become clear when we consider them in the light of occult science.

Theosophy is thus spreading light on the world around us. We redeem everything which has become matter from its frozen state. That is the concept of redemption in its most profound nature. Humanity has evolved; certain realms were always left behind in the process. Humanity will grow powerful and redeem all that has been left behind, and they will redeem the earth, too. They must not despise it, however, but must connect with it in order to redeem it.

LECTURE 12

YESTERDAY we sought to trace human evolution cosmically and also on this earth. Today I will merely add a few things on the subject and then make the transition to theosophy and what it has to say on Christianity and also on Christian initiation. To begin with I would ask you to turn the mind's eye once more to the very beginning of human evolution.

We have been saying that when the present-day moon separated from it the earth was surrounded by a kind of prime ocean, describing how the physical human being did at that time unite with the human being of spirit and soul. We then followed the evolution right to the present day, seeing that our time is the one when humanity has gone down deepest in mind and spirit into matter. We realized that there has to be an ascent now, growing spiritual, and have also spoken of the mission which theosophy or the science of the spirit is believed to have with regard to this evolution.

We have also pointed out that the separation into two genders happened in ancient Lemuria. Two genders did exist for lower life forms on the Moon, but the human being who dwells in each and every one of you was only divided into two genders then, when entering into a physical form. We have to think of the earlier human being—before division into two genders, one male and one female—as a condition where sexuality as we know it did not exist at all as yet, or at least took a very different form. A great deal depends on our understanding the great significance which the things I have just been saying had for the whole of human evolution.

For if the separation into two genders had not happened, if present-day humanity had not completed its evolution in the world with male and female working together, the human being would have been configured in a completely different way. The individual element in us is due to the male influence. Yesterday I explained the difference between group soul and individual soul. This is very different in animals. Animals have gender even on the astral plane. Man simply did not have two genders on the astral plane before he entered drop by drop into the individual human beings; he had not yet fallen into gender division, as we are wont to say. If the genderless state of humanity had reproduced itself in the physical world, that is, if a kind of non-gender state had taken the place of the two-gender state, it would not have been possible to give the human being individual nature. The whole point of human evolution is that human beings grow more and more individual.

If we were to go back once more to the time of which I spoke yesterday, we would see how human beings were very much like one another in their outer form. The two genders then worked together to create the individual differences, and these individual differences are getting more and more individual the further humanity moves into the future. Without separation into genders the generations would always look much the same. We actually have to say that it is due to having two genders that human beings are getting progressively more independent.

In those very early times and on into Atlantean and indeed post-Atlantean times you see dominance in humanity of 'close marriage', as we call it, and this was only gradually replaced by 'distant marriage'. In the far distant past people would marry close blood relatives and within small clans. You will find that among all nations it was considered unusual for a member of the tribe or clan to marry into another tribe or clan, and that it was always considered an important event.

The further we go back we find that it was moral for people to marry within tribes that belonged together, blood only mingling with related blood. We can best show this by looking at a comparison—lame like all comparisons but nevertheless to the point. Let me tell you a bit of a story.

You will have heard of Anzengruber and Rosegger. Rosegger[45] is a writer who shows great devotion in telling stories about the people in the village. Anzengruber[46] also knows his subject well and is able to present country people in his plays that are true to life. Rosegger and Anzengruber went for a walk one day,[47] and Rosegger said, 'I know you never really look at the country people; you might present them even better if you were to visit them in their village.' Anzengruber said, 'It would probably send me round the bend if I were to do that. I actually have never made the closer acquaintance of farmers; the fact that I am able to present them the way I do is due to the fact that my father, my grandfather and all my forebears were farmers, and so I have farming in my blood. It is out of this farming in the blood that I create my figures, not bothering with the others; I've still got it in the blood, as it were.'

This is an interesting fact which takes us to the subject we are considering. If the blood stays unmixed, as it was in the early tribal communities or the Anzengruber farmers, you get the kind of powerful phenomenon which also existed as a last embodiment in the writer Anzengruber. He had inherited the power to create those figures and was well aware of this. The power had come down through the blood of generations. That is how it truly is where blood mingles only with related blood. Mixing in other blood extinguishes the creative power in the soul. If Anzengruber had married someone who belonged to a completely different class his children would no longer have had this power to configure.

We can observe this phenomenon in the early days of almost all nations that have a long history. Marriage within small blood-related clans always meant extraordinary powers of memory. It was connected with the faint, dim clairvoyance. You will remember what you have lived through from birth and consider it part of your individual nature. Before close marriage was replaced with distant marriage, people would literally remember what their grandfather and forebears going a long way back had lived through; they would say 'I' and remember the lives of their grandfather, great grandfather and so on. The further we go back the more do we find a memory that extended back through generations.

And the interesting thing is that people did not feel themselves to be individual Is; they would say 'I' to their grandfather by adopting the same name as all the others. Just as you have the right to take a name today which refers to you as an individual, so these people gave themselves a name that extended far back through centuries, because birth did not mean a break in memory. The individual human being did not have a name, for birth was no special event. People would have one name for everyone as far back as the thread went. The Bible documents this for you. All disputes over the significance which the names of the Patriarchs had are just academic. Adam was Adam and the age he was because any descendant of such a figure would feel himself to be at one I with him. Thus everything where the blood flowing through the centuries generated such memories would have borne the name 'Adam'. For as long as the memory continued through the generations and people remembered the events their forebears had known as if they'd been there themselves, for that long would one say that Adam was still present. People did not feel themselves to be individual physical entities, but felt themselves to be something which was there in the spirit and held people together.

Then distant marriage became more and more common and the mixing of the blood would increasingly kill off the memory that went beyond a single human individual. The narrowing down of memory was a consequence of distant marriage. That was the progress of humanity, that the individual was growing more and more beyond the tribe. In the common blood shared in the tribes lay also the common expression for this blood—love. Those of the same blood loved one another. In the course of time, however, that love, which we may call the prime love, bound to the blood, which had led to a whole family being created, would die away. That love in the past was very different from the love that shines out to us from the future. Love through the blood was still dominant in post-Atlantean times—those who have the same blood flowing in their veins loved one another. But this will disappear more and more; people are increasingly moving away from close blood relationships and growing individual.

The prime love, which arose when the souls descended into the physical bodies, was therefore diminishing in the course of time. It had flowed into human beings at the moment which in the Bible is referred to in the words 'And the Lord God ... breathed into his nostrils the breath of life and man became a living soul.'[48] Something else also came into being at that time. Man had become a living soul and with this a lung-breather. The air he inhaled gave him his red blood, and I nature came to expression in the red blood. For as long as the blood was common, the I was common, as in the case of the Jewish people where a whole nation was governed by one group soul. But human beings matured more and more so that they no longer depended on blood relationship. When the breath had entered into man, that was the first potential for the ability to form blood. It took long periods of time, however, before humanity was ripe to work this blood through to the point where general love of humanity could take the place of that prime love.

Think of the progress of humanity, as I have just described it. Prime love would gradually die out; love within the family—a mother's love for her child and so on—would have to grow less. The influence of the blood was no longer such that a bond of love might embrace the whole of humanity, and the power of the I, the power of egotism would grow and grow. An event then had to come which called up a love other than the prime love, a spiritual love. That event was Christianity. With the coming of Christianity the development which would have had to come was held back—the whole of humanity splitting up into individual people. Human beings have to grow more and more independent. That is part of the evolution of the blood. But now there was need to bring together in a spiritual way what had been driven apart in the natural course of events. The new power which could now come into play without the love in blood relationship—that was Christianity. The Mystery on Golgotha thus gains fundamental significance for the whole of human evolution. If we understand this we also understand the significance of the words 'the blood of the Christ'. It is not something we can learn and explore in purely external ways but something which must itself be seen as a mystic fact. Because of this my book has in full awareness been given the title—not 'the mysticism of Christianity' but *Christianity as Mystical Fact*.

To understand what Christ Jesus himself was on earth, to understand that Christianity has fundamental significance, we need to consider the preparations that preceded Christianity. They had gone on through all

the ages that went before. You can really see how a Christian of old saw
this if you take a passage from the works of St Augustine. 'Christian
religion, as it is called today,[49] has always been the true religion, it is
merely that the true religion of earlier times is now called the Christian
religion.' Augustine still knew that Christianity had a precondition—
the things done in the ancient mysteries. And it is exactly this which is
to be revealed to humanity through the theosophical movement. Let me
characterize it in a few words.

Schools existed that were at the same time also church and art centre.
These schools were run by the leaders of humanity, individuals who
were most advanced in their development. People considered to be
mentally and spiritually ready to gain their own view of the spiritual
world around us were admitted to those schools. They were carefully
prepared in that they must first get to know the facts of the spiritual
world theoretically, more or less the way we learn things in spiritual
science today. Then came progressively higher levels. Learning became
living, the exoteric esoteric. They were taught everything in a living
way. A strict rule stated how the disciple had to arrange his life so that
he might slowly rise to vision of the spiritual world. Disciples first
learned the facts and laws of the spiritual world, and then did prescribed
exercises to create the organs that would allow them to see into this
spiritual world.

I'll now tell you the last act in this. You have to remember that
human sleep means that the astral body is outside the ether and physical
body, and that death consists in the physical body being left on its own,
with the ether and the astral body united. What happened was that the
head of the mysteries, the hierophant, would use the special methods
they had to treat the human being in such a way that the physical body
would lie there as if dead for three and a half days, and the ether body
would be outside with the other principles that made up the human
being. It was neither sleep nor death but a third thing. Everything had
been arranged so that the individual would during those three and a half
days move through the higher worlds. Thanks to the directions given by
the hierophant initiator he would now get to know the things that we
have described in the previous lectures. He would get to know it from
direct perception. After the three and a half days he was a twice-born

individual. On his return he would remember everything he had lived
through in those other worlds; he was now a living witness of the reality
of such worlds. His words would be different now from the way they
had sounded before. He was one of the 'blessed' [in harmony with the
spiritual world] and the words 'Blessed are your eyes because they see'[50]
would apply to him.

On his return he would be given a completely new name; he laid
aside his name and as an initiate continued under his new name. And a
strange thing happened when he descended again into his physical
body, when he was again able to live in the physical world. The words
would break forth from all new initiates—this was law—'My God, my
God, how greatly have you glorified me!'[51] This was what someone who
had advanced so far would feel. He would say of himself: 'Everything
that remained of that prime love, something which had to be implanted
in human beings through the blood, has to be replaced in me by a love
that knows no difference between mother, brother, sister and other
human beings.' He had in the spirit left parents, wife and child, brother
and sister, and had become a follower of the spirit. In him, it was said,
the Christ had come to life.

All this had happened in the seclusion of the mysteries. People like
that bore witness of the spiritual world. People like that were also
prophets, for they would point to a coming event, and that was indeed
the Mystery on Golgotha. What had happened for individuals in the
occult schools then happened once and for all in the physical world and
was for all humanity. If you were able to know the rules for the initiates
of old, you would see that they concluded with those three and a half
days. The event had never before happened on the physical plane. But a
new age then began. So you may be able to say to yourself: 'All those
initiations were prophetic forecasts of what would happen in the Mystery on Golgotha; it could only have happened because an individual as
all-embracing as the regent of the sun spirits had incarnated in the body
of Jesus of Nazareth. No human I of the kind we have in us could have
done what was done on Golgotha. This needed an I which had already
advanced that far on the sun.'

In this way we grasp the God-and-man nature of Christ Jesus which
is so much denied today because people are no longer able to enter into

the depths of the spiritual world. And so we see, if we consider the matter in the right light, how something happened on Golgotha the significance of which goes far beyond anything else that ever happened.

Among the great minds of more recent times, only Richard Wagner has had an inkling of the significance of blood. I explained to you how human glandular life reflects the ether body, the life of nerves the astral body, and the life of blood the I. I have shown you that if the Christ had not come the blood would have developed towards greater egotism; the I would have increased self-seeking, dominance of I nature more and more. The blood that was in excess in humanity had to flow out, be sacrificed, lest they gave themselves entirely to self-seeking. A true mystic saw the blood that flowed from the redeemer's wounds as the excess blood flowing out. It had to flow so that humanity would not fall into utter egotism but a brotherly love in mind and spirit might take hold of the whole human race. That is how the spiritual scientist regards the blood flowing from the cross which had to be taken in by humanity so that they might rise above the material. The place of the love that was held together by the blood had thus been taken by a future love that goes from one human being to the other. This alone allows us to understand the words of Christ Jesus: 'Anyone who comes to me and does not disregard his father and mother, his wife and children and his brothers and sisters ... cannot be my disciple.'[52] This has to be taken to mean that through the deed on Golgotha everything which before had to be given substance by related blood, by love among relatives, has been overcome. Someone who put the new love, love in mind and spirit, in its place was entitled to say that the old love had to be let go. That is the situation.

The coming of the Christ itself is a profound mystical fact and can only be understood if one does not apply the standards of natural science. Anyone who did this would be like someone who sees a tear fall and wants to consider it only according to the law of gravity and not as something which reflects the state of mind.

Such insights can only be gained through the science of the spirit. Because of this, the coming of the Christ on earth differs from the coming of all other founders of religions. The others have given doctrines. When it comes to Christ Jesus we can truly say: 'Almost every word he said had been said before in one context or another. With Hermes and the Buddha it was important what they said. With Christ Jesus what matters is that he was present on earth, lived on earth, and that the Mystery on Golgotha did happen.'

Those who wish to be Christians in the true spiritual-scientific sense are Christians because they believe in the divine nature of Christ Jesus. The first disciples did not only say, 'We have been sent out to proclaim the words,' but they were meant to be witnesses of his existence, 'which we have heard, and have put our hands in his wounds'.[53] It is the fact of his presence which matters. Think of the other religions without their founders—you would not lose anything. Think of Christianity without the Christ—and there would be no Christianity. That is the difference. People like Darwin, Strauss, Drews and so forth may say as much as they like that the teaching of all other religions may be found in Christianity, but that is not the point. The point is that the Christ came to earth, and that he enacted the things foretold by the prophets so that they were reality, fact. Christianity is not a doctrine but a power. If you were able to ascend from here to another planet, you would see not only the earth but also the earth's ether and astral body, the spiritual earth as well as the physical; and if you had been able to stay on that planet for millennia, starting from the time before the coming of Christ Jesus, you would have seen how the colour of the astral body in the earth's spirit changed because the Christ was there. The earth has truly changed, and the human beings who have been living since the coming of the Christ have lived in a changed world and this has given them the ability to overcome the deepest descent of the spirit. In earlier times people had to be raised into the spiritual world in order to know about it; with Christianity the mystery itself has descended. For physical eyes it was a historical event. The god had to descend to guide humanity back to the spiritual from the physical world.

This is how Christianity is described for you in the purest of the Gospels, the Gospel of John. It is not fiction but a book of life. Only someone who has lived it knows what the Gospel of John truly is; living it you are able to proclaim everything that has been said today as your own truth.

I'd now like to tell you briefly how human beings can gain insight into Christianity.

The Gospel of John is the one among the many books which gives the methods that can help us to fathom the depths of Christianity. Christianity was taught in the schools even when it did not yet exist in its present form, for instance in the school of Dionysius the Areopagite, a disciple of the apostle Paul. In those earlier times it was customary to give the same name to the actual bearer of the mysteries, so that the individual to whom the secrets had come down and who wrote them down also bore that name.

Entering into the first words of the Gospel of John from the esoteric point of view one has the experience that they are a power of awakening within one. One must, however, use the Gospel of John the way it was used originally, and have the patience to take up the first sentences in the Gospel as material for meditation, letting them pass before one's soul every morning. It is then a power which will bring forth powers that lie hidden deep down in the soul. One must, however, have a correct translation. It must express approximately in the words of one's own language what was really said in the original. Let me show you in a translation which is as correct as possible that the Gospel's actual life in the spirit is presented in the words:

> In the Beginning was the Word, and the Word was with God, and the Word was God.
> This was in the Beginning with God.
> Through the same everything entered into existence, and without this nothing entered into existence.
> What existed was life in this, and the life was the light of mankind.
> And the light shines in the darkness, but the darkness has not taken hold of it.
> There entered into existence a man sent out from God. His name was John.
> He came as a witness to bear witness to the Light so that everyone might believe through him.
> He was not the Light but a witness of the Light,
> the true Light who enlightens every human being coming into the world.

It was in the world, through it the world entered into existence but the world was not aware of it.

It came to individual human beings, all the way to the I-endowed human beings, but the individual human beings, human beings endowed with I, did not take it in.

Those who did take it in were able to show themselves through it to be children of God.

Those who put their trust in his name were born not of the blood, nor of the will of the flesh or the human will, but of God.

And the word has become flesh and has dwelt among us, and we have heard its teaching, the teaching of the only-born son of the father, full of dedication and truth.

I might now tell you many things about how you would have to enter into the individual chapters of the Gospel of John. Let me give you just a taste of how you would need to use the chapters from the thirteenth onwards if you were a genuine disciple of Christian initiation. I am telling it to you in words, but it has actually taken place. To help you to understand I'll put it in the form of a dialogue. This might give you an idea of what happened between teacher and pupil.

The teacher said to the pupil: 'You must develop a feeling in you; think in the following way. Enter into a plant. If it were able to have conscious awareness as you do, and if it were able to look down at the stones with this conscious awareness, it would say: "Dead stone, you are at a lower level than I am in the ranks of entities; I am at a higher level. But would I be able to exist as a plant today if it were not for you being there as a stone? I get the juices that feed me from you. I would not exist without something which is lower than I am." And if the plant were able to feel it would say, "I am at a higher level than the stone is, but I bow down to it in humility, for the stone has made it possible for me to exist." In the same way the animal would have to bow down before the plant, saying, "If you, plant, did not exist I could not exist either. I bow down before you in humility." '

If you now move on to human beings, many different ones, those lower and those higher, what would anyone who is a bit higher up on the ladder of evolution have to say? Like the plant before the mineral, the animal before the plant, every human being who is at a higher level would bow down before those who are lower, saying, 'You may be at the lower level, but I owe it to you that I am able to exist.'

Now think of this being done all the way up to the highest, to Christ Jesus, and you have the relationship that the Christ had to the apostles who were with him. He bent down like the plant to the mineral and washed their feet: 'I have come forth from among you and I bow down before you.'

The pupil had to go through such feelings at all different levels for long periods. And the feeling had to come more and more alive; then he would awaken at the first level of Christian initiation. It could be felt through an outward and an inner symptom. The outward one was that the pupil was truly sentient of this for a time, feeling as if the watery element was flowing around his feet. And the inner symptom would have been that he lived the thirteenth chapter of the Gospel of John as an inner vision on the astral plane.

They would then move on. The teacher would say to the pupil: 'You must experience something else; you have to imagine that suffering and pain in mind and body come rushing up to you from all sides. You have to be strong to face them all so that you might be able to say to yourself: "Whatever pain and suffering beset me, I stand erect and will not be thrown down on the ground." ' This was called the 'scourging'. The outward symptom for it was that you felt something like pain in your skin, a sign that the soul had come this far. And the inner symptom was that you saw yourself as being scourged on the astral plane. But it was the inner experience which the soul had gained which mattered.

The third thing the pupil would hear from the teacher was: 'Now you must develop a feeling that you not only stand firm against all pain that besets you, but you must stand firm also when that in you which is most sacred to you is dragged into the dust. You must remain so strong that people might say, "It's not worth anything." You must know its value even if they crush it and be able to stand up to a whole world.' When the pupil had achieved this, one would say that he had gone through the 'crowning with thorns'. The outward symptom was a feeling as if of a certain pain in the head, and the inner symptom was that one saw oneself in the situation of the redeemer crowned with thorns.

The fourth then was this. The teacher would say to the pupil: 'You must gain a completely new relationship to your body. You inhabit your body; but now you must consider it to be something completely alien, just as a table out there is not you, and you must even know how to say: "I am carrying my body through the world." It has to be as foreign to you as all objects out there.' Then one would say that one had lived through the 'crucifixion'. Just as the redeemer bore the cross so one bore one's own body, more or less like a piece of wood. The outward symptoms of the crucifixion itself were the stigmata. The pupil was able in his meditation to call forth the blood marks on himself, on the hands, on the feet and on the right side of the chest; there the red marks would appear that recall the wounds on the cross. This 'blood trial' was an outward symptom indicating that one had come to know the inner nature of Christianity. And the inner experience would be that one saw oneself hanging on the cross in an astral vision.

The fifth level was called the 'mystic death'. One can give only an approximate description of this. The mystic death consisted in it actually seeming to the individual concerned that the whole world was immersed in deepest darkness; it would be like a black wall before them. The whole world perceived through the senses would be wiped out, gone from existence; this is what one might experience. At that moment one came to know—and one can really only come to know it through this event—all things bad and evil that might exist in the world. To come to know life one also had to go through this. It was called the 'descent to hell'. There followed a strange event. You would see it as if spread before your eyes. That wall would fall apart. It was the 'curtain in the temple tearing apart' and you would then look up into the spiritual world. This was called the 'mystic death' and the 'tearing apart of the curtain'.

The sixth level was the 'entombment and resurrection', when the individual would be adding another feeling to those gained before, namely that the other objects outside became something which now seemed to belong to his body, with the whole earth also being part of him. As a finger might say 'I am a finger only because I am part of the organism of the hand', so the human being is on earth only by virtue of being part of it. Human beings are able to walk about on earth and because of this consider themselves to be independent. When one fills oneself with the feeling that everything is part of one, the condition would arise that was called the 'entombment'; in mind and spirit you rested in the earth, and it was only after this that you would rise again, as it were, in the spirit. It is only then that you would understand the deed of Christ Jesus who in his death united with the earth and became the spirit of the earth where before he had been the regent of the sun. And the words 'He who eats my bread has lifted up his heel against me'[54] must be taken literally. If you know Christ Jesus to be the most sublime planetary spirit of the earth and the earth his body, you will also understand that you are literally raising your heel against the body of Christ Jesus. And you were united with him when you lived through the entombment at this sixth level.

Then came the seventh level, the 'ascension', which we are quite rightly unable to describe for only someone able to think without using his brain would be able to understand it.

I have told you how people went through Christian initiation. The pupils would gain the 'Christ eye', as it is called. If you did not have any eyes, darkness would reign all around you; just as you cannot see a sun unless you have eyes, so you could not perceive the Christ unless you had the Christ organ. The eye is born of the light for the light. The light is the cause of seeing. The sun has to be there outside as the real sun, and in your eye you live this real sun itself. It is the same with the spiritual eye. It is nothing but empty talk to merely speak of the 'inner' Christ. It would be just like talking of the eye where there was no sun. Human beings can gain the ability to see the Christ by doing the exercises of which I spoke, but it is thanks to the historical Christ himself that they will have the strength to do this. The Christ relates to the development of the Christ organ in the human being as the sun does to the eye.

The aim has been not to give instructions but to present facts. But one should come to know what there is in the world. And these lectures are meant for this, that one comes to know the depths on which the true Christian spirit is drawing, and how the Gospel of John itself provides the methods for Christian initiation by which human beings gain the eye which is able to behold the Christ. Those who wish to proclaim the

Christ, however, must have lived with him in a particular way, really so and not in mere belief.

To tell of the things that exist in the world consider what has been said today—that Goethe has most marvellously characterized the way things are in the spiritual world. He spoke the beautiful words which hold true for the whole of natural science and for the whole of spiritual science:

> If the eye were not like the sun,
> How could we ever see the light?
> If the god's own power did not live in us,
> How could all things divine be such delight?[55]

The things and living entities must be out there in the world; it creates the organs and abilities. Without the sun, no eye, nor any ability to see the sun. Without Christ Jesus, no organ to behold the Christ, nor any way of developing that organ!

LECTURE 13

KASSEL, 28 JUNE 1907

TODAY and tomorrow my aim will be to show you the way to the higher worlds that is particularly suitable for the present time. It has been cultivated in occult training, as it is called, especially from the fourteenth and fifteenth centuries, and is the most suitable for modern humanity. We'll find it easier to understand what this is about if we first take a look at the future evolution of humanity.

We have spoken of human evolution through the Saturn, Sun, Moon and earth states. It is difficult for someone whose thinking is wholly in the here and now to think of how one might know something about the future. But you must understand that some major laws will apply just as much in future as they do now. Anyone who is familiar with these laws can take a look into the future. In the field of material reality no one will doubt today that it is possible to predict things, calculating eclipses of the sun and moon and other stellar events far into the future, for instance. No one will be in doubt about this any more in the field of material reality. Everyone also knows that when you speak of particular substances being brought together in a retort it will be possible for a scientist to say what will happen when they are mixed. This kind of prophecy relates to external facts that can be perceived with the senses; one can prophesy because one knows the laws according to which the substances act. In the same way we get to know the laws in spiritual science according to which human life proceeds, and it is therefore possible to know something in advance that will happen in future.

People will, of course, raise an objection at this point, one which philosophers have raised through the ages. It is that if we are able to foresee what will happen there will be no chance for human freedom. What is happening here is that people confuse foreseeing future events with predetermination. You will therefore find the oddest things said about this in all philosophies, for all philosophers have been unable to make that distinction. Except for Jakob Boehme, really. Let me give you an example to illustrate this.

I want to compare time with space. Consider yourself to be standing here, and two people standing out there in the street. You see what they are doing from a distance. Does this also make you the person who is to say what they should do? No. You see it, but the two people are perfectly free to act. The fact that you are watching them does not govern anything they do. Consider the clairvoyant now who sees what will happen in future. If those events were determined by the future, which is fixed already at the present time, this would not mean seeing into the future. You will only clearly understand the distinction if you think for a long time about the difference between predetermination and pre-science.

Today I do not really want to tell you how things will be on earth when the Jupiter and Venus times have been reached. I want to tell you something else that will give you a picture for human evolution towards the future; I want to present something to you that comes from the earliest Christian mysteries, from the same Christian school of the real Dionysius, as a doctrine that has always been taught in esoteric Christian schools. They would start from the following comparison. I am talking to you here. You hear my words, you hear the thoughts that are in my mind, thoughts which I might also keep hidden from you by not putting them in words. When I say some word here, the air in this room moves; my words do every time set up waves in the air; the whole body of air vibrates according to the way in which the words are spoken. Let us now take this a bit further. Imagine you were able to make the air liquid and then solid. It is actually possible to make air solid today. You know that water may exist as vapour, that it can cool down and then be liquid, and that it may be solid when it is frozen. Consider me speaking the word 'God' into the air. If you could make the air frozen at the moment when the sound waves are here, a form would drop down—the form of a shell, for instance. A different wave would drop down if the word 'world' was said. You would be able to capture my words, and there would be a crystallized air form corresponding to every word.

This was an actual example given in the Christian schools. Something is first a spoken word, then it grows solid, turning into a solid form. Earlier, before it became solid, it was a thought hidden within the speaker. The Christian would then think: 'Creation in the world at large is like the creative act here in this room. It started from the thought of things; then the divine spirit spoke the thought into space. The plants and minerals you see out there are such divine words grown solid. You could think of everything resolved into the sound waves of the divine world word. I see the word of God grown solid in everything I see.' This is what the Christian would say to himself. And he would make distinction in a certain respect between the 'Father who is hidden' who has not yet uttered, the 'word'—or the 'Son'—sounding through space, and then the world grown solid, the 'Revelation'. You thus gain a deep understanding of the beginning of John's Gospel: 'In the Beginning was the Word, and the Word was with God and the Word was God. It was in the Beginning with God. Through it everything entered into existence, and without it nothing entered into existence.' Everything that has come into existence has arisen from the Word. We must take things as literally as possible and then we will easily recognize the creative nature of the Word or Logos. In Christian terms this Word or Logos comes in second place. 'Logos' must not be translated as anything but 'Word'; for the way it is meant is that the unuttered creative Word is behind all creation out there, that it sounded out as Word and that in it lies the source and origin of all that is. If we were to go back far enough in the course of time we would hear all things we know as animals, plants, minerals, human beings sound through cosmic space as 'Word' just as you hear my words today, for the air had then not cooled down enough for them to drop down as figures and forms.

If you keep that in mind you'll be able to say to yourself: 'The human being is a beginner today compared to what his forebears were doing, the gods that were above him. There was a time when the gods spoke the word into space, and then this creative activity became creation, everything we have around us. Anything we are able to produce in the plant, animal and human worlds by sexual reproduction is but a changed form deriving from that creator word of old. Human beings have a higher and a lower nature in them. The most finished aspect has the sexual element in it; and human beings have the beginnings of a new way of procreating in their larynx. When they send out the word it is a beginning of what they will achieve at a later time. The human being is today just beginning with the work that the gods once did.' The old way of procreating will be replaced with something else. And where human beings produce words with their larynx today, the larynx will one day be a generative organ; it will produce ever higher, ever denser creations. What is mere air today will in future be an entity, a spirit. When the earth has changed into Jupiter the Word will be creative in the mineral world; at the Venus stage the larynx will bring forth plants, and that is how it will continue until man will be able to reproduce himself. Man only arose in the form we have today when he was able to send out air from his lungs to be sound outside. Things we can today only say to ourselves we will be able to produce in such a way at future stages of earth evolution that it will persist. And ultimately the larynx will be the organ by which human beings can reproduce themselves in purity, with no sexuality. They will then have reconfigured their larynx into an organ of procreation.

We get a glimpse of what the future human being will be like, and the potential that lies in the larynx. A puzzling phenomenon can give a pointer to the way in which the life of the larynx is connected with certain developmental states. In the male gender, sexual maturity also means that the voice breaks. The larynx is in its beginnings, sexuality at its end. Such subtle connections exist between things in the natural world. Our sexual life is dying; our larynx, our word, will in future be an organ to reproduce ourselves.

We might refer to many other things to show how human beings will gradually develop the organs which today exist only in their beginnings, which we have made our own as our breathing system on earth, though this does belong to the system of the heart.

Let us now see how with the training that has been introduced in Europe from the fourteenth century we can indeed anticipate further states of humanity, how one can also make one's inner development go faster than if one simply gives oneself up to the course that the world is taking. The training which we call Rosicrucianism is something which has really got a bad name with people who have only once heard of it. If what the books say and scholars know about it were true, Rosicrucianism would be no more than the fraud which it is said to be. But the truth is that the people who judge Rosicrucianism in that way do in fact only know the fraud. We will consider the genuine Rosicrucianism today which came into existence through the individual who hides behind the name Christian Rosenkreutz and who initiated the Rosicrucian movement in 1459.

Let me say emphatically that what I am saying has been selected as an example, just as I said yesterday with regard to the Christian training. I will therefore give you the seven main points of Rosicrucian training straight away. Not everyone goes through them in the same sequence, but we'll begin by listing these stages which apply to everyone with regard to Rosicrucianism.

The first stage is called 'study': 'gaining insight in images' comes second. The third is 'reading the occult or secret script'. The fourth is 'preparing the Philosophers' Stone', the fifth is what is called 'correspondence between the small world, the microcosm, and the large world, the macrocosm. The sixth is 'living with the macrocosm', and the seventh is called 'being in harmony with God'.

The Rosicrucian way is the one which takes one in the most certain and profound way to insight into Christianity. However, the Christian way is more suited to those who are able to stay firm in the faith and are able to bring the feelings of which I spoke yesterday inwardly to life. The Rosicrucian way is more for those who are able to connect the Christian truths with the truths of the outside world. It is exactly in this case that Christianity can be defended against any attack from outside. Christianity is a philosophy of life where one can never be wise enough to understand it adequately. There is no degree high enough to fully understand how Christianity exists for the most wise among the wise. But the Rosicrucian way is the one most suitable for people today.

We 'study' in the Rosicrucian sense when we have thoughts that have nothing at all to do any more with the world we perceive through the senses. In the western world people really only know 'thinking in free thought' when doing geometry; Christian gnostic schools therefore also used the term 'mathesis' for something that referred to the higher truths, to God and the higher worlds, for these must be seen free from all sensuality, just as mathematics must also be seen to be free from all sensuality. A circle drawn with a piece of chalk is most imperfect; the true circle exists only in thought, and everything you are able to learn about the circle can only be thought. It is exactly in mathematics that you learn to think in a way that is independent of the senses, learning from the circle that you construct in your thoughts, from a mentally constructed triangle, its angles adding up to 360 degrees. It is not all that comfortable to learn to think without the things we perceive outside, and for most people the only field of study for this is theosophy. As I told you in our very first session, theosophical knowledge is perfectly logical. But anyone wanting to find the truths for himself will need to be clairvoyant. Logic is, however, enough for insight.

Computing machines, which do not teach us to learn independently of the senses, could only be the fruit of our materialistic age. Yet the very thing which children must learn is to grasp things without recourse to the senses. It will be particularly and tremendously valuable for education to bring in the influence of insight in the spirit. Spiritual science actually is good training in thinking without recourse to the senses. For everything I have been telling you about Saturn, Sun, about the levels of human existence, is something you cannot see; you have to grasp it in thoughts free from sensuality, and no one should think that they can train well unless they first grasp things in theory. That is indeed the good thing, that these things do not exist for the sensual approach; for we then learn a way of thinking that goes beyond sensuality. It will therefore be enough for many that they first simply enter into what theosophy tells about the things which one cannot grasp with the senses. Essentially those have also always been the thoughts presented to people in the Rosicrucian schools, and they were made to impress those thoughts thoroughly in their memory.

If you want to go further you'll find a good way of learning pure thinking in my books *Truth and Science/Truth and Knowledge* and *The Philosophy of Spiritual Activity/The Philosophy of Freedom*. These books are sheer mental gymnastics free from sensuality. With other books you will not, as a rule, make much of a change if you move a thought to a different place. With these books the thoughts cannot be put in a different place. These books came about in that my person merely provided the opportunity for these thought edifices to be made perceptible to the senses. One simply had to give oneself up so that these thoughts generated themselves, extended themselves. Anyone who wants to go into them more deeply and give half a year to them—it is not easy but this effort and what can be achieved in this way is the best of all things—and read them right through will have drawn on a power in himself that has so far been hidden.

The second thing is Imagination, insight gained in images, and this is wholly in the light of the beautiful words of Goethe: 'All that must pass away is but a parable.'[56] Only those who have gained certainty in their thinking should really do this. Otherwise one might easily give in to fantasy. The precondition is therefore that one has first become a clear thinker; nothing is more likely to prevent aberration than clear thinking. And nothing is more likely to lead us astray than lack of clear thinking, lack of logic.

In the wider sense we might say that with Imagination you look at everything around you the way you look at a person. Look at a person's face. You see lines, creases develop and disappear again; you do not merely describe them but call them 'smile' or 'sadness'. The human smile tells you of a cheerful inner mood. You do not just draw conclusions from outer appearance as to inner life; it actually is a sign for you of an inner life. Or you see a tear develop—you're not just a physicist who judges a tear merely according to the law of gravity, but you know that the teardrop reflects some sadness in the soul. All outward things are thus a reflection of the inner mood of soul to you. And the Rosicrucian pupil enters into a mood where everything he sees outside does in the same way reflect for him the earth spirit, let us say— a certain plant, the autumn crocus, in reality becomes a reflection for him of mournful earthly existence, other plants a reflection of cheerful earthly existence. Just as a smiling face reflects a cheerful mood so do the flowers reflect for him the earth's cheerful or sad mood. Goethe was not just referring to an outward image when he spoke of the earth spirit in his *Faust*:[57]

In life like a flood, in deeds like a storm
Up and down I flow!
Birth and the grave
An eternal wave,
Turning, returning,
A life ever burning:
And thus I work on Time's whirring wheel,
God's living garment I weave and reveal.

The earth spirit gradually became something to him that lives in the earth, and he developed a relationship in mind and soul to the whole of nature around him. Let me quite specifically tell you of *one* mood.

The Rosicrucian pupil would walk through the fields and see the small dew drops on all plants. He had to recall ancient Niflheim (home of mists) then, where the air was full of dewy mists, and where human beings related to the natural world in a very different way. Walking through the fields and meadows the Rosicrucian pupil would say to himself: 'In ancient Niflheim this was dissolved in the air atmosphere.' And a profound memory would arise in him of Atlantean times.

Imagination was taken to a particularly high level for the pupils of medieval Rosicrucian schools, and also by those who were pupils of the Holy Grail. I'll put that teaching in the form of a dialogue, being unable to formulate it in any other way.

The teacher would say to the pupil: 'Look at the plant as it sprouts from the ground, how it opens the calyx with the organs of fertilization, and how the sun's rays come down, get the flower to open and the fruit to ripen.' The pupils of Rosicrucianism and those of the Holy Grail had to call this image, this idea, to mind. Even in materialistic science we find something that is highly significant—which is that the plant is compared to the human being. But you would have to compare the root to the head and the flower with the organs of fertilization in human beings, something they hide in shame. The root is the plant's head. The human being is an inverted plant, an animal is only a half-inverted plant. The Rosicrucians would therefore say: 'Look at the plant, its root in the soil, its organs of fertilization chastely held out to the sun. Look at the animal—its spine horizontal, and then the human being—completely transformed. Plant, animal and man in their evolution symbolized by the cross! The cross is plant, animal and man.' We will now understand Plato's words: 'The world's soul is stretched on the cross of the world.'[58] The soul of the world which fills everything is stretched out across plant, animal and man.

So the Rosicrucian pupil would be exhorted: 'Look at the plant. Of its kind it is lower than you are; it does not yet have conscious awareness and power of thought. But its substance is pure and chaste; it holds up its calyx to the sun, extending its organs of reproduction towards the sun, without want or desire to the sun's ray, the sacred lance of love. Now, however, matter is being filled with desire. Do create the idea for the future in your mind that matter shall be cleansed again, that it reproduces in pure chastity.' And his attention would be drawn to the larynx, where human beings will have regained the chastity of the calyx in purity. 'Think of the calyx of the plant; it is still free from desire. It goes through desires it develops but will be pure again, bringing forth again in chastity, letting itself be fertilized by the sun's ray which has been made spiritual, the sacred lance of love.' The portent of this sacred lance of love was the lance used to pierce the heart of Christ Jesus on the cross.

Yesterday we saw how this blood from the redeemer's wound banished egotism from the earth. That lance was therefore a portent for the higher lance which is the sun's ray made spiritual. And the Holy Grail points to humanity's chalice which evolves from the larynx and will be the great reproductive organ of the future, as it is with plants today.

That is the deeper concept of the Holy Grail, and this was made clear to pupils at the Imagination level of their initiation. Take the images you now have before you—calyx of the plant, sexuality immersed in desire, Holy Grail, calyx or chalice free from desire—and compare them with the dry, sober rational concept provided in modern science. This gives you the difference between Imagination and mere rational thinking, all cosmic events seen in images! This is important because mere rational concepts of the kind people have today are not creative. These images are truly creative for those who bring the concepts together in an image. People felt this in earlier times, and it must be taken into account when raising children.

I'd like to discuss a current issue at this point. People are much inclined to say, 'Think of the silly things our forefathers taught us when we were children. The story of the stork bringing babies, for instance. Today we have to tell children the truth.' If our descendants are going to treat us the way we treat our ancestors, they will laugh at us and say, 'Our ancestors thought that human beings come into existence through material interaction.' And they'll consider the time when people explained this to children in a spiritual way. The ancestors believed in the stork story themselves when it first came up, for they knew full well that when someone is born the soul comes down from the spiritual world. They would always connect it with something that had wings. You'll also find it in children's songs today, like the song:

> Fly, ladybird, fly!
> Your father is in the war!
> Your mother is in podge land,
> Podge land has burned down.
> Fly, ladybird, fly!

'Fly' is meant as an image for the human soul, for people still had an inkling of astral space, of bodies that were flying there and came into the physical world from there. And 'podge land'? 'Podge' is nothing but the name for an infant, and 'podge land' is the land of the children where the mother goes to fetch her infant. We merely have to explain it wholly in terms of the spiritual world. If you then recall that this image of the stork bringing babies is an image for a spiritual process, for reincarnation, you will see how tremendously important it is that people first take in things in images, for their state of mind will be very different if we teach children first the image for the spiritual process so that they will then hear of the physical process in holy awe.

You yourselves will be able to believe in the stork again if you know that this stork is an image you have for the soul flying down! Your teaching will give wings to the child's powers of imagination, and if you perceive the truth, a mysterious aura will come from this and be transmitted to the child. That is how it is with all things seen in images. You can teach the children anything.

If the question to be considered is about life after death, you take the child to see a butterfly chrysalis. As the butterfly flies from the chrysalis so does the soul fly from the body, only that we don't see it. But you'll only speak to the child with conviction if you believe it yourself, and the emergence of the butterfly from the chrysalis is the same, though at a lower level, as what happens to the soul at a higher level. When spiritual knowledge takes people again into understanding the spiritual world, so that images live in their hearts, children will be brought up in a very different way again and not given the dry intellectual truths that coarsen the mind. We must not, however, make it grotesque or comical but understand clearly the important aspects of life that are behind it.

The third thing to be acquired so as to pave the way is 'getting to know the occult script'. This does not mean learning a script the way we do in ordinary life. The characters of our alphabet do in many ways go back to occult images, but they are far removed from what we call the occult script. There we have a way of finding one's way into the genuine great powers that come into play out there in the world. Everything we record there has to be such that one developmental process leaps to the next. Take a plant. It bears seed. In the seed you have the starting point for a new plant. But if you were really able to see into the whole process you'd see that nothing of the old plant becomes part of the new one. In reality the whole of the old plant perishes as far as matter is concerned. The new plant is completely new as it develops. There is just a process of movement evolving the new plant. Here you have sealing wax, and here a seal. You press the seal into the wax, but no part of the seal remains in the wax. Only the form is transferred. That is how it is with every development process. The old matter as it is dying merely provides occasion for the new form to rise again in the manner of the old one. This is represented as two intertwined spirals which never come together. This kind of transition came after Atlantean civilization; it disappeared and a new one arose as the Indian civilization. This, too, would need to be shown as two spirals. I have told you that in the year 800 the sun rose roughly in the sign of the Ram, before that in the Bull, even earlier in the Twins and before that in Cancer. Graeco-Roman civilization, which held the beginnings of ours in it, was at the time when the sun rose in the Ram. The preceding civilization, the Chaldean, Assyrian, Babylonian and Egyptian, came at the time when the sun rose in the sign of the Bull. Before that you have the Persian civilization which was at the time when the sun rose in the Twins. The ancient Indian civilization evolved when the sun was in Cancer, and that was when the sign of Cancer, the two intertwined spirals, was first written.

I could explain the true meaning of every sign of the zodiac to you in this way. The signs have been created out of the natural world and reflect the powers and laws at work out there in nature. Getting to know the occult characters one begins to go out of oneself and penetrate the hidden roots of the natural world.

Thus you have the first three stages of the Rosicrucian path briefly outlined—'study', 'insight in images' and thirdly 'learning the occult script'.

Tomorrow we'll consider the other stages, starting with 'preparing the Philosophers' Stone'.

LECTURE 14

KASSEL, 29 JUNE 1907

Yesterday I spoke of the Rosicrucian initiation, as it is called, up to the third stage, 'learning the occult script'. We also came to know the Rosicrucian way of 'study', the 'gaining of insight in images' and then 'finding one's way into the occult script', the signs that have been taken from the natural world. We must now move on to the fourth stage which is called 'preparing the Philosophers' Stone'. Please leave aside anything you may read about this in old books and understand that it is only at the present time that one can say something about what Rosicrucians actually meant by 'preparing the Philosophers' Stone'.

Certain rules had been given for getting up into the higher worlds since the well-known founder of Rosicrucianism[59] had established it in 1459. You have to understand that this stream has always been treated with the greatest care and always kept secret. It was somewhere towards the end of the eighteenth century and at the beginning of the nineteenth century that there was a kind of betrayal and some of the Rosicrucian secrets came to be publicly known. Various publications appeared then and it was evident from them that those concerned had heard something but did not understand it. They did at least hear proper words, picking up something, also concerning the Philosophers' Stone. Some reports even appeared in the *Reichs-Anzeiger* paper[60] at the time about a society which had set itself the task of 'preparing the Philosophers' Stone', and one item was such that only those who knew what it was all about were able to understand. It said: 'Yes, the Philosophers' Stone does exist. Most people actually know it. Most have even held in in their hand; it is not that difficult to find, though most people do not know this.'

The idea behind this concept of the Philosophers' Stone was that it would gradually teach one to know the immortal part of man, the part that is not subject to death, and would guide one to the higher worlds. When human beings come to realize that this immortal part cannot be subject to death and are in possession of the Philosophers' Stone, this means that they attain to eternal life, overcoming death. The interpretation that was put on this was that one would never die. The real meaning was, however, that this allows human beings to get to know the world in which they will live after death. Apart from this the Philosophers' Stone was also considered to be an elixir of life. All this made the Philosophers' Stone something to be greatly desired. Those who knew what it was about had to consider these words to be true in a strange way, for they are true, but those who did not know the secret could make little of them.

Let me now show you, briefly, what is meant by them. To understand this, you'll have to follow me in a very simple natural-scientific fact. You have to know the nature of the relationship between human beings and the plant world. The facts are that everything which breathes the way human beings do could never exist were it not for the plants. You need to familiarize yourselves with the process that occurs between you and the plants.

You inhale the air; you need the oxygen from it. You'd never be able to live without oxygen. When you take in the air and use the oxygen in your organism, you exhale carbon dioxide, a compound of carbon and oxygen. So you have to say to yourself, 'Human beings are all the time taking in oxygen to maintain life and exhaling carbon dioxide. They are therefore all the time producing a poison which would kill them. So you are all the time filling the world around you with poison.' What does the plant do? It is in a way doing the exact opposite. It takes in carbon dioxide, retains the carbon and releases the oxygen which is of no use to it. So you are giving the plant what it needs, and the plant gives back the oxygen in return. This process of carbon dioxide breathing and release of oxygen far exceeds the plant's uptake of oxygen. What does the plant do with the carbon it retains? It uses it to some degree to build up its body. You are, as it were, giving the plant occasion to build up its body in the way that is appropriate for it. And you will have the same substance thousands of years later when you dig up the plant as anthracite.

The plant gives you oxygen. You take this in. You give it the carbon dioxide; it keeps the carbon, building its body with it, and gives the oxygen back to you. It is a wonderful interaction which takes place there. This is how it is today. Humanity is, however, evolving and in future the human body will be such that it will have the organ in itself which changes carbon dioxide into oxygen, and will retain the carbon itself.

Here I am pointing to a future condition of man in a different way than I did yesterday when speaking of Rosicrucian training. In future human beings will have a desire-free body of a higher order than that of the plant, which is at a lower level. They will be able to build a body for themselves that will be plantlike at a higher level. The organ which today is the human heart will then be an apparatus that will do what the plant is doing today. Today plant and human being belong together; neither could live without the other. If there were no plants, all oxygen-breathing life forms would have to die out in a short time, for the plants give us our oxygen. We cannot think the human being without the plant. But in future the organ into which the heart will develop will do in us what the plant is now doing outside us. It will then be a voluntary muscle. We spread our conscious mind out over the plants, we grow together with the plant world so that the function the plant has outside today will later be inside us. We will then also retain the carbon which we give off today, using it to build our own body. We shall be plantlike at a higher level of conscious awareness.

In occultism all this has from time immemorial been given the form of a wonderful legend, for truths have for centuries been preserved in images and legends. Here it is the Golden Legend. And the things I have told you today were taught to students of occultism in images, more or less like this:

When Seth, the son whom God had given to Adam and Eve in place of their murdered son Abel, entered into Paradise on one occasion he found the two trees, the tree of knowledge and the tree of life, intertwined. They wound their branches around one another. At the behest of the angel who was with him Seth took three seeds from this tree. He kept them safe and when Adam died he put the three seeds into his mouth. A tree then grew from Adam's grave. For those who knew how to look, this tree showed writing in letters of fire—the words 'Ehyeh asher ehyeh—I am the one who was, who is and who will be'. Seth then took wood of that tree growing from Adam's grave and made various things of it—including the staff which was Moses' magic rod. And it was reproduced further; the portal to the Temple of Solomon was made of it, and later, when it had gone through various other fates, the cross on which the redeemer did hang.

Thus the legend brings together the wood of the cross on Golgotha and the tree which grew on Adam's grave from seeds taken from the tree in Paradise.

The secret at which I hinted today is also hidden in this legend. It was meant to tell us that in times immemorial the human race was such that it had not yet come down to being flesh filled with desire but was chaste and pure, like the plant holding up its calyx to the sun. Then came the Fall and humanity's flesh was filled with desire. Yet human beings shall have again everything that was theirs when they were in a state of innocence, if they have taken the path of insight and created the desire-free body, the body as it has once been, before man entered into knowledge. Remember where the I comes from. Man no longer has the body of old because he has become a lung-breather and is able to develop red blood. The present form of human beings is therefore connected with breathing and blood circulation, and because of this they have been able to become the bearers of insight which they are today.

Put yourself into the present-day body. There you can get a picture of the way the oxygen flows in, how it stirs up the red blood, how the red blood flows through the whole body like in a branching tree, how the blue blood then flows back, full of carbon dioxide.

You have two trees in you—the red blood tree and the blue one. Without the two, human beings could not be bearers of an I. This is why the red blood has to be taken up; it is the way in which our present-day insight is called forth. But death was also part of this, for you are changing the red blood into blue blood full of carbon dioxide. And so the occult teacher in the Old Testament said, 'Look at yourself. You have the red blood tree in you. If you had not been given this tree you would never have been a human being rich in insight. You have eaten of the tree of knowledge; but this did at the same time take away your ability to give life to yourself out of yourself.'

The tree of life had turned into a tree that killed; this is why the blue blood tree in us is the tree of death. That is the present condition. The initiate's soul does, however, have a future condition before it when human beings will have plant nature in them, when the blue blood will be changed back into red blood through the heart apparatus. They will then have changed the tree of death into a tree of life. Human beings will then have become immortal; they will be once again at a higher level what they have once been at a lower one. They will then have the apparatus in themselves which today exists in the plant.

Paradise thus represented an end stage for man. And Seth's mission was understood to be that he saw what comes at the end of time—when the two principles will be in balance in man himself. The tree of life and the tree of knowledge thus intertwine in Paradise; they can only find one another in the human being when the human being has recourse to the plant. But how do human beings gain the ability to have the two trees intertwined in them? By developing the three higher levels of human nature in themselves.

We have got to know the human being, made up of physical body, ether body, astral body and I, and we have seen how by working on the astral body the I achieves the first of the higher constituent principles, by working on the ether body the second one, and how it works on the physical body to gain the third. The future human being will therefore have seven constituent principles, the higher ones being Spirit Self, Life Spirit and Spiritual Human Being. When man has thus transformed his lower nature he will have the tree of knowledge and the tree of life in himself. From the beginning of his evolution, man was therefore given the preconditions for the three higher constituent principles as a potential in his I.

Seth took the seeds, and Adam, the first human being endowed with I nature, let those three seeds grow into a tree. In this tree there was the principle that goes through all your incarnations. At the first incarnation your I was at a very low level. It then rose to higher and higher levels as incarnation followed incarnation. The symbol for the eternal in us was growing there, and it will reach its highest level of perfection by the end of the earth stage of evolution. Human beings will, however, only be able to attain to it if they connect with all the most sublime which they have come upon on the path of the spirit. Everything that has guided humanity on that upward path—the rod of Moses, the Temple of Solomon, and finally the cross on Golgotha—all this helps human beings to give full expression to the three higher principles. And it was the cross on Golgotha which pointed the way to man's greatest perfection. To begin with it had been put in Adam's mouth as the seed from which the tree then grew—one could not put it in any better way than has been done here—and was made from the wood which Seth had obtained in this way. This shows the road followed by humanity going through the ages, humanity's road through time. Today the plant is able to do the things which human beings must gain in future—transforming their essential nature, the ability to use their own powers to produce their own carbon. At a future time, humanity will be able to master this alchemy of the plant.

In alchemy, the process I have just been describing consists in giving the Rosicrucian pupil certain directions as to how to regulate his breathing. This, too, can only be understood according to the principle that 'a steady drip hollows the stone'. But the Rosicrucian pupil would work away at it. As a drop, being small, tiny, will need a long time to hollow the stone, so is progress made in human bodies with this process of regulating one's breathing. The directions which the pupil has to follow are such that they put him in the way of making preparations today for his I to gain the ability to develop future bodies in a different way. It does mean, however, that the things which will be your physical surroundings at a later time will be there for you even now in the spiritual world. The advice given to Rosicrucians is to prepare for one's future condition in a slow process, gaining the ability to behold this condition even now in the higher worlds. So the Rosicrucian pupil does two things. In the first place he prepares in advance for the future of humanity, and secondly he sees what will later descend into physical reality.

Now you will also understand the directions which that strange man had printed though he did not understand them. The Philosophers' Stone is ordinary black coal; but you have to learn the process in which you are able to process carbon using your inner powers—that is how humanity progresses. Today's coal is the model for what will one day be the most important substance for man, though it will look very different then. Do you remember the bright diamond? That, too, is merely carbon!

This, then, is what Rosicrucians call 'preparing the Philosophers' Stone'. Behind it lies a process of human transformation and a challenge to work on the future conditions of humanity. All who do the work are working for the human bodies of the future, for the bodies which our souls will later need.

There are words which express this most beautifully and we'll understand them when we are clear about the difference between the evolution of souls and that of races. You have all been Atlanteans once, and those Atlantean bodies of yours looked very different, as I did describe it for you. The same soul which has once been in an Atlantean body is in your body today. But not all bodies that are like yours today have had the preparatory work done that was done by a few colonists—people who went from the west to the east at that time. Those who stayed behind, who 'connected with the race', as it is put, have degenerated whilst those who were advanced established new civilizations. The last stragglers in the migration to the east, the Mongols, have retained something of the Atlantean civilization. The bodies of those who will not progress and continue to evolve will grow beyond the next turn of an era and be the future Chinese people. There will be peoples again that fall into decadence. Today souls are living in the bodies of the Chinese which will need to incarnate once again in such races because they have felt too much drawn to the race. The souls which are in you today will later be incarnated in bodies that come from individuals who are today working in the way I have indicated and who are generating the bodies of the future, just as the first Atlantean colonists did in the past. Those who really cling to the familiar, who do not want to have anything to do with the things that point to the future, will become welded to the race. There are people who want things to stay the way they have always been, who do not want to know about progress, who do not want to listen to those who take us beyond race to ever new ways and forms for humanity.

This tendency has been wonderfully well preserved in mythology. There can be no better way of presenting this than in the words of one of the greatest spirits who said, 'Anyone who does not disregard his father and mother, his wife and children and his brothers and sisters cannot be my disciple,' and instead showed how sad it is when a person says, 'I don't want to know about such a master and guide!' and rejects him. There can be no clearer way of putting this than in the image of someone who rejected the master and guide and was unable to rise higher. This is the legend of Ahasver, the wandering Jew, who sat and rejected the greatest leader, Christ Jesus, did not want to know of further development, and therefore had to stay with his race, returning to it again and again. Myths and legends like this have been given for humanity to remember for ever so that human beings may know about these things.

This is how we should see this fourth level of Rosicrucian training, as something tremendously profound, and it is the way in which 'preparing the Philosophers' Stone' becomes part of human evolution.

The fifth is 'correspondence between microcosm and macrocosm'. The whole, complicated human body the way it is today has arisen in a particular way. I have guided you through the Saturn, Sun, Moon and earth states. Of everything there is in your body today, only the first beginnings of your sensory apparatuses existed on Saturn, embedded in the Saturn mass the way crystals are today embedded in rock masses. Your eye was then like a rock crystal in the mountains. On the Sun your highest organs, all of them glands, were such that they covered the Sun's surface. On the Moon the organs which make up your nervous system today were spread out over the Moon's surface. The Moon had a nervous system, and the individual human animals which were there did on the Moon for the first time enjoy a nervous system. On earth human beings were given their skeletal system, for there had of course been no mineral system as yet on the Moon.

You see how marvellously the human being was made up. The eye in us today was spread over the whole of Saturn as an eye; having been out in the world at large it has now become part of us. Occultists can tell you how every single organ relates to the great world out there—liver, spleen, heart and so on—with the corresponding elements in the world outside, and what had to happen in the outside world so that they might develop. There are ways and means known to Rosicrucians of entering deeply into ourselves, with the sense organs our point of reference, inwardly entering into eyes, ears, and so gain clairvoyant insight into the development of these organs.

I have taken you to the time in Atlantean evolution when the ether body was still so far outside that it could not connect with the point that is above the root of the nose here in the head. We have seen how the ether body then moved into the physical body, how the physical body then assumed its present configuration. There is only one method of entering deeply, using a specific formula which is passed on by mouth. If you use this and enter deeply into the place where the head is connected with that place in the ether head of which we are talking, then insight arises for you into that time on earth, into the way the earth looked at that time when this part of the ether head moved into the physical head. In this way you can enter into every part of your microcosm and so get to know the powers of the macrocosm, the work which the world's architects did to put you together. According to the directions given in occultism you can therefore get to know the macrocosm; for all things in the world, out there in the macrocosm, have a corresponding organ in the microcosm. Human beings are highly complex. When you get a telegram you can draw conclusions as to the sender from its content. When it comes to the human body, you can enter deeply into the organ to draw conclusions as to its creator.

With this we have already touched on the sixth level, known as 'entering deeply into the macrocosm'. Having thus come to know how the microcosm relates to the macrocosm, one has extended oneself into insight into the whole world. This is what is behind the ancient words 'Come to know yourself'. Much damage has been done by theosophists who said, 'The whole of God, the most sublime principle, does already exist in you. You only have to look inside yourself and you'll come to know the whole world.'

This turning inward and brooding is the most foolish thing you can think of. All you get to know in this way is your lower I, something you do already have. In this way no one learns more than he has learnt already. Genuine self-knowledge is only gained in the complicated way described and is at the same time also knowledge of the world. Genuine theosophy is not designed to make things easy for people; it has to say, 'You must come to know even the most complicated entity there is by entering into this calmly and in all seriousness. There is no other way of coming to know the god than by coming to know him bit by bit in the world.' Patience and endurance are part of this. Advance calmly and slowly and you'll come to know the world. Theosophy can provide no formula, no cure-all, to gain full insight. All it can do is show you the way which will take you to self-knowledge and thus also knowledge of the world. And human beings will then also come to know God.

The insight which human beings gain on the sixth level is not dry rational understanding; it is such by nature that it brings us closely together with the world. Those who have gained it will have a close relationship with all things in the world, something people of today know only in the mysterious relationship of love between man and woman, and this is based on a mysterious insight into the nature of the other person. Such a relationship where you do not only understand but feel connected with all creation, just as the lover feels connected with his love, is gained as you behold the macrocosm. You will then have a close relationship, a kind of love relationship, to the plant, to every stone, to all life in the world. Your love for all life forms will grow specialized; they will tell you something which they will otherwise only tell you when you have not yet descended to knowledge. Animals feed on things that are good for them, leaving anything that is not; they relate in sympathy to the one and antipathy to the other. Man had to lose this direct relationship to things in order to gain his present-day knowledge but will regain it at a higher level. How does an occultist know today that the flower of a plant has a different action in man than its root does? How does he know that the action of an ordinary root differs from that of a carrot? Because things are telling this to him again in the same way as it is with the animals. This close relationship exists at the lower levels where the rational mind does not come into it. At the highest levels humanity will have it in conscious awareness again.

When one has come this far, the seventh level is something which arises of its own accord. You have been able to see from the above that this is a matter of gaining insight into impressions gained in the mind and feelings. There is nothing here that would not move the human heart in the liveliest way; because of this you must not make a distinction in this between ideal and intellectual and spiritual insight. Occultists do not seek to move you, to tell you all kinds of nice things. They tell you the facts of the spiritual world; they would think it shameless to seek to touch directly on your feelings. They know, however, that the facts when told speak for themselves; they themselves are there to evoke the feelings. Because of this, the person of the teacher has no significance in Rosicrucianism. The doctrine has nothing to do with the person. The teacher merely provides the opportunity for the facts to speak to people. And he'll be all the more correct the more he makes himself the means of expression for beholding the higher worlds. People who still believe and have opinions and views of their own do not make suitable occult teachers. For if feeling were to decide things and not objectivity you may well end up saying that two and two makes five!

You see, therefore, how Rosicrucians gradually come to gain insight into the higher worlds by developing a number of things in themselves. It does need instruction but everyone who is earnestly seeking will find this at the right time.

It would be wrong to say that in being given personal instruction one works through these seven levels one after the other. The teacher will select whatever is most suitable for one person or another. It has also been my intention to give you the preliminary stages. Now I'll just take two things to show you that other things have to be developed before one moves on to the more serious exercises. One thing one has to practise from the beginning is concentration, concentration in the life of thoughts. Just think how thoughts flit about in your mind from morning to night. They come from here or there and take you along with them. As a Rosicrucian pupil you have to set aside a time when you are master of your thoughts, when you take the most uninteresting object you can think of and reflect on it. This will prove enormously beneficial for you. Time does not matter; energy, patience and endurance are what is needed.

The other thing is 'positive thinking', as we call it, where we look for something in life that is best described in a Persian legend about Christ Jesus.[61] One day when Christ Jesus was walking with his disciples they saw a dead dog by the roadside that was already decomposed a great deal. The disciples, not being as far developed as Christ Jesus, turned away from the ugly sight. Christ Jesus stood still, looked musingly at the carcase and said 'Surely the creature has the most beautiful teeth!'

Ugly as many things in the world may be, there is always something beautiful in the ugliness, a grain of truth in all untruth, something good in all things evil. People often think that one should no longer consider anything to be bad, and so on. What is meant, however, is that in anything that is ugly there is always still a grain of beauty, and there is some good in every evil. This raises up the higher powers of the soul. All this is part of the preparation.

My intention has been first of all to give you an idea of the spirit which reigns in Christian gnostic training. In Rosicrucian training you have the deepest, most genuine Christianity and can be a Christian in the truest sense of the word, in spite of all modern life. It was possible to be a Christian in the old style for as long as there were more opportunities for withdrawing from the world and for as long as the thought forms had not yet entered into us that make it so hard to be a Christian today. The ideas coming from the natural-scientific way of thinking do make it hard for people to accept Christianity in its original form. Indeed it is the noblest minds who say, 'I cannot reconcile anything today with Christianity.' The spiritual world lives all around us but so do the thought forms produced in our materialistic age. We are always surrounded by the thought forms of material life. A conscientious person therefore has to say to himself or herself: 'Our age needs something which can hold its own in the midst of the ideas that come flooding in, so that we may stand tall in the face of everything that comes flooding in from the world.' Spiritual science provides it for us. We are egotists if we reject it and do not wish to make it our own.

Spiritual science is like the executor for something which was the will even in medieval theosophy. It can, however, be understood by everyone, even those who know all the justifiable objections raised in natural science. Today everyone will be able to find in theosophy with Rosicrucian orientation the things that guide one to insight into the world and also to peace in one's soul, to being secure in life. The theosophy of the Rosicrucian is no mere theory, something to enter into dispute about, giving mere reasons; it is an insight that must flow into the whole of our civilization. A theosophist trained the Rosicrucian way knows all the objections that may be raised; he is fully aware of all the counter-arguments. If we were to counter them using reason, things might go for us the way they once did for Eduard von Hartmann[62] with his *Philosophy of the Unconscious*. Eduard von Hartmann published this work. He had said things in it about Darwinism and so on that appeared to be like a more elevated point of view compared to the materialist one in scientific research. All the academics then rose against him, and a flood of criticisms appeared. Eduard von Hartmann was called the worst of all amateurs. Among the many brochures was one written by an anonymous author. It was a brilliant refutation of *The Philosophy of the Unconscious*, giving consideration to everything someone would know about who masters the knowledge of our time. This brochure was much praised by everyone. Oscar Schmidt,[63] the great zoologist, said for instance, 'What a pity that we don't know who has written this rejoinder, for that is someone who is at the very summit of present-day natural science!' Ernst Haeckel[64] said, 'Let him give us his name and we'll have him in our ranks!' The brochure did indeed make a great impact. A second edition then appeared bearing the author's name— Eduard von Hartmann! Now the scientists fell silent, and the story has not come to be widely known. But it did indeed happen.

You see how when one has gained a higher point of view one can oneself mention all that speaks against it; one only has to get oneself down to a different point of view. If there had been enough time we, too, could have gone into some such counter-arguments. But it was important, time being short, that we were able to learn what can already be said today about the realities of the higher worlds. What matters is that these things can benefit people, and that one is able to show how spiritual science can enter more and more into all the branches of human life and make them fruitful. And when it is able to do so, then the very fact will be the best proof of its justification. This should be the kind of proof we look for in spiritual science. A theosophist won't be greatly shocked, therefore, when people are still saying today that it is all mere fantasy. Everything which has gone on to be a blessing for humankind has always been called fantasy at first.

An example from the 1840s: Stamps as we know them did not exist at that time. They were only introduced by someone called Hill[65]—an absolute amateur really. The member of parliament asked to present the idea gave a most peculiar speech. 'In the first place,' he said, 'it cannot be that traffic increases to the extent which this man has calculated, and if that were the case, one would have to increase the size of the building.' Nowadays it appears perfectly normal to enlarge the building if traffic increases, but that is how the idea was put down at that time. When the first railway[66] was to be built, the medical experts in Bavaria were consulted, and those gentlemen said that one should not build a railway, for it would have the worst possible consequences for the passengers. But if they were going to build a railway then they must put a tall wooden hoarding around it so that others would not suffer concussion from it.

Everything was considered fantasy when it came up for the first time. However, if spiritual science is to be a fact of life it will have to penetrate directly into our everyday world. It will be a power that lends wings to the whole of our life, entering into our most ordinary activities; then, and only then, will it have shown itself to be fact. Rosicrucian theosophy takes this as its starting point, and I would ask all of you to take this standpoint with regard to everything said in these lectures. In future it will be able to develop into something that influences human creative powers, giving people new impulses in the fields of medicine and education, in art and academic knowledge, and this will bring soul and life to all branches of life.

Lectures like these are given from this point of view, and I would ask you to accept them from this point of view.

THE GOSPEL OF JOHN

LECTURE 1

Someone taking a careful look at cultural life will find that many souls are in deep conflict. People are in their earliest youth presented with not one but two philosophies of life, one through religious instruction, the other through natural science. As a result they are in doubt about the correctness of religious teaching from the very beginning.

We might think that theosophy is intended to be yet another religious belief system. That is not the case, however. Theosophy is not a new religion, nor a new sect; it is more than religion.

In these lectures the aim is to show, with the aid of theosophy, the significance of a religious document such as the Gospel of John. A look at this Gospel is particularly apt to show how theosophy relates to religious documents in general. It helps us to understand the religious streams that exist in the world. Someone who is familiar with theosophy takes Christianity as it is for a fact that is of the greatest significance for the whole cultural and spiritual life of humanity. However, it is impossible in modern cultural life to plumb the depths of Christianity. Theosophy is the instrument, the means, without which nothing can be done. Using this instrument we can enter deeply into the wisdom of the religious documents. We might compare theosophy with philology. Philology also makes it possible for us to study the religious documents. Theosophy does, however, take us into the spirit of these documents. Euclidean geometry is properly interpreted not by someone who merely knows Greek but by someone with knowledge of the facts of geometry.

Theosophy is not meant to be a new religion for modern humanity but the means of bringing Christianity closer to them again in its true content. Christianity is the most sublime of all religions. All other religions merely point towards Christianity. It is the religion of all our future, and none other will take its place. The source spring of truth bubbling forth in it is inexhaustible. It is so powerful that it will reveal ever new aspects to itself as humanity continues to evolve. Theosophy is intended to show us Christianity in a new aspect.

We can approach religious documents in four different ways, firstly from the point of view of naive belief, with people going by the actual words they are given. Many people are unable to reconcile this approach with modern thinking. They then take the second approach—critique, doubt, rejection. This is the approach of clever, enlightened people who consider religious truth to be something which has been overcome. Many of these enlightened people investigate further and find that these religious documents are after all rich in content. They win through to the third approach, which is that of symbolism. They produce many or few interpretations, depending on their cast of mind and their knowledge. Many former freethinkers in Germany have won through to this approach. Theosophy finally offers a fourth approach. One learns to take the religious documents literally again. We will have notable examples of this in our study of the Gospel of John.

The Gospel of John has very much a place of its own among the four Gospels. Those of Matthew, Mark and Luke provide a historical picture of Jesus of Nazareth. The Gospel of John is considered to be an apotheosis, a marvellous poetic work. It contradicts the other three Gospels on a number of occasions; but those contradictions are so evident that we cannot assume that the early defenders of the Gospel of John did not take note of them.

At present the Gospel of John is considered to be the least credible. The reason lies in the materialistic mentality of our time. Human beings grew materialistic in their feelings in the nineteenth century and in consequence of this also in their thinking. People form their opinions on the basis of their feelings. Materialism is a philosophy of life which is put forward not only in the works of Buechner,[67] Moleschott[68] and Vogt;[69] even people who want to take a certain academic position as exegetes of the scriptures do so in a wholly materialistic way. An example would be the dispute between Karl Vogt and Professor Wagner[70] at Goettingen University. This dispute was published in the *Augsburger Zeitung* newspaper, and it was Karl Vogt who gained the complete victory. Wagner stood for the existence of the soul, but did so in a wholly materialistic way.

As our theologians are also materialistically minded, the three Gospels of the three synoptists suit them better, for with them, materialistic exegesis is permissible. It goes against the grain in materialistic thinking to accept a spirit that is vastly superior to all humanity. It is more to their taste to see Jesus of Nazareth as a noble individual, the 'simple man' from Nazareth. In the Gospel of John it is quite impermissible to see in Jesus only the principles which are also to be found in any other human being. The soul of the Christ in the body of Jesus is something completely different. The Gospel of John shows us the Christ not only as an outstanding human being but also as a spirit that embraces the whole earth.

Translated not literally but in the spirit, the first 14 verses of the Gospel of John read:

> In the Beginning* / Was the Word / And the Word / Was with God / And the Word / Was God.
> He was in the Beginning / With God.
> Through him / Everything entered into existence / And without him / Nothing entered into existence.
> What existed / Was life in him / And the life was the light of mankind / And the light / Shines in the darkness / But the darkness / Has not taken hold of it.
> There entered into existence / A man sent out from God / His name was John.
> He came as a witness / To bear witness to the Light / So that everyone / Might believe through him.
> He was not the Light / But should bear witness to the Light / The true Light / Who enlightens every human being / Coming into the world.

---

* In German, the term for Principalities [*Urbeginne* (first beginnings)] is also used in John 1:1—'In the first beginning'.

He was in the world / Through him the world / Entered into existence / And the world / Was not aware of him.

He came into his own / And those who were his own / Did not receive him.

To all who accepted him / He gave the authority / For their existence as children of God.

For those who believe in his name / It was not of blood-streams / Nor of the will of the flesh / Nor of the will of mortal man / But of God / That they were born

In the flesh / The Word entered into existence / And made his dwelling among us / And we beheld the glory of his revelation / Revealed as an only-born from his Father / Full of grace and truth.

For John,

Truth	αληθεια (aletheia)	=	Manas
Devotion	χάρις (charis)	=	Buddhi
Wisdom	σοφία (sophia)	=	Atman

The very first word is taken as an abstract term by modern people. The beginning is seen as an abstract start or beginning. To grasp the real meaning of this term you have to bring to mind what was taught in Dionysius the Areopagite's[71] occult school: mineral, plant, animal and human being are the developmental sequence of entities that need a physical body; above them are others that exist without one. These are the Angels, Archangels, Principalities or Rulers, Powers or Authorities, Virtues or Strongholds, Dominions or Lordships, Thrones or Ophanim, Cherubim, Seraphim and beyond.

The Principalities or first beginnings are real entities, therefore. The name was given to spirits which at the beginning of our world evolution had developed as far as humanity will go at the Vulcan stage. If we consider the first verse: 'In the Beginning was the Word—Logos . . .' we could picture the situation by using the following analogy. Before we utter it, the word lives in us as thought. When it is uttered, waves are created in the air around us. If we think of some process in which these waves are frozen, we would see the words drop to the ground as forms and configurations. We would see the creative power of the word with our own eyes. The word is creative now; in future this will be the case to a much greater degree. People today have organs that will only gain their full significance in future times, whilst others are already decadent. The latter include the reproductive organs, the former the heart and the larynx, both of which are only in the early stages of their evolution. The heart is an involuntary muscle in spite of being striated like all voluntary muscles. This striation gives a hint that the heart is in transition from an involuntary to a voluntary organ. The larynx is destined to be the human reproductive organ in the far distant future, however paradoxical this may seem. Today human beings can use speech to convert their thoughts into waves in the air; one day they will be able to use the word to create their own image.

The Principalities had this creative power at the beginning of our present world evolution and may thus rightly be considered to be divine spirits. When world evolution began, a divine word was spoken, and this has become mineral, plant, animal and human being.

LECTURE 2

IN spiritual science, the human being we have before us is considered
to consist of seven principles. The physical body, perceptible to our sense
organs, is only one part of the essential human being. We have this
physical body in common with the whole mineral world around us. The
forces active in our physical body are the same as those in seemingly
inanimate nature.

The physical body is penetrated by higher powers, rather like a
sponge that is full of water. The difference between inanimate and
animate bodies is this. In an inanimate body the matter of which it
consists obeys merely the laws of physics and chemistry. In an
animate body the substances are linked to one another in a complex
way and need the help of the ether body to stay linked in groupings
that are not natural to but imposed on them. Physical matter can at
any moment return to its natural grouping and that would mean the
decomposition of the living body, and the ether body is at all times
struggling to prevent this decomposition. When the ether body
leaves the physical body, the substances in the physical body assume
their natural grouping, and the body decomposes, turns into a corpse.
The ether body is therefore constantly fighting the decomposition of
the living body.

The ether body is the power that underlies every organ. Human
beings have an ether heart, an ether brain and so on to hold the relevant
physical organs together. One is often tempted to think of the ether
body as a material entity, perhaps a very subtle mist. In reality the ether

body is a sum of energy currents. Clairvoyants see certain currents in the human ether body and these are of the greatest importance. One rises from the left foot to the forehead, goes down from there to the other foot, then to the opposite hand, from there through the heart to the other hand and then back to its point of origin. This creates a pentagram of energy currents.

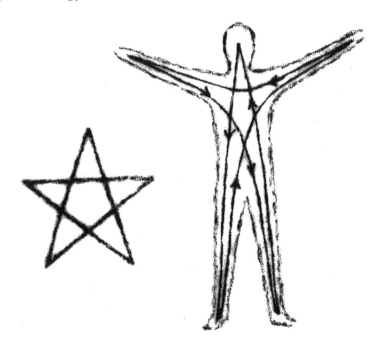

These energy currents are not the only ones in the ether body; there are a great many more. Human beings specifically owe their upright position to this one. Animals are bound to the earth in their forelimbs, and we do not see this kind of current in them. As to the configuration, form and size of the human ether body we may say that in its upper parts it is an exact likeness of the physical body. In its lower parts it is not congruent with the physical body. There is a great secret behind the relationship between ether body and physical body, providing deep insight into essential human nature—the ether body of a male is female, that of a female male. This explains why we see much that is feminine in a man's nature and much that is masculine in a woman's nature. The ether bodies of animals are larger than their physical bodies. In a horse, for instance, a clairvoyant sees the ether body project like a cap sitting on the physical head.

There is something in human beings that is much closer to them than blood, muscle, nerves and so on. These are the sensations of pleasure and suffering, joy and pain, in short everything human beings call their inmost life. In occult science it is called the astral body; human beings share it with animals only.

Someone who is born blind only knows the world around him incompletely. The world of colour and light does not exist for him. Ordinary people are in the same position with regard to the astral world. It exists, fills and surrounds the physical world, but is not perceived by them. The astral world becomes visible for those in whom the sense for the astral opens up. The significance and importance of this moment in human development is much greater, however, than when sight is given to someone born blind with an operation. We all know this astral world, though only incompletely so, for our astral body enters into it every night. We rest in the astral world in order to restore harmony to our astral body, for from the spiritual-scientific point of view being tired is merely a disharmony in the physical and astral body. An analogy may throw light on the relationship between physical and astral body. If we take a sponge, cut it into a thousand pieces and let those pieces absorb the contents of a glass of water, that is analogous to an ordinary person when awake. If we express the little sponges and collect the water in its container, it will form a single body again. That is how human astral bodies, made individual during the day, like the absorbed drops of water, enter into the common astral substance to gain strength and energy there. We realize this from the fact that the tiredness has gone by morning. The astral bodies of people who are not yet seers mingle with the other astral bodies when they have gone out in sleep. It is different in the case of seers.

Individual plants do not have astral bodies of their own. The whole plant world has one common astral body, the astral body of our earth. The earth is a living entity, plants are its members.

The fourth principle of the human being is the I. The word 'I' is one which people can only use in reference to themselves. It can never reach our ear from outside if referring to ourselves. When this I sounds in an individual it is the god in him who speaks. The animal world, the vegetable and mineral world are in a different position with regard to the I. An animal can no more say I to itself than a finger on our hand can do. To refer to its I the finger would have to point to the I of the human individual. In the same way an animal would have to point to an I belonging to an entity which lives in the astral world. All lions, all elephants and so on have a common group I—a lion I, an elephant I, and so on.

If a plant wanted to refer to its I it would have to refer to a common I at the centre of the earth, in the mental world. It is known that when we stab an animal this animal will feel pain. It is different with plants, and the seer is able to tell us that picking flowers or cutting wheat is as pleasurable a feeling for the earth as that felt by a cow when her calf sucks her milk. But when a plant is pulled out with its root, it is as if you were to cut flesh from an animal. The pulling out gives a sensation of pain in the astral world.

If we were to ask where the I of the world of rocks is to be found, it would no longer be possible to find an entity that has a centre in the spiritual world. The I of minerals is a power spread out over the whole cosmos that is to be found in the super-spiritual world, the 'higher devachan world' in theosophical terms.

In esoteric Christian teaching the world where the I of animals is to be found, the astral world, is called 'the world of the Holy Spirit'; the world where the I of plants is to be found, the spiritual or devachan world, is 'the world of the Son'. When the seer begins to feel something in this world, the 'Word' speaks to him, the Logos. The world of the mineral I, the super-spiritual world, is known as the world of the Father Spirit in occult teaching.

Human beings are evolving all the time. We have now come to know all four principles in essential human nature. Pythagoras spoke of them as the lower four in his school. The savage, the civilized person, the idealist and the saint; these four are to be found in everyone. The savage is, however, a slave to his passions; the civilized person no longer obeys his drives and desires indiscriminately; the idealist does so even less, and the saint has gained full mastery of them.

The I works on the astral body, differentiating out a part of it. In the course of human development this part gets bigger and bigger, whilst the inherited part gets less and less. In Francis of Assisi, the whole astral body had been worked through and transformed in activities coming from the I. This transformed astral body is the fifth principle in essential human nature—the Spirit Self or Manas.

The I can also gain mastery over the ether or life body. The part of the ether body which has been transformed by the I is called Life Spirit or Buddhi. Impulses in art and religion influence the ether body and transform it, religious impulses to a particularly great degree because they are repeated daily; repetition is the magic which transforms the ether body. Working consciously on occult training, meditation and concentration are the means used for this. The rate of change differs in ether body and astral body rather like the movement of the hour and the minute hand on a watch or clock. If it has been possible to make even the smallest change in one's temperament, which depends on conditions in the ether body, this is worth more than making however many spiritual theories one's own.

The greatest strength is needed to make conscious changes in the physical body. The means for this are only made known in occult schools. The physical body consciously transformed by the I is called the Spiritual Human Being or Atman. The power to transform the astral body flows to us from the world of the Holy Spirit. The power to change the ether body flows to us from the world of the Son or the Word. The power to transform the physical body comes to us from the world of the Father Spirit or the divine Father.

LECTURE 3

BASEL, 18 NOVEMBER 1907

THE terms used in the Gospel of John have such depths that we will only understand the document properly and in all its parts once we have established an adequate basis for this by knowing the evolution of our planet.

There is a strange agreement between the beginning of the Gospel of John and the beginning of the Bible. In the Bible we read, 'In the beginning God created the heaven and the earth,' in the Gospel of John we read, 'In the beginning was the Word.' These first words strike the basic chord for the whole of the Gospel. Earth evolution can only be rightly understood if we bring to mind that the same laws applied as in the development of the individual human being. From the spiritual-scientific point of view the planet that is visible to us is but the body of the spirit that dwells in it. This spirit goes through repeated embodiments just as human beings do. Spiritual investigation reveals three embodiments before the earth reached its present state. This is not to say that it had not gone through further embodiments before that; but even the highest of clairvoyants is able to perceive only the three embodiments that came before and three that will follow. Together with the present embodiment this makes seven. There is nothing superstitious about this number seven. Standing in a distant field I see equally far in all directions. It is much the same for the clairvoyant; he, too, sees equally far looking ahead in time and looking back. In occult science these seven embodiments are called Saturn, Sun, Moon, Earth, Jupiter, Venus and Vulcan. The names merely refer to the states in which one and the same entity finds itself.

Saturn was a state of our earth in a far distant past. The present planet Saturn relates to the present earth the way a child does to an old person. The earth has once been in the Saturn state just as the old person has once been a child. The next embodiment of the earth also should not be taken to mean that humanity would ever walk on Jupiter. In its next embodiment the earth will reach the state in which the planet Jupiter is at present.

Between two planetary embodiments comes a kind of heavenly or spiritual devachan, a pralaya. The time between two planetary states is no more a period of rest than the time between two lives on earth is for human beings. It is a time of spiritual activity and preparation for the next future, the next life. Outwardly this state appears shadowy and dim. When the earth emerged from pralaya to enter into the Saturn state, it was not yet the way it is today. If we were able to mix up everything by way of substance and spirit that makes up earth, sun and moon, making it into a single body, we would have the earth as it was when it emerged from that dim and shadowy condition into its Saturn state. It emerged not as a body from which all entities had gone. Even present-day humanity was present then, but in a condition adapted to the state of the planet at the time. The potential for the physical body was created on Saturn. We get an idea of the physical nature of human beings at the time if we try and grasp the material consistency of the planet. On Saturn corporeal states of the kind we know today did not exist. There were no solids, fluids or gases; matter was in a state which modern physicists would not even consider to be physical or corporeal.

Four states of matter are known in occult science—earth, water, air, and fire or heat. Earth means everything that is solid; frozen water or ice is also 'earth' in occult science. Water is everything fluid; molten iron or rock would thus also be 'water'. Air is everything gaseous, including water vapour. Fire or heat is only a property of matter for modern physicists, a state where its smallest particles are in extremely rapid vibration. In occult science, heat is also matter, but much more subtle than air. When a body is heated, it takes up heat matter, according to occult science; when it cools down, it gives off heat matter. Heat matter can condense into air, this into water, this into earth. All matter did once exist as heat matter only. When the earth was in its Saturn state, only heat matter existed on it.

The first beginnings of the human body also consisted only of heat matter, though some organs were already hinted at. But it was not only the germ of the physical body which was there but also the spirit, the inmost depth of the human being which is known as Spiritual Human Being or Atman. This Spiritual Human Being rested in the womb of the Godhead which made up the spiritual atmosphere of Saturn. This Spiritual Human being was no more an independent entity than our finger is. It will only gain independence by the end of the Vulcan stage.

During the Sun period which followed Saturn, the materiality and also the human bodies condensed from the heat state to the airy state. In consequence, human beings developed the ether body as well as the existing physical body, and where the spirit was concerned the Godhead went down a step, as it were, developing the Life Spirit or Buddhi.

During the Moon period, materiality condensed to fluid, and we might compare the densest form of matter there to wax as far as consistency is concerned. Human beings also continued to evolve, on the one hand developing the astral body and on the other, on the spiritual side, the Spirit Self or Manas. Human beings of that time did not yet have an I; they may be compared to the animals of today, though different in appearance.

When the earth emerged from the rest period that had followed the Moon phase, entering into the present period of evolution, the matter and entities in it were everything that makes up the present sun, earth and moon. In material terms humanity had been refined to the point where the astral body was able to take in the I, developing into a vehicle for the I. On the other hand the spirit had condensed so that, rather like a drop of water, it was able, as an I, to fertilize the lower bodies.

Atman	Atman	Atman	Atman, Spiritual Human being
	Buddhi	Buddhi	Buddhi, Life Spirit
		Manas	Manas, Spirit Self
			I
Saturn	Sun	Moon	Earth
			vehicle for the I
		astral body	astral body
	ether body	ether body	ether body
physical body	physical body	physical body	physical body

The first significant cosmic event was the separation of the sun from the earth. This was necessary so that the higher spirits which until then had been connected with humanity and were now ready for higher functions would have the kind of arena they needed. These higher spirits had reached the human level of development at the Saturn stage. They had then been at the stage of evolution which human beings will reach only in the earth's distant Vulcan period. Other, higher spirits had during the earth's Sun stage reached the degree of evolution to which humanity will attain in the Venus period. These particular spirits are the ones which now send their powers to us with the physical light of the sun. Both types of spirits separated from the earth, taking the most refined powers and substances with them to create the present sun.

Those were miserable times, when the sun had left the earth—but the moon continued to be part of it. Human beings were in danger of giving themselves up wholly to form, with all things spiritual, all potential for development, dying away. Together, sun and earth would have caused humanity to develop so rapidly on the spiritual side that they would not have been capable of physical development. If the moon powers had continued to be connected with the earth forces, all life would have been frozen in sheer form. Human beings would have turned into statues, 'crystallized humanity', as Goethe put it in *Faust II*.[72]

Separation of sun and moon from the earth established the balance between life and form that was needed for human evolution. It is only with those powers now acting on humanity from outside that human beings were able to evolve in the right way. The powers coming from the sun create and fructify life. The powers that cast this life in solid forms come from the moon. We are indebted to the moon for the development of the physical body as it is today; but the life which comes down into this body is from the sun.

These two streams from sun and moon are always acting in the right way because one of the sun spirits has connected with the moon. The spirits that were at the level of gods had departed with the sun; one of them has however gone its own way, making the present moon its dwelling place. This spirit is called Yehovah or Yahweh, the god of form or the moon deity. Yehovah or Yahweh shaped the three bodies of

human beings in such a way that they were able to take in the I droplet.
Yehovah made the human body in his own image, 'So God created man
in his own image' (Genesis 1:27).

This was the theory of evolution taught in mystery schools through
the ages. In the Christian school of Dionysius the Areopagite, disciples
would hear something like this: 'Consider the realms of life forms on
earth. You see stones. They are dumb. They do not express pain or
pleasure. See the plants. They are dumb, too, not expressing pleasure or
pain. The animals have risen above the dumbness.' If you were to follow
evolution with an eye sharpened by the spirit, you would see that the
same quality came to expression in the sounds produced by animals in a
far distant past as also sounds through the whole cosmos. The more you
move up towards the human being, the more will you find that sound
expresses individual pain and individual pleasure. Only man has succeeded in putting something that comes from the individual spirit into
sounds. Animals roar out what is happening in nature; but sound
became word when Yahweh had formed human bodies so that the sun's
spirits were able to enter into them. When sound becomes word, the
spirit sounds into the astral body. Meaning and significance came into
sound when the higher sun powers entered into the forms created by
Yahweh. When the first word sounded in man, this marked man's
actual beginning as a spirit.

We have now come to the point which the evangelist touched on in
Chapter 1, verse 1: 'In the beginning was the word ...'. The most
sublime spirit connected with the sun who sent the Is down to earth is
called the Christ in occult terms. The Is as members of the sun Logos did
however only flow gradually into the forms. The light streamed out
from the sun Logos but in those times only a few accepted it. Those who
did accept it came to be different from others. They were called the
children or the sons of God (Chapter 1, verse 12). They were made up of
four principles—physical body, ether body, astral body and I, though
the fourth, the youngest of them, was still weak and dark. The light is to
come to all humanity, but it needs time to do so. Reference is made to
this in verses 8 to 14. Individual people had already taken in the light to
a high degree and therefore knew of it and were able to bear witness.
They taught others. Those who bore witness from personal experience

and not from being taught, telling people that the one would come who would for the first time bring the light to all, were called 'John' in occult teaching (Chapters 6 and 7). The writer of the Gospel of John was one such 'John'. In verse 18 of Chapter 1 we read, 'No one has ever had sight of God . . . ,' which means no one before John, for it was only with Christ Jesus that he became personified. The greatest event for the evolution of the cosmos and of humanity was the event on Golgotha.

LECTURE 4

TODAY we must begin our studies with an important spiritual-scientific term. In Christian occult science the Moon is called the cosmos of wisdom and the earth the cosmos of love. Moon here means the Moon stage of Earth evolution. The reason why the Moon is called the cosmos of wisdom is that everything which had evolved by that stage was filled with wisdom. When the Moon stage was followed by the earth stage, the cosmos of wisdom was followed by the cosmos of love. As the earth emerged again from the dimmed-down stage of pralaya, the seeds of the human physical, ether and astral bodies germinated. On the Moon, wisdom had been placed in these three bodies and their mutual relationships. This is why wisdom is to be found in the construction of these three bodies. The greatest wisdom exists in the structure of the physical body, less in that of the ether body and still less in that of the astral body. Contemplating the bodily nature of man not only with the rational mind but reflectively, we discover this wisdom in every organ, every part of the body. Looking at the human thigh bone, for instance, we find there a real network of bars going one way and the other, seemingly at random; but no engineer would be able today to create these two columns which support the human upper body using the smallest amount of energy and material. Only wisdom was put in there when the divine spirits were still constructing the human body. The human physical body is usually considered to be the lowest principle, but unjustly so, for it is in this very body that we see the greatest wisdom. It is only thanks to this wisdom that the physical body is able to withstand the attacks which the astral body is making on it all the time, and does not break down ahead of time. The passions active in the physical body, the drinking of coffee, tea and so on, all these are attacks which the astral body makes on the physical body and especially the heart. This had to be so wisely made that attacks continuing for decades will not destroy it. It did, of course, take many reconfigurations before the right form was found for the heart.

It is only because it is the basis for the way the world is built that our rational mind can seek and find the wisdom in the world. Wisdom did not come suddenly into the world, however, it was poured in slowly and gradually, and the world will just as slowly and gradually be filled with love. The whole point of earth evolution is to fill the earth with love. Love has begun to be on earth to a very small degree; it spreads more and more, however, and by the end of the earth stage everything will be imbued with love just as it was imbued with wisdom by the end of the Moon stage.

When the moon left the earth, the power of love existed only as a seed. Initially only blood-related people loved one another. This went on for a long time, and the sphere of love slowly grew. It needs a certain independence of spirit to be sentient of love and use it. Two powers had always been active in human evolution—one that brought together and one that separated, power of Sun and power of Moon. Under the influence of these powers human beings developed to the point where their three bodies with the vehicle for the I inclined towards the Spirit Self, Life Spirit and Spiritual Human Being. It was not yet possible, however, to have a final union; that needed a new cosmic power. This power, which had a particularly strong effect following the separation of the moon, came from one of the other planets, which entered into a strange relationship with the earth. This planet, Mars, made a kind of passage through the earth mass when the earth began to evolve. Until then one particular metal had been missing on earth, and that was iron. Its appearance on earth abruptly changed the process of evolution. It is the planet Mars which gave iron to the earth. From then on the possibility existed for human beings to develop warm blood that contained iron. The astral body was also given a new principle by Mars—the sentient soul, the soul of courage. The quality of aggression developed in the soul as Mars entered. We now have to distinguish physical body, ether body, astral body and sentient soul in the human being. The influence of the sentient soul on the physical body led to the development of red, warm blood. The fructifying I was then able to integrate itself bit by bit.

'Blood is a juice with curious properties,' Goethe said in his *Faust*.[73] The god of form, Yahweh, played a particularly important role in this. He did above all take hold of the newly developed organ, the blood, imbued it with his powers, transforming the aggressive properties of the soul of courage into the powers of love, and made the blood the physical vehicle for the I.

Not every human individual had his or her own I to begin with. The same Yahweh power, the I power of the same I, was active in all who were related by blood, preserving the same blood by marrying within the family. Such a small group would therefore have a common I. The individual related to the whole family the way a finger does to the whole body. Initially there were group souls. The individual felt himself to be merely part of the tribe. People were sentient not only of the I of those who were alive at the time; it lived on through the different generations for as long as the blood was not mixed and people only married within the tribe. The I was thus not felt to be something personal but something all members of the tribe had in common. Where we remember things we have lived through from birth, the people of those times remembered what the ancestors of the same blood community had been doing, remembering it as if it had been their own experience. Grandchildren and great grandchildren felt the same I within themselves as their grandfather and great grandfather. We are thus able to understand the great age of the patriarchs. 'Adam', for instance, was not the term for a single individual but for the common I that ran through generations. I said earlier that Yahweh made the blood into the vehicle for the I. He did this by causing blood to form. He brought his power to expression in the way of breathing. Human beings became Yahweh human beings in that Yahweh gave them breath. We have to take it literally that the breath of life was breathed into the human being who had now been provided with the necessary preconditions. 'Yahweh breathed into his nostrils the breath of life; and man became a living soul' (Genesis 2:7). This did not happen suddenly, however. It must be seen as a process that took a very long time. It made man into an air-breather.

Something else took the place of the breathing process on the Moon. Where human beings breathe air in and out today, which gives them an inner source of warmth, their ancestors, who consisted of physical body, ether and astral body, breathed heat matter or fire in and out. On the Moon, human beings were fire-breathers. Occult science calls them fire spirits, and human beings on earth, air beings. In spiritual science, all matter is seen as spirit coming to expression. We do not only inhale and exhale air but with it also the spirit. Air is the body of Yahweh, flesh the body of man. Remembrance of this lived on in the Germanic legend of Woden riding the wind. On the Moon, too, it was the spirit which was breathed.

The same spirits existed on the Moon as on the earth. There they lived in fire, on earth they have become air spirits. In cosmic evolution, some spirits lagged behind, like schoolchildren who have to repeat a year. The spirits that had made the sun their dwelling place had developed more rapidly, managing the transition from fire to air spirits, though large numbers of spirits did not manage this transition. Those did now act on human beings as spiritual powers from outside, from the sun and the moon. Human beings take them in with the breath. Between human beings and these highly evolved sun spirits are spirits that did develop a great deal further than human beings on the moon but have not got as far as the sun spirits and the god Yahweh. They were not yet able to influence human beings in the breath but nevertheless sought to influence them. These were fire spirits that had not achieved completion. Their element was heat which in human beings existed only in the warm blood. They had to live on that warmth.

In the course of their evolution human beings were thus between the air spirits that live in the breath, the highest spirits that fill them with spirit, and the fire spirits that sought out the elements of their blood. They acted as opponents to the god Yahweh. Yahweh sought to keep human beings together in small groups by means of love. He wanted to fill them with a sense of belonging together. Yet if only love had been available, human beings would never have grown independent. They would have had to develop into automatons of love, as it were. The fire spirits directed their attacks in this direction, with the result that human beings gained personal freedom. The small groups of people were driven apart. The god Yahweh was only interested in bringing people together in love. He was active in the blood as the god of blood love. The action of the fire spirits was different; it was they who gave human beings art and science. They are also known as the luciferic spirits. Human evolution then continued under the influence of Lucifer who gave human beings freedom and wisdom. Under the guidance of the god Yahweh, people were brought together according to the principle of being blood brothers. Human beings owe their existence as free earth citizens to Lucifer. Yahweh placed them in the paradise of love. There the serpent, the fire spirit appeared in a form which human beings had had when they still breathed fire, opening their eyes to things that still remained from the moon. This luciferic influence was felt to lead man astray. People raised in occult schools, however, did not see this enlightenment as a way of leading astray. The great initiates did not degrade the serpent but elevated it, as Moses did in the desert (Numbers 21:8–9).

The things to be revealed to man were for a long time revealed as blood love by Yahweh. The spirit of wisdom, a principle which served to prepare for something else, was active at the same time. Love gradually spread from relatively small to larger groups, from families to tribes. A typical example is the Jewish nation who felt themselves to be a coherent group, referring to all other people as Galileans, that is, people who were not of the blood. Humanity was to be given not only blood love but spiritual love, embracing the whole earth with a brotherhood bond. The time when humanity were held together only by love among those who were related must just be considered a period of training for what was to come later. The influence of Lucifer, driving apart the bonds that were too narrow, was also in preparation for the influence of a higher spirit who was to come. This higher spirit was called the true bearer of light, the true Lucifer, the Christ, in Christian occultism.

Let us go back to the time when Atlantean humanity was on earth. The earth did look very different then. Between Europe and America, where there is a great ocean today, was land, a continent which is now at the bottom of the ocean. People are gradually also coming to realize in modern science that there used to be a continent where the Atlantic Ocean is today. People who were very different from people today lived on Atlantis. The relationship between ether and physical body was very different then. A clairvoyant sees two points in the head of human beings today, one in the ether brain, the other in the physical brain, about a centimetre deep between the eyes. The two points coincide in people today. It was different with Atlanteans. The ether brain projected well beyond the physical brain and the two central points of the brains were not coincident. There can be exceptional cases today where the two points do not coincide; idiocy is a consequence of this. It was only in the last third of the Atlantean age that the two central points came together, and only then did human beings learn to say I to themselves in full awareness. Atlanteans also had not been able to reckon, count, judge things and think logically before that. But their memory was vast, extending through generations, and they had some dim clairvoyance. They did not see the outlines of physical bodies clearly, but they perceived what went on in the soul. Meeting an animal, an Atlantean would be clairvoyantly sentient of the animal's attitude to him. If he saw a reddish brown colour he'd step aside, knowing that a hostile element was present. But if he saw a reddish violet, he'd know that something was coming towards him that was sympathetic. The value of foods was also recognized with the aid of clairvoyance. Present-day animals, which have retained that dim clairvoyance, use it to judge different plants in their pasture for their benefit or harm.

The experiences human beings still have in their dreams are a decadent residue of ancient Atlantean clairvoyance. Atlanteans did not make clear distinction between sleep and waking consciousness the way present-day people do. Their daytime consciousness was less clear than ours. Sleep and dream consciousness was brighter then. In early Atlantean times, states of complete unconsciousness would be filled with mighty dream images. Very early Atlanteans knew nothing of the act of reproduction. It would proceed in states of complete unconsciousness. When the Atlantean woke up he would know nothing of that act. It was only shown to them in symbols. The Greek legend of Deucalion and Pyrrha who went to Greece throwing stones behind them which then turned into human beings reminds us of this.

The act of procreation was veiled in unconsciousness for as long as people only married blood relatives. Under the influence of the luciferic spirits, who 'opened people's eyes', human beings developed conscious awareness and recognized the act of procreation in full awareness. They learned to distinguish good from bad. No longer just concerned with blood relationship but knowing of their love, human beings grew independent. The Christ then took the place of Yahweh, bringing a higher form of life into the world and making human beings independent of others in their tribe and blood relations. This universal love is only in its early stages. One day the earth will have given its entities over to Jupiter and they will then be quite full of this spiritual love. The Christ's words 'If anyone comes to me who does not disregard his father and mother, his wife and children and his brothers and sisters as well as his own soul-bearing life, he cannot be my disciple' point to this (Luke 14: 26). The spirit that is pouring out this universal love more and more over the earth is the Christ spirit. With the coming of Christ Jesus earth evolution was divided into two parts. The blood that flowed on Golgotha signifies that spiritual love took the place of love within blood bonds. That is the connection between Yahweh, Lucifer and the Christ.

LECTURE 5

'THE law was given through Moses, but grace and truth entered into existence through Jesus Christ' (John 1:17). When we fully understand these words we also grasp the profound, significant change which the coming of the Christ brought in human history. In the previous lectures I gave a rough outline of human evolution, showing the way in which awareness of I nature developed. In the far, far distant past whole groups and generations of people were sentient of being an I. The great age of the patriarchs thus becomes understandable. The sense of I gradually came to be limited to single individuals. I have also shown how two spiritual streams made themselves felt in this evolution—one being blood relationship, endeavouring to keep people together in a natural way; the other, luciferic stream making people independent and preparing them for the purely spiritual bond that was to come.

Through the period of the Old Testament, the law was something that imposed order from outside in human society. When blood relationship had lost its power to bind, people had to be brought into some kind of connection through external thoughts creating order among them. The law was felt to be something coming from outside. This law given to us from outside will pertain until the devotion, the grace and truth given to us by the Christ has created an understanding for true insight that comes from within. Grace and truth can only develop gradually. Christianity, seeking to bring devotion instead of the law, is still in the early stage of its evolution. The further earth evolution progresses, the stronger will also be the influence which Christianity has on humanity. Humanity is to rise to a level of living together where promptings from within make every individual relate to whoever is nearest as brother does to brother. Humanity would not be able to rise to this level of their own accord, and it is the mission of Christianity to help them with this. Human beings will no longer need external law when they have the inner impulse to let devotion and truth be the guiding principles in their actions.

This is not to say that humanity has reached the point where no more law is needed; it is an ideal to strive for. Humanity will gradually come to where voluntary actions establish harmony in the world. To achieve this goal the power had to intervene which in the terms of the Gospel is the Christ. Those who have found the inner strength to relate to all others in such a way that they fit in freely, without compulsion, with the harmony are in the occult schools said to 'bear the Christ within them'.

To understand what follows we need to call to mind again the principles or levels of existence that make up the human being:

I

astral body	Spirit Self
ether body	Life Spirit
physical body	Spiritual Human Being

The work that the I does on the astral body transforms the latter into Spirit Self. This happens in stages, with the sentient soul developing first, then the rational soul, then the spiritual soul [translation suggested by Rudolf Steiner; 'consciousness soul' in other translations]. The Spirit Self pours into the matured, purified spiritual soul. The I also works on the ether body, and the impulses which are most effective there are those of art, religion and occult training.

Occult schools existed also in pre-Christian times. They were able to take their disciples so far that they could look into the higher worlds. Such vision existed however only for the true disciples in the most secret occult schools and even then only during the actual act of initiation, when the ether body had been separated from the physical body. Initiation means raising the individual to the point where he can see into the spiritual world. All initiation procedures of pre-Christian times involved getting the initiand into a kind of sleep state. The sleep of initiation differed from ordinary sleep in that in the latter the ether body remains connected with the physical body, whilst in the former the ether body was separated from the physical body for a brief period. The hierophant had to keep the body alive during that time. Taking out the ether body made it possible to take it into the higher worlds together with the other bodies so that it would learn things there which could later be conveyed to the physical brain. Those were the only methods of initiation in pre-Christian times.

Something quite new relating to the method of initiation came with the coming of Christ Jesus. Imagine that the human being had transformed the whole astral body into Spirit Self. This Spirit Self then came to be impressed into the ether body like a seal in sealing wax, imposing its form. This transformed the ether body into Life Spirit. When this had been done completely, the Life Spirit would be impressed in the physical body, making it into the Spiritual Human Being. It was only with the coming of Christ Jesus that it became possible to impress the principle which was the Life Spirit directly into the life body. Things learned in the higher worlds could not be embodied in the physical brain without first separating the ether body from the physical body. The first individual who had an ether body wholly filled with Spirit Self and a physical body wholly filled with Life Spirit was Christ Jesus. It was because Christ Jesus had come to earth that it became possible for those who are connected with him to go through the same initiation without separating the ether body from the physical body. All pre-Christian initiates thus had experienced initiation when out of the physical body, had then returned to the physical body and were thus able to tell from personal experience what had been going on in the spiritual world.

Buddha, Moses and others were such initiates. With Jesus, a spirit came to earth for the first time which was able to see the life in the higher worlds whilst remaining in the physical body. The teachings of Buddha, Moses and so on were entirely independent of the personality of their masters. People are Buddhists or Mosaists because they observe the teachings of Buddha or Moses. It is irrelevant if they acknowledge Buddha or Moses, for these originators merely passed on what they had learned in the higher worlds. It is different with the Christ. His teaching becomes Christianity because of his personality, and it is not enough merely to follow the teachings of Christianity to be a Christian. True Christians feel deeply connected with the historical Christ. Individual tenets of Christianity existed before. But this is not the point, but rather that the Christian believes in Christ Jesus, takes him to be the one who represents the perfect human being in the flesh.

In earlier times people still knew the saying that the initiate is a divine individual. This was because the initiate was up in the spiritual world and with the spirits or gods during initiation. There he was the divine human being. But the 'divine human being' could only be seen in the physical body through Christ Jesus, never before that. The passage in John 1:18, 'No one had ever had sight of God; the only-born Son who is within the being of the Father, he is the interpreter,' must therefore be taken literally. In earlier times only those who had made the ascent themselves were able to perceive the godhead. With the Christ, the Godhead had for the first time visibly come to earth. This is proclaimed in John 1:14 and was also taught in the school of Dionysius. The Christ came to show human beings the way; they were to follow him, were to prepare themselves to impress all that is in the ether body into the physical body, that is, develop the Christ principle in themselves.

The Gospel of John is a book of life. No one has understood it who has explored it with the rational mind, only those who have lived it. If you repeat the first 14 verses day after day for a period of time, you will discover why those words were written. They are material for meditation, enabling us to see the individual parts of the Gospel, such as the wedding at Cana in Chapter 2, the conversation with Nicodemus in Chapter 3, as personal experiences in the great astral tableau. These exercises make human beings clairvoyant, so that they can know the truth for themselves of what is written in the Gospel of John. Hundreds have gone through this. The writer of the Gospel of John was a high-ranking seer who had been initiated by the Christ himself.

No mention is made anywhere in the Gospel of John of John the disciple. He is merely called 'the disciple whom he loved', in 19:26, for instance. This is a technical term referring to one whom the master himself had initiated. John wrote of his own initiation in the raising of Lazarus in Chapter 11. The most secret connections of the Christ with world evolution can only be revealed in that the writer of the Gospel of

John was initiated by the Lord himself. As said earlier, the old initiations took three and a half days—hence the raising of Lazarus on the fourth day. Of Lazarus, too, it is said that the Christ loved him (11:3, 35–6). This is again the technical term for the beloved disciple. As the body of Lazarus lay in the tomb as if dead, his ether body was taken out to go through the initiation and receive the power that is also in the Christ. He thus became one raised from the dead, the one whom the Lord loved, and the Gospel of John is his work. Reading the Gospel with this in mind you will see that not a single line contradicts this fact, except that the process of initiation is covered with a veil.

Let us consider another image in the Gospel of John. In 19:25 we read: 'But beside Jesus' cross stood his mother and his mother's sister, Mary the wife of Clopas, and Mary Magdalene.' To understand the Gospel we need to know who those three women were. In those days you would no more find two sisters having the same name as you would today. Looking through the Gospel of John we find no indication anywhere that Jesus' mother was called Mary. In the story of the wedding at Cana (Chapter 2) it says merely that the mother of Jesus was there, for example. These words refer to something which is important, though we will only understand it if we know how the writer of the Gospel chose his words. What did the term 'mother of Jesus' mean? As we have seen, human beings consist of physical body, ether body and astral body. The transition from astral body to Spirit Self should not be considered in too simple a way. The I transforms the astral body slowly and gradually into sentient soul, rational soul and spiritual soul. The I continues its work and it is only when it has taken the astral body to spiritual soul level that it is able to purify it so that Spirit Self may arise in it.

Father	7 Spiritual Human Being	
Son	6 Life Spirit	distant future
	transformed ether body	
Holy Spirit	5 Spirit Self, spiritual soul	Virgin Sophia, purified spiritual soul
	4 rational soul, astral soul	Mary, wife of Clopas
	3 sentient soul, sentient body	Mary Magdalene
	2 ether body	
	1 physical body	

The Spiritual Human Being will only evolve in the distant future. The Life Spirit, too, is still at the germinal stage in most people. The evolution of the Spirit Self has now begun. It is inseparably bound up with the spiritual soul, rather like a sword in its sheath. The sentient soul on its part is in the sentient or astral body. We thus have nine principles making up individual human nature. Spirit Self and spiritual soul are, however, inseparably bound up with one another, as are sentient soul and astral body, and reference is therefore usually made to seven principles in theosophical literature. Spirit Self is also Holy Spirit, in Christian terms the leading spirit on the astral plane. The Life Spirit is called the 'Word' or the 'Son' by Christians. Spiritual Human Being is the 'Father Spirit' or the 'Father'.

People who had brought the Spirit Self to birth within themselves were known as 'children of God'; for them 'the light shone into the darkness' and 'they received the light'. Outwardly they were flesh and blood, but they bore a higher human being in them. Within them the Spirit Self had been born out of the spiritual soul. The 'mother' of such an individual who had become spiritual is not a biological mother; she is within him; it is the purified spiritual soul that is now spirit. She is the principle out of which the higher human being is born. This spiritual birth, a birth in the highest sense, is referred to in the Gospel of John. The Spirit Self of the Holy Spirit pours into the purified spiritual soul. The words 'Thus I beheld the Spirit descending as a dove from heaven and remaining on him' (John 1:32) also refer to this.

The spiritual soul is the principle in which the Spirit Self has developed and is therefore called 'the mother of Christ' or in occult schools 'the virgin Sophia'. The Christ could be born in Jesus of Nazareth following the insemination of the virgin Sophia. Rational soul and sentient soul were called 'Mary' and 'Mary Magdalene' in the occult schools of Dionysius.

The physical human being is born from the union of two human beings. The higher human being can only be born from a spiritual soul that encompasses the whole nation. Among all peoples, the method of initiation was the same as far as the essential stages were concerned. Every initiation is in seven stages. Their names in Persian initiation were the same—first the Raven. Someone who is at this level has to bring news of the outside world to the temple. The Raven is everywhere known as the messenger of the spirits, for instance also in the German legends of Odin and his two ravens. Secondly the Occult One. Thirdly the Fighter. He would have permission from the occult schools to go out and proclaim the teachings. Fourthly the Lion, firmly rooted in himself, who had not only the Word but also the magic powers, who had come through the trial and so offered a guarantee that he would not abuse the powers granted to him. Fifth the Persian. Sixth the Sun Hero and seventh the Father. Here it is the name of the fifth grade, the Persian, which interests us. Initiates of the fifth grade bore the name of their nation in all occult schools, for their mind had broadened so far that it encompassed the whole nation. All the suffering of his nation he would feel to be his own. His mind had been purified and broadened to be the mind of his nation in general. Among the Jews an initiate of this grade would be called an Israelite. We need to know this to understand the conversation which the Christ had with Nathanael (1:47–9). Nathanael was an initiate of the fifth grade. The surprising words of the Christ that he had seen Nathanael under the fig tree refer to a particular part of initiation, receiving the spiritual soul.

The following will be helpful for understanding the inner aspects of initiation. Individual awareness of I nature is in the physical world. Human beings walk about with their I. The I of animals, on the other hand, is on the astral plane. Every group of animals has a common I awareness there. It is not only the I of animals which exists in the astral world but also the I of the body which human beings have in common with animals, that is, the I of the human astral body. In the devachan world we find the Is of plants and also the I of the body we have in common with plants, the I of the ether body. Going up even higher to the upper devachan we find there the I of minerals and the I of the part which human beings have in common with minerals—the I of the physical body. We are therefore connected with the upper devachan through our physical body. With our individual I we are here in the physical world. When the I of an initiate's astral body is imbued with and worked through by his individual I he gains conscious awareness in the astral world. He is then able to perceive things there and take action. He meets the spirits that are incarnated in the astral bodies, including the group souls of animals, and the higher spirits which in Christianity are called angels. Following initiation to an even higher grade, the I of the ether body is imbued with the individual I. With this, conscious awareness extends up into the devachan world. There one meets the plant Is and the planetary spirit. Initiation reaches an even higher level when the individual I imbues the I of the physical body. The human being will then gain personal conscious awareness also in the super-spiritual world. There he meets the I of the minerals and yet higher spirits. Initiation thus means moving up into higher worlds where one meets higher and higher spirits.

Upper devachan world I of minerals	I of the physical body	Super devachan level of conscious awareness
Devachan I of plants	I of ether body	Devachan level of conscious awareness
Astral world	I of astral body	Astral level of conscious awareness
Physical world	Individual I	Daytime level of conscious awareness

We might use the following analogy:

> The I of the ether body may be compared to the mechanic.
> The I of the astral body may be compared to the driver of a car.
> The I of the individual I, physical body, may be compared to the
> owner of a car.

When the individual I has gained full control of the three bodies, it will have developed inner harmony. A spirit who had this harmony in full was the Christ. He came to earth so that human beings may be able to develop that power of inner harmony. We see the whole of human evolution in this son of man, all the way up to the highest spiritual level. Before that, this inner harmony did not exist; external laws took its place. Inner harmony is the new impulse which humanity has received through the Christ. Human beings are meant to gain the Christ capacity, that is, develop the inner Christ. But just as Goethe said that 'the eye develops in the light for the light',[74] so this inner harmony, the inner Christ, is ignited only because the external, historical Christ exists.

Before he came it was not possible for human beings to reach this level of spiritual development.

The human beings who lived prior to the Christ's historical life are not excluded from the blessing that his coming meant for humanity. For we should not forget that they have to return according to the law of reincarnation and therefore will have opportunity to develop the inner Christ. It is only when one forgets about reincarnation that one might speak of injustice. The Gospel of John shows us the way to the historical Christ, to the sun which ignites the inner light in human beings, just as the physical sun has ignited the light of our eyes.

LECTURE 6

BASEL, 21 NOVEMBER 1907

O<small>NE</small> of the most important secrets of all occult schools, including that of Dionysius, is the 'secret of numbers'. No one is able to read occult writing unless able to decipher the secret of numbers. When you have numbers in religious documents, there is always some deep meaning behind it. The school of Pythagoras[75] was also based on the secret of numbers. It may be true that the letter kills, but in the exegesis of occult scripture we do have to attach some value to the letter, otherwise we are in danger of imposing the spirit we want to see in them on those scriptures. In the Gospel of John we find many numbers of occult significance. In the fifth lecture I spoke of the three women who stood beside the cross, the virgin mother Sophia, Mary and Magdalene. In today's lecture we'll first of all make another study of numbers our basis.

Let us recall the conversation Christ Jesus had with the Samaritan woman (4:7 ff.). The Christ spoke the important words: 'You have had five husbands and he whom you have now is not your husband.' The figure five also appears in the story of healing the man who had been sick for 38 years (5:5). The Bethesda pool had five colonnades. Let us go a bit more into the meaning of this mystic figure five. Consider the essential nature of the human being in connection with human evolution. As we have seen, human beings are made up of nine parts, though these can be reduced to seven. These seven bodies evolved gradually in the course of evolution. Not all seven have developed at the present time. The average person has evolved as far as the spiritual soul; the

Spirit Self is in the early stages of development. Going back to the time in human evolution when human beings learned to say 'I' to themselves in full awareness, this was preceded by the ancient Atlantean period when human beings still had dim clairvoyant powers. In the region of Atlantis which is Ireland today lived people who had progressed so far in evolution that the ether head and the physical head were congruent.

These were the people who were most advanced at that time, and it was their destiny to be the bearers of future evolution. One very advanced spirit, Manu, lead this group eastwards through present-day Russia to central Asia, in the region of today's Gobi desert. A colony was established there and groups were sent out from there in many different directions to spread the culture of the group. This happened at the time when the continent of Atlantis was gradually sinking. Present-day Africa and Europe gradually emerged from the floods. Another group of Atlanteans went from their dwelling place to the west and became the original population of present-day America. They were found there when America was rediscovered by Europeans. One group also went to the north of Europe. All these groups have preserved their clairvoyant memories in old legends and myths. When we come to understand these legends and myths properly much of the darkness that is still covering up human history will be lifted; we shall then get to understand much that is still incomprehensible to us. We must not be pedantic, however, in explaining these legends and myths. We have to know the complex way in which clairvoyant experiences and fantasy played a role in creating these ancient legends. At this time, when the I first came to shine out in the individual nature, human beings lived in their surroundings to a much greater degree than later. They did not so much perceive the definite outlines of objects around them but rather the inner qualities and their attitude to them, if they were beneficial or harmful, friend or foe. The more the I came to be enclosed within the individual nature of human beings, the more did clairvoyant powers decline, and the forms in the outside world then appeared more and more clearly to the physical eye. Putting this before our mind's eye we can easily understand that the entry of the I brought a great change. Before, human beings did not see their own body; now they began to refer to it as their I or self.

Towards the end, Atlantis was a land of mists, covered with dense mists; there was no alternation of rain and sunshine, nor the rainbow phenomenon. This could only develop in post-Atlantean times, when the mists parted. This event has stayed alive in folk memory as the legend of Heimdallr and in the story of Noah and the Ark. The land of mists is remembered in the Nordic term Niflheim, home of mists. The people of northern Europe have also kept the memory of the entry of the I into individual human nature alive in the legend of the Nibelungs. There gold serves as the symbol for the I. The gold was dissolved in water but came together in the ring, the treasure of the Nibelungs—the I, until then dispersed all over the world, had come together and entered the solid human form. In Wagner's version of it one can be aware of the unconscious sentience of the creative artist. Wagner was not fully aware of what he was creating in the work, but subconscious knowledge was his guide. One may well think that Wagner characterized the I which had come to awareness in the drone heard throughout the prelude to *Das Rheingold* (Rhine Gold).

In the Far East, the first civilization developed under the guidance of a highly developed individual; the ancient Vedas still bear witness to this. The first impulse of this civilization was given towards the south in ancient Indian civilization. These facts are preserved in the ancient Indian myths and legends, in religious writings. Clairvoyants are able to read them. Seemingly contradictory parts show themselves to be the most profound truth. This civilization still had definite memories of the earlier ancient clairvoyance and there was still a deep longing then for something that was felt to be a precious heritage, sadly lost. People were still so full of the reality of the spiritual world that they referred to the physical world as Maya, delusion. They sought to regain the lost heritage by turning away from the earthly world and always focusing on the spirit. This was the origin of the yoga exercises, seeking to enter into the spiritual world by reducing conscious awareness. They wanted to return to the old twilight state; they were looking for a way back to their lost paradise. For the whole Atlantean period, the outside world had only been seen in blurred outlines. The Atlanteans were still living mainly in the spiritual world. For the spiritual investigator, the whole post-Atlantean period signifies merely the gradual conquest of the physical plane. The first period of post-Atlantean civilization, Indian, had little feeling as yet for anything in the natural world; initiates considered it to be an absolute illusion and sought to escape from it into their only reality, spiritual reality.

The second impulse was the ancient Persian civilization. The Persians were closer to the outside world than the Indians; they knew the phenomenon of good and evil, represented by the gods Ormuzd and Ahriman. They sought to connect with the former in order to fight the latter. The earth was to them a place for work, to integrate the spirit into physical existence. The third period of civilization was the Egyptian, Assyrian, Chaldean and Babylonian civilization. Human beings had taken another step forward in conquering the physical plane. To the Persians, the world was physically still an undifferentiated place of work. Now human beings were already using their knowledge to make the forces of the soil serve them. They knew geometry and used it to divide up the land; they also looked beyond the earth to the stars, and that was when astronomy developed.

The fourth was the Graeco-Roman period of civilization. Until then people had applied science to outward civilization; now they put their own inner being, the specifically human aspect, into matter. We see the human form in works of art; epic poems and drama described people's own inner qualities. The Roman was the citizen who projected his own laws outwards, creating the state and jurisprudence.

In the fifth period, in which we are now living, human beings have gone even further in controlling the outside world. Our age marks the extreme descent of the spirit into matter since Atlantean times. This descent had to come if humanity was to progress. The spirit must descend all the way down into matter before it can begin its ascent. Our age has developed a highly scientific approach. In primeval times, when human beings ground their grain in primitive fashion between two stones, it did not need much mental energy to satisfy their modest needs. It is very different now. Just think of the enormous expenditure of mental energy needed to meet the material needs of modern man. We have railway engines, steam ships, telephone, electric light. A vast amount of mental energy has been expended on material things. Yet the cultural interests of people lose all significance. So we see that the whole cultural development in post-Atlantean times has been the descent of the human mind and spirit into matter. The purpose of this descent is, however, to overcome matter, this great adversary of mind and spirit. For the deep descent must now be followed by humanity rising to conscious spiritual life.

The diagram below may serve to show the progress of human history in post-Atlantean times.

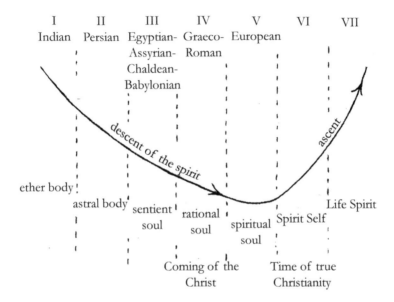

The power of Christianity was to bring about the ascent. The star of Christianity rose in the middle of the fourth period of civilization, long before the lowest point in the descent was reached. Christ Jesus appeared as the sublime individual who will provide humanity with the strength needed for the ascent to the spirit. All preceding periods of civilization may be considered to have been in preparation for Christianity. In the fifth period of civilization Christianity has to face its greatest trial of strength, for materialistic thinking is obscuring its spiritual truths.

In the sixth period, Christianity will be uniting humanity in one great brotherhood, and theosophy may be seen as a herald of that future time, preparing for the spiritualization of humanity. The teaching which

Christianity gives to humanity is so profound and full of wisdom that no future religion will be able to replace or displace Christianity. Christianity has the power to adapt to all future forms of civilization.

There is another aspect of human evolution to be considered. The physical body evolved in Atlantean times, and when the continent of Atlantis became submerged human beings had approximately the form they have today. There followed the evolution of the non-physical principles. The ether body evolved during the Indian period of civilization. The Indian people, the first branch of civilization in post-Atlantean times, were highly receptive to spiritual life. This has to do with the special development of the ether body.

Incidentally, our present-day European civilization differs greatly from both the ancient Indian and the present-day Indian civilization, and so we can understand why different ways and means are needed to guide an Indian and a European to spiritual life. The yoga exercises which are helpful for Indians do not serve the purpose for Europeans. The masters who indicate the ways of initiation always adapt them to the current stage of human development. A method which is excellent at one level may actually be detrimental at another. Religions also have not succeeded one another without reason. All have a common core of truth, yet the different ways of presenting this truth are based on the differences in periods of civilization. From root to blossom, a tree is a single whole, yet the root needs a different kind of sustenance than do the leaves or flowers. Humanity, too, needs different religions and methods of initiation in different stages of civilization.

The astral body evolved during the Persian civilization. The Egyptian, Assyrian, Chaldean and Babylonian civilization was the time when the sentient soul evolved in the astral body. The rational soul came to evolve during the Graeco-Roman period. Our own civilization is the time when the spiritual soul evolves. The Spirit Self will evolve during the sixth period. Today it is still germinal. It will need the tremendous driving force of the Christ spirit to let this seed develop. True Christianity will only come into flower once the Spirit Self has evolved. Then humanity will have made itself ready to receive the Buddhi, Life Spirit. Initially only a small group of people will develop this inner power, but they will attain to a wonderful life in the spirit. Today Christianity is only in the beginnings of its evolution. Those who are today preparing themselves to develop the Spirit Self within themselves will in the next era make this deeper, spiritual Christianity more and more accessible to human beings.

We see how in the third age a small group, the Jewish people, created the preconditions that would make the coming of the Christ possible; how in the fourth age the power of the Christ entered into the physical world; how in the fifth age humanity descended more deeply into the physical world; how, once humanity has gained mastery of this physical world, they will in the sixth age gain all the more strength and powers to take in the spiritual life which the Christ spirit has brought. The Christ appeared as the first-born who as a human being was far ahead of his time, having reached the level which the rest of humanity will only reach in the sixth age. The fifth age is the most material in the evolution of humanity.

Spiritual sentience is the basis for physical conditions, and every disease in the body reflects some kind of spiritual aberration. Leprosy, for example, the most horrible disease of medieval times, reflected at the physical level the fear which European peoples had of the Huns. The Huns were descendants of the Atlantean race in decline. Their physical body was still sound, but their astral bodies were full of rotting matter. Fear and terror are an excellent medium for the rotting material of the astral plane. This rotting material of the Atlantean tribes could establish itself in the astral body of European peoples and from there cause leprosy in the physical bodies of later generations.

Everything lives first in a spiritual way and later comes to expression in the physical body. The nervousness we see today is also a consequence of the materialistic attitude in our time. Those who are wisely guiding humanity know that if the great flood of materialism were to continue yet further, great epidemics of nervous diseases would appear in our world; children would be born with limbs already atremble. The theosophical movement has been brought into the world to save humanity from the dangers of materialism. People who spread materialistic thinking and feeling are therefore promoting these disastrous diseases; people who fight materialism are fighting for the health and positive development of our nation. Individuals cannot do much for their health; they are part of the whole of humanity and draw on a source common to all for the material they need to survive. If we look more deeply into the laws of human evolution we have to look on, and it makes your heart bleed, as individuals suffer and how their suffering is but a reflection of the spiritual aberration of the whole of humanity. Theosophy is not so much called on to help individuals but rather to give the whole of humanity fresh impetus for the things of the spirit and thus for the physical well-being of humanity.

During the sixth and seventh ages the power of the Christ will make the Spirit Self and the Life Spirit develop in those who lean on him. They will also gain sound thinking and sound feeling. Christianity is the bringer of great health and great healing. The vital strength of the Christ will overcome all sickness and death. The human body has developed from the fluid state into a solid body, and in occult science the fluid element is therefore considered to be the bodily element. The five colonnades surrounding the pool of Bethesda signify the five ages used by man to enter more and more deeply into bodily nature, being wholly subject to matter in the end. It will only be when these five ages have been gone through that human beings will gain health. Those who have fallen victim to these five colonnades cannot be healed unless the Christ, the great healer, comes to them. Then the event described in the fifth chapter of the Gospel of John will happen. The story of the man who was sick for 38 years is therefore a prophetic announcement of what will happen in the sixth age, when human beings will no longer need medicinal agents for they will be their own healers.

Remnants of blood relationship did still persist at the beginning of the post-Atlantean age. The words of the Christ that whosoever does not leave his father and his mother . . . cannot be his disciple refer to the stage humanity will reach in the sixth age. Then spirits of nations, tribes and races will have given way to the one spirit of all humanity. Then man will no longer be the son of his tribe or nation, but the son of humanity, the son of man. Once again the Christ was the first who rightly bore that name (John 3:13–14). He did already show the attitude which human beings will show when they are sons of man.

This is shown in that the Christ went to the Samaritan woman. Samaritans lived separate lives from the Jews. Human beings have a feminine passive element in them that makes development possible, the counterpart to the spirit which is the inseminating, active, male principle. The consequence of this continuous influence of the male on the female principle was initially the unfolding of the ether body, then of the astral body, the sentient soul, the rational soul and the spiritual soul. In the last of these the Spirit Self is then configured. This is hinted at in the talk which the Christ had with the Samaritan woman (4:18) in the words: 'Because you have had five husbands and he whom you have now is not your husband.' The five husbands the woman had had are the five spiritual bodies that acted on the physical body; the sixth is the Spirit Self and no longer a husband in the old sense. The other five were lower, transitory stages of development. The sixth, the Spirit Self, represents the divine, eternal principle. We see how in the talk with the Samaritan woman, too, the time which is to come through Christ Jesus is announced.

The five bodies need purification from outside; the Spirit Self will itself keep human beings pure. The body of the Christ is already filled with purity. He wanted to cleanse humanity as well and because of this went and cleansed the temple from traders and money changers (2:14–22), that is, he cleansed the temple of the Holy Spirit, the body of man, from lower principles that were attached to it, making it fit to receive the spirit.

What I am saying here should, however, never be taken to mean that things written in the Gospel of John should be taken to be symbolic only. The giving of names was not at all arbitrary in antiquity but strictly related to the character of the person. Although it is absolutely true that the three women who stood by the cross signified the three qualities of spiritual, rational and sentient soul, it is also true that those three people stood below the cross in their physical form. When we read the Gospel of John, we are therefore seeing symbolic images of what will come to realization in the next age on this earth and at the same time something which truly happened at the beginning of the Christian era. The historical facts have all been put there by the wise powers that guide humanity as symbols of the future evolution of humanity.

LECTURE 7

EVERYTHING written in a document such as the Gospel of John is significant and important, and nothing could be put in a different way from how it is written there. Why, for instance, does the Holy Spirit appear as a dove? To explain this would need a number of lectures. But we can at least get some idea if we look at the evolution of humanity from a point of view that differs from the one taken so far. Something said in an earlier lecture which must seem outrageous to those who think in terms of natural science is that man existed from the very beginning of evolution and that humanity have made the evolution of the earth also their own. Evidently we must not forget that earlier human beings were organized and constituted in a very different way compared to present-day humanity. Even the Atlanteans looked very different from people today. The difference is much greater for people of the Lemurian age and still greater for human beings at the time when moon and sun were still connected with our planet.

To find our way into the spiritual-scientific view of evolution we have to start close to home. Not all human beings living on earth today are at the same stage of development. Let us take the nations that have become known with the discovery of America, for example, and refer to an episode[76] that gives us some insight into the thinking of those nations. As you know, the white people had pushed the native American population further and further inland, failing to keep their promise that they would give them land. A native American chief once said to the leader of a troop of European conquerors: 'You palefaces have taken our land, promising to give us other land instead. But the white man has not kept his word to the brown man and we do know why. The white man has small signs that have magic spirits in them, and uses these to look for the truth. But what he is learning is not the truth; it is not good. The brown man is not looking for the truth in such small magic signs. He hears the "great spirit" in the wind soughing in the woods, the sound of the brook. The great spirit tells him what is right and what is wrong in lightning and thunder.'

Native Americans [have] preserved belief in a monotheistic spirit that speaks to them from all the sounds of nature. The native American is so closely bound up with nature that he still hears the voice of the sublime creative spirit in all natural sounds. Both races have the same origin, both are descendants of the Atlanteans whose faith was monotheistic, deriving from a spiritual clairvoyance. This development must always be taken into account. It may be put as follows. Our planet has been changing through the millennia, and this change also played a role in human evolution. Lateral branches that were no longer fitting in with conditions grew decadent. So we have a main trunk in evolution and side branches that deteriorated.

Going further back from the time on Atlantis when Europeans and native Americans were still one, we came to a time where human bodies were still relatively soft, jelly-like in density. There again entities were branching off and lagging behind. Those entities continued to develop but in a downward direction, and those were the tribe of monkeys or apes. Branching occurred at a point where this original form had opportunity either to ascend and be human or to fall and be a caricature of a human being. We'll only look at the theory of evolution as much as is necessary to find the connection with things said in earlier lectures. In the people of ancient Atlantis, the ether body was still outside the physical body. Today only the human astral body is outside the physical body, and this only in sleep. Today people are therefore only able to overcome the physical body's tiredness in sleep, for then the astral body is outside the physical body and thus has opportunity to work on it. Other influences on the physical body are now no longer possible. Only remnants of such activity still exist in the phenomena of turning red for shame, pale with fear and shock, and so on. Yet the further we go back in Atlantean times and the more the ether body was outside the physical body, the more was it able to reconfigure the physical body. The ether body's mastery over the physical body was so great in those times because the physical body was still much more supple and flexible than it is now. At a time in human evolution when the physical body was only a finely differentiated first beginning of the skeleton, the power of the ether body over the physical body was so great that human beings were able to lengthen an arm, a hand, at will, let fingers project from them at will, and so on. This seems absurd to modern people. It would be quite incorrect to imagine Lemurian man to have been like modern man. The Lemurian human beings did not walk on their limbs the way we do today; they were more or less creatures of air. All the organs of modern man were only hinted at; Lemurians were able to metamorphose. It is quite incorrect to imagine that Lemurians were similar, grotesquely so but still similar, to modern man.

In Atlantean times, too, the human body was still capable of being shaped and could be reconfigured from inside, using the will. The reason was that the ether body, as I said, was still partly outside the physical body. The ether body therefore worked on the outer form and the entities that did not work on their body in the right way developed into what we call monkeys or apes today. That is how these caricatures of the human being of today arose. They are descended from us, not we from them. The question may be raised at this point as to why it was the apes that split off, why did some remain behind at a lower level as entities without a soul—I am speaking of the higher soul, not the astral body. You see, conditions changed. Human beings adapted, but they were not able to do so. Their physical body hardened, whilst human beings were able to keep their physical body soft and supple.

For the beginning of earth evolution we have to think of human beings having a subtle etheric body. They refashioned it more and more. A clairvoyant would have seen the human being as a sphere at that time.

It was relatively late in the Atlantean age that the genus branched off which later became the apes of today. Certain higher mammals had branched off earlier on in Atlantean times; certain lower mammals branched off in the earliest Atlantean age. The physical human being was a mammal in developmental terms at that time; however, the mammals remained at this stage whereas human beings continued to develop. At an even earlier time, the human being was at the reptile level of development. The body was completely different from that of a present-day reptile, but today's reptiles evolved in that their bodily development grew decadent. Human beings developed their inner principles, but reptiles remained behind. A reptile is a retarded brother of the human being. Even earlier than this the future birds branched off. And before that the human being was at the level which has been preserved in the fishes of today. Nothing higher than complicated fish forms existed on earth at that time. In the far distant past human beings were at the level of an invertebrate creature. And the unicellular creatures, called Monera by Haeckel, branched off first of all, one of the oldest brothers of man. If we use this sequence to create the genealogical tree of man, it will agree with the one which Haeckel presented in his books:[77]

1	Monera	13	Ganoidei
2	Unicellular forms	14	Protopteridae
3	Polycellular forms	15	Perennibranchiates
4	Hollow spheres	16	Scaly amphibia
5	Archenteron	17	Proreptiles
6	Placozoa	18	Mammal-like reptiles
7	Nemertina	19	Protheria
8	Tunicata	20	Marsupialia
9	Early chordata	21	Prosimiae
10	Acrania	22	Cercopithecidae
11	Cyclostomata	23	Hominidae
12	Semionotus	24	Cryptids

25 Human beings capable of speech

We might actually adopt Haeckel's tree, the only difference being that he let the animal forms arise first and then develop all the way to the human stage, whilst we see the very first form as man, with the animal world branching off as human forms that had grown decadent. Man is in fact the first-born on earth; humanity continued to develop in a straight line, leaving the other life forms behind at various stages.

If we consider the time when birds and reptiles branched off we see that physical human forms truly existed at that time which were similar to the later bird species and others similar to the later reptiles. The seer looks back to that distant past when the spiritual nature of man had not yet taken possession of his body. He sees the generic soul of the human being floating around the birdlike body. The spiritual entities that had no need to descend onto the physical plane stayed behind at this point. Having come down to this level in the physical world they developed further spiritually. These are spirits of the astral plane, the world of the Holy Spirit, which have reserved the airy sphere for their realm, just as human beings took possession of the physical earth, the earth sphere, for their realm. We have to think of these spirits assuming the bird form if they are to be physically visible to us. This is why the writer of the Gospel of John had to use the dove as the symbol for the Holy Spirit which comes down into the spiritual soul of Jesus, filling it as Spirit Self. This symbol gains most marvellously in depth when we consider it in connection with the evolution of humanity.

Let us connect the words in the Gospel of John with human evolution on earth from a different point of view. For this we'll briefly recapitulate an idea of Rosicrucianism. At a certain stage of development the pupil was told: 'Let us consider the plant in relation to the human being. The plant directs its root downwards, towards the centre of the earth, which is the seat of its I. Chastely it turns its organs of pollination to the sun, the light. It opens its flower and lets its fruit ripen in the light of the sun. This fructifying action of the light is called being touched by the sun's sacred lance of love in occult science. It calls forth the flower and makes the earth fruitful. The root which the plant sends down into the soil corresponds to the human head. Human beings turn their head to the sun, the light. And they modestly turn the organs of fertilization, which the plant turns to the light, down to the earth. The human being is the inverted image of the plant. The animal is between the two. We draw the plant in the vertical, directed down into the earth, the human being equally vertical but turned away from the earth, and the animal horizontally. This gives us the form of the cross. Plato put it like this: The world's soul is crucified on the most ancient world cross.'[78] The cross is a cosmic symbol, put there into world evolution.

The pupil would be profoundly moved when thus able to look into the process of world evolution.

We thus see the plant, too, as a brother spirit from a far, far distant past. Originally man, too, had been an etheric entity and plantlike in substance. At that time the human being had the material nature which plants still have today. If man had not transformed the plant substance into flesh, he would have remained as chaste, as pure as the plant. He would never have known desire and passion. But that state could not be maintained, for human beings would then not have awoken to self-awareness. They would have stayed for ever in the dream life in which plants still are today. Human beings had to be filled with desires and passions, had to be taken to existence in the flesh.

Not all organs were transformed at the same time from plant to flesh substance. The organs which give expression to the lowest drives were last to be drawn into evolution in the flesh. And they are already getting decadent. The reproductive organs preserved their plant nature longest. Old legends and myths still tell us of hermaphrodites; those were entities with sexual organs that were not flesh and blood but had plant nature. Some people believe that the fig leaf that the first human beings had in paradise reflected their embarrassment and shame. Quite the contrary. The story reminds us that human beings had reproductive organs of plant nature rather than of flesh.

Now a look at the future. The organs in the human body which are even today of a low nature, having been the last to be included in fleshly nature, will also be the first in the human body to drop away again, to disappear, shrivel up. Human beings will not continue at their present level. They have descended from the pure chastity of the plant to the sensuality of the world of desire and will rise again from this to be chaste again, their substance cleansed and pure.

Some organs in the human body are breaking down, others are at the peak of their developmental potential, and others again are in the early stages of development. The reproductive organs belong to the first group, the brain to the second; organs that are still in the germinal stage are the heart, the larynx and everything connected with creating the word. The organs developing from them will replace the reproductive organs in their functions and go far beyond them. They will be voluntary to the highest degree. When human beings produce forms in the air as they speak and the word will be creative, that will be the time in the future when humanity has regained the chastity that plants have preserved; but it will be a deliberate chastity. For the spiritual investigator the heart, too, is only in the early stages of evolution. It is not the pump which people thinking in materialistic terms say it is. Belief that the heart is the cause of blood circulation is erroneous. Horrible though it may sound, the movements of the heart are the consequence of blood circulation. In future times, when humanity will have reached a higher level of evolution, the heart, too, will be subject to their conscious will. The potential is there, evident in the striation which heart muscle shows, like all voluntary muscle. Human beings will then deliberately create their own kind through the word, and human substance will be chaste and purified. The calyx opening to the sun at a lower level, taking in the sun's ray as love's arrow, will at the higher level reached by future humanity be the chalice open to the cosmos, a chalice fructified by the spirit. This is represented as the Holy Grail, the luminous chalice which medieval knights were seeking.

Let us consider how the plant relates to the earth. Plants have only a physical and an ether body, and so their level of conscious awareness is like the one human beings have in sleep. Animals have a group awareness, the conscious awareness of plants is concentrated in the centre of the earth. Plants are bound up with the earth in such a way that they have to be regarded as parts of it. Individual plants do not have an astral body; instead they are embedded in the earth's astral body. The earth's astral body interrelates with that of the sun. We also find a process similar to the alternation between sleep and waking consciousness of human beings in the higher organism of the earth. In consequence plants sprout in summer; they germinate, grow, open their flowers to the sun. In winter the sun's astral body withdraws from the earth. The earth's astral body is left to itself; it withdraws to the centre of the earth, and the earth's vegetation is at rest. The seer is able to observe this relationship between the two astral bodies in detail. The withdrawal of the astral body causes vegetation and vital activity to come to rest, and conscious awareness was also interrupted; because of this human beings had to be given their own astral body in the course of their evolution, for this alone would give them continuous conscious awareness.

So far we have been considering the significance that the Christ had for human evolution. Let us now also consider the significance of this spirit for cosmic evolution. The spirits which at the very beginning of earth evolution had already achieved the state of perfection which humanity will only achieve by the end of earth evolution have their seat on the sun. The Christ as cosmic power is one of them. At the beginning of our present earth evolution his astral body was therefore connected with the sun's astral body. His seat was in the sun. With the coming of the Christ on earth, the astral body of this cosmic power of the Christ spirit also came down to earth, and since then his astral body is continuously connected with the earth's astral body. With the coming of the Christ on earth the earth's astral body was given a completely new substance by the sun's astral body. Someone looking down on the earth from another planet at the time of the Christ would have seen this new substance being added to the earth's astral body, for the colours shining out from it would have changed. By connecting his astral body with that of the earth, the sun spirit Christ became the spirit of the earth. The Christ spirit is sun spirit and at the same time also earth spirit. From the moment when the Christ walked on the earth, he has continued to be connected with the earth. He has become the spirit of planet earth. The earth is his body, and he is guiding earth evolution. This connection was established on Golgotha, and the mystery on Golgotha is the symbol for what happened for earth evolution at that time.

Four main races share possession of the earth's surface—the white, yellow, red and black race. But the atmosphere which surrounds the earth is the same for all. This is indicated in John 19:23: 'When the soldiers had crucified Jesus they took his clothing and made four shares, a share for each soldier. There was also the tunic. Now the tunic had no seam but was woven in one piece.' The Christ's clothes are symbolic of the earth's surface, but the tunic, woven in one piece, symbolizes the atmosphere, undivided and indivisible, encompassing the earth on all sides. It has to be stressed once again that this symbol, too, is at the same time also historical fact. This also explains the words of the Master. He said: 'He who eats my bread has lifted up his heel against me' (John

13:18). If the Christ is the spirit of the planet, if the earth is his body, is it not fair to say that people eat his flesh and drink his blood and in doing so lift their heel against him? And are people not walking about on the body of the spirit of this planet, lifting their heel against him? When this spirit points to the fruits of the earth, surely he may say, 'This is my body,' and pointing to the pure juices of plants, 'This is my blood' (John 6:56). And people are surely lifting up their heels against him as they walk about on the earth. This was not spoken of as something bad but merely to mention the fact that the earth is the true body of the Christ. This passage in the Gospel must therefore also be taken literally. And the mystery of Holy Communion serves to remind us of this great truth. You only know how to give Holy Communion its true value if you are sentient of the importance of the Last Supper for the whole of cosmic evolution. You see the power of the Christ as the plants shoot and sprout from the ground in spring, turning to the light of the sun. You know that when the Christ became man this was not just a human but a cosmic event.

LECTURE 8

T HE writer of the Gospel of John said in conclusion that the Christ also did many other things which are not included in the book. 'Jesus also did many other things; indeed if they were all written down I expect that the world itself would not contain the books being written' (John 21:25). In the same way we have to say that even quite a long series of lectures would not be enough to explain everything written in the Gospel.

Today we'll take a closer look at the two concepts 'Father' and 'I'. They will provide an explanation for the human evolution which has been discussed in the preceding lectures. Humanity started out from an I awareness that was very different from the one we know. 'Adam' should not be taken to be a single individual but an I awareness spanning several generations. The one who starts such a generation is the 'Father'. In Old Testament Judaism Abraham was indeed felt to be the father, and every Jew in those times said to himself, 'I am not an independent I; but *one* I flows down from Abraham and branches out into all members of the tribe, including me.' If you have a great tree, the vital sap flows from the root to every individual branch and twig, and so the vital sap of Abraham, the I which the Jewish peoples have in common, flows through the whole Jewish nation. When a Jew spoke the name of the father in Old Testament times he would be pointing to the whole blood line. He would call this I awareness which encompassed all generations 'the divine consciousness'. Addressing the I as God he would call it Yahweh. When the name Yahweh was heard the people were reminded that a common I flows through the whole nation that began with Abraham, the father of the tribe.

Mixed blood meant that this relationship changed in time. Awareness of the I AM has been individualized, and the Christ is the power appointed to make humanity aware of this change. For the human beings of earlier times the I AM meant something which flowed on through generations. To people of later times it is something which flows through their own inner body. The former meant the god who flowed through the whole community as the divine awareness of I nature. The others are sentient of a spark in them, a drop of the divine substance. Think of a power sent to earth which makes humanity very much aware that this I AM can live in every individual human being, a power which makes it clear that God has put a drop of his substance into every human being. This power would say: 'This I AM is something which is there in every one of you; it is one particle of the *one* divine power. The individual I AM of which you are sentient is one with the Father's I AM. If you have gained awareness of this fact you are able to say, "I and the Father are one." Look up all the way to Adam. You see I awareness flow through generations, for centuries and millennia. But there is an even higher awareness, one given to man in the human quality at his very source and origin. It is the awareness of a humanity that encompasses not individual generations but the whole of humanity. Then came the awareness which human beings individualized in the I AM.' Thus the Christ was able to say: 'Before there was Abraham there was the I AM.'[79]

To elucidate the concept of the I AM still further, let us go to the Golden Legend which is known in all Christian schools.[80] There it says:

> When Seth, given by Jehovah in place of Abel, came to the gates of paradise one day, the cherub with the flaming sword admitted him to the place from where human beings had once been driven out. Seth saw two intertwined trees, the Tree of Life and the Tree of Knowledge. And the cherub indicated that he should take three seeds from the two intertwined trees. Seth put these three seeds into the mouth of his father Adam when he had died. A threefold tree grew from the grave, and some would see it in fiery letters

making up the words 'I AM he who was, who is and who shall be'. The wood from this tree which had grown from Adam's grave was put to many uses. The magic rod Moses used to perform his miracles was made of it. The wood was also used in the gates to Solomon's temple. The bridge which Jesus crossed when he was taken to his death was also made of it, and finally the cross on which he was crucified on Golgotha.

The explanation of the legend given in the occult schools was this. You see two trees in the human being, the tree of red blood and the tree of blue-red blood. The red blood tree reflects knowledge and insight, the blue-red blood tree life. The two trees were separated from one another, according to the most ancient teaching. 'There was a time when no red blood did as yet develop in man. It was only when the I came down into the human body that the red blood developed. The life reflected in the blue-red blood had been there for a long time. It developed through higher development of the juices of life. And from the Christian point of view the time when it had been given to human beings was the time of paradise, when the first dawning of the I settled in the human soul, when the Godhead came down and human beings, only endowed with a group soul, nevertheless had in this the first beginnings of the individual I.'

According to the paradise myth, 'Having been given the red blood, human beings gained insight, learned to look up; their eyes were opened and they came to know the difference between man and woman.' This insight had its price, however. Awareness of I nature can only arise if the blood dies. Life is continually used up and renewed in the human body. The blue blood has done what it was made for when it is used up, and the annihilation of the blue blood leads to awareness of I nature. Powers are going to develop in the human soul that will enable human beings to master and unite the two trees. Human beings are sentient of I nature only because they are all the time bearing murder, the dying process, in them.

In the state in which they came to earth, human beings are depen- dent on plants for it is only they which provide the conditions for life. Just consider, for instance, that people are all the time inhaling air containing oxygen and exhaling used-up air that contains carbon dioxide. They use up the oxygen, converting it to carbon dioxide. We are unable to live without oxygen and we get this only from plants. They change the carbon dioxide produced by human beings back into oxygen and thus make the air breathable again. The plant keeps back the carbon which it has split off from the carbon dioxide, giving it back to human beings thousands of years later in the form of coal. The earth is a single organism and if just one part of it were missing, life as it now exists would be impossible. We may consider plant, animal and human being as one system, and indeed if you take away the plant, life will no longer be possible for the other two. This will change in a far distant future. People in general do not yet know about this, but the seer can perceive the time when the stream of carbon dioxide will no longer be transformed with the help of plants but by human beings themselves producing useful oxygen. That is the great future ideal of the occult schools, that human beings will consciously achieve within themselves what plants are doing for them today, making a function their own which is today performed by plants. Organs will develop in them that will permit them to convert carbon dioxide themselves. The initiate sees how at a future time the two trees, the carbon dioxide and the oxygen tree, will merge their crowns into one. Then the principle of which it is said 'I am the one who was, the one who is and the one who will be' will live in every human being as something that is eternal. The I did live in Adam, but it had to be fructified first. In the beginning, the tree of life had to be made into the tree of death. It could not be put together with the tree of knowledge, and so the two trees were separate from one another, with the plant put between them. Awareness of eternity had to be gained first. Christ Jesus bore this within him and transplanted it to the earth. The three seeds are the three divine principles Manas, Buddhi and Atman. The eternal part of them all was placed in Adam's grave. From that grave, awareness of eternity was proclaimed; from that grave grew the tree which showed writing in fire. 'I am the one who was, the one who is and the one who shall be.' The Christ taught human beings to ignite this 'I am an individual human being' in human nature when he said: 'Seek to lean more and more on the spirit of the I AM and you will have the element that lets you be in communion with me. It is only through this I AM that you get to the divine Father, for the Father and I are one.' Only one seer was able to grasp this, and that was the writer of the Gospel of John. He did not want to record just historical fact but something which one perceives on looking into the spiritual world.

To know what was happening in the spiritual world, a seer who was a contemporary of the Christ had to enter into the sleep state. This is hinted at in Chapter 3. Nicodemus, a leader among the Jews, came to the Christ at night. He came to him because he wanted to be a seer. He had achieved the state where he could be a seer, and he 'came at night' because his daytime consciousness has been extinguished. In the fifth verse of the chapter we also find the important teaching that the human being can be born 'out of the spirit'.

The Christ said (John 14:6), 'I am the way, the truth and the life.' Where is the way which takes us to the highest Godhead through the Christ? The I AM is working on the astral body, creating the Spirit Self; it is working on the physical body, creating the Spiritual Human Being. When the I of man works on the human being, the Spirit Self is worked out and the Life Spirit then arises. That is how the human being finds the true life, for the I AM is working through the lower bodies, letting the true life arise in them. We can represent it like this:

I AM	the way	the truth	and	the life
Direction	Spirit Self	Life Spirit		Spiritual Human Being

The I AM shows the direction which human beings must take to get Spirit Self, Life Spirit and Spiritual Human Being to unfold.

Theosophical teachings may also be found in the Gospel of John. The fact that an individual I lives in every human being, that there is a spark of divine substance in this I, and that this spark must become the 'God in us', is touched on by the writer of the Gospel (Chapter 9). Most translations of the Bible give the answer that the Christ gave when asked who had sinned, the man born blind or his parents, as 'Neither has this man sinned nor his parents: but that the works of God should be made manifest in him.' But is it reasonable for a Christian to say that God lets someone be born blind in order to reveal his glory in him? The notion of a god who is capable of such a conclusion is impossible. The passage reads much more simply and clearly if we base it on the theosophical view. The Christ's answer was: 'Neither he nor his parents have sinned; he fulfils his karma so that the divine spark in him may be visible, so that the deeds of God within him may be outwardly apparent.' The Christ's answer (John 9:3) should be translated as: 'He was born blind so that the deeds of the god in him shall be visible in the body.' Every human being goes through repeated lives on earth. We see someone who was born blind. He does not have to have sinned in this life, but may have brought the sin that has led to this birth with him from an earlier life. It is karma as taught in theosophy, active throughout incarnations, which is described in this event. It is clear that with this the Christ would be in conflict with the accepted Jewish view, and this also explains the difficulties which he then had with the Jews (John 9:22).

Another passage in the Gospel also relates to the karma concept. A strange passage in Chapter 8 says that when the Pharisees questioned Jesus on his views concerning adultery, he bent down (verses 6 and 8), not saying a word, and wrote with his finger in the earth. The earth, as we have seen, is his own body. He did not condemn the woman taken in adultery but inscribed her action in his own organism. He was indicating that, just as a seed put in the earth germinates and bears fruit of its kind, so will everything a human being does germinate in a later life on earth and bear fruit of its kind and that no power on earth can remove the consequences of an action. Theologians believe in expiation, believe that the Christ died for us, and believe that they must not accept the karma concept because it goes against the view that the Christ took on all the sins of the world with his death. This disharmony between theosophical and theological views does, however, resolve in harmony if seen in the right way.

The karma concept is the same for life as the accounts ledger is for the merchant. According to karmic law we have to assume that anything we have caused in earlier lives will have its effect on us in the present life, and that anything we do now will have its reflection in later lives. We thus have a complete balance sheet in life. Good deeds are shown on one page, bad ones on the other. If someone thinks that it is not possible to act freely under the rule of karmic law, every way of doing things being a consequence of earlier actions, he'd be like the merchant saying that having drawn the balance I must not do any more business, otherwise the balance sheet would be incorrect. That is not the right way of thinking in business, and the conclusion drawn above about karmic law is equally incorrect. Rightly understood the karma concept does not have any fatalism to it. Free will and karma can be reconciled most beautifully and, rightly understood, karma is never something that cannot be changed. And if someone were not prepared to assist another person in his misfortune, saying that he must not intervene in his karma, that would be just as wrong as refusing financial help to a merchant who is facing bankruptcy. The merchant would enter that financial help as a debit in his ledgers which he will have to repay, whilst the individual who has helped out would enter it as a loan in his books. In the same way every good deed is like an entry on the credit side of the balance sheet, and a debit in the records of the individual given that help. Karmic law therefore does not ignore any help given, and it seems perfectly appropriate to relieve the karma of one's neighbour with acts of mutual assistance. People can do something good for a single individual, but there are also actions that benefit many people, that is, ease their karma, and these are recorded in the ledgers of many people. And an act as mighty as the one performed by the Christ is recorded in the karma of all human beings, for it eases the karma of all the people who inwardly respond to it. We see, therefore, that the karmic law is almost mentioned in the Gospel of John, and that its existence does not in any way limit freedom of action. Christ Jesus entered into a relationship with the whole of humanity in an act of self-sacrifice.

According to karmic law, every act is recorded in life's register of debts. It is then connected with the body of the Christ, with the earth. This is why he did not judge the adulterous woman on the spot but inscribed her action in his own body. He receives into his own body everything that can happen between one individual and another, for karma must always come to fruition in the earthly world. The story makes us deeply aware that with his deed the Christ has made himself part of the whole karmic evolution of all humanity. He is leading the future evolution of humanity.

Recalling again the five periods of civilization—Indian, Persian, Egyptian, Graeco-Roman and European—we see that the basis for the

Christ power that will bear fruit for the whole of humanity was established during the third period. The foundation then laid within human evolution will only emerge into life in the sixth period. Then the Spirit Self, which has evolved from the spiritual soul, will connect with the Life Spirit. From the third to the fourth period the Christ power shone out prophetically. In the sixth period, the great marriage of humanity will be celebrated as the Spirit Self unites with the Life Spirit. Then humanity will come together in the great brotherhood, with I joining I, brother joining brother—in that brotherhood forecast in the wedding at Cana in Galilee, which was not only a historical event but also shows symbolically how the sons of man will in the sixth period of civilization come together in one great brotherhood that encompasses the whole of humanity. Three periods have to pass from the third period before this will come to pass—the third, fourth and fifth. In esoteric teaching a period is called a day, which is why Chapter 2 begins with the words 'on the third day a wedding took place at Cana in Galilee'. The words indicate that the story of the wedding which follows refers to something that will happen in the future. The mother of Jesus, the spiritual soul, was present at the wedding. The Christ said to her, 'This is between me and you, woman, my hour has still not come.' This clearly shows that reference is made to something at the wedding in Cana that is due to happen only in the future. What did Jesus do, his hour not yet having come? He transformed the water into wine! One keeps coming across the explanation that this was to indicate that new fire, new vital energy was to be given to a Jewish nation that had fallen into decadence, changing 'insipid' water into fiery wine. One might imagine that wine drinkers have thought this up as a justification for what they are doing. But in grasping the true significance of this act we gain deep insight into the great evolution of the world.

Alcohol has not always been connected with humanity. Everything spiritual that evolves has its corresponding reflection in matter, and conversely all forms of matter also have their counterpart in the sphere of the spirit. Wine, alcohol, only made its appearance at a particular time in world and human history. It will disappear again in due course. Here we see the profound truth of occult investigation. Alcohol was the bridge from the generic or group I to the independent individual I.

Human beings would never have made the transition from group to individual I without the material effect of alcohol. This generated the individual, personal conscious awareness of human beings. Once humanity has reached this goal it will no longer need alcohol and this will disappear from the physical world. You see, everything that happens has its significance in the wise guidance of human evolution. Because of this we should not say anything against anyone who takes alcohol, though on the other hand human beings who have rushed ahead of the rest of humanity and taken their inner development to a point where they no longer need alcohol should also avoid it. The Christ has come to give humanity powers so that the highest level of I awareness can be reached in the sixth period. He wants to prepare human beings for the time 'still not come'. If he had let the water be the offering, humanity would never have got as far as having an individual I. Transforming the water means raising human beings to the level of being individuals. Humanity had reached a point in its evolution where it needed the wine; this is why the Christ changed the water into wine. Once the hour has come when humanity no longer needs wine the Christ will change the wine into water again. How could the Christ develop the power needed to change water into wine? Because the earth itself is his body he was able to make the earth's powers active in himself. In the earth, water changes into wine as it flows through the grapevine. As a person the Christ was also able to do the process that happens in the earth, for all the powers and forces of the earth must also be present in him as soon as the earth comes to be his body, ensouled by his astral body.

What does the earth do with its powers? If we put seed in the ground it will germinate and bear fruit. It multiplies, one becoming many. In the same way reproduction makes one animal into many. The same power of increase, of multiplication, is also active in the Christ, as indicated in the feeding of the five thousand. The Christ has the power of multiplication of seeds that is inherent in the earth. If we keep hold of the idea 'the body of the Christ is the earth with its powers' and apply it to the story in the Gospel of John, many of the details begin to make sense.

What, in fact, are Gospels? In the Gospel of John we have to see a presentation of the initiation principles that existed throughout antiquity. The things an initiand did outwardly did not set the standard for the school to which he belonged; it was the experiences he went through in one level after the other, from one degree of initiation to the next, that set the standard. Academics are most surprised to discover elements similar to those of the evolutional history of Christ Jesus in that of the Buddha. The explanation is that the authors of such biographies recorded not the circumstances of external life but those of the inner life, the spiritual facts. These are the same for all true initiates, for they have all taken the same course and gone through the same experiences. The things initiates had to live through in the process of initiation were laid down in the rules for initiation, and all initiates of the same degree had to go through the same experiences. The biographers were therefore only writing a biography of the different stages of initiation. The Gospels are nothing but ancient initiation rules that go to different depths. A process that in earlier times had gone on at a reduced level of consciousness was gone through openly on Golgotha. Death, until then overcome in the ether body during initiation, was now overcome in the physical body. The event on Golgotha was the initiation of an initiate of the highest degree who had not been initiated by someone else.

The writer of the Gospel of John was therefore only able to describe the life of the Christ in the way given in the initiation codex. Living through the Gospel of John you will awaken the power of vision in you. It is a seers' book, written to train visionary powers. Living through it sentence by sentence, the great, tremendous result you get is that you come spiritually face to face with the Christ. It is not made easy for human beings to gain conviction; they have to work their way through to the goal where insight arises that the Christ is a reality. The Gospel of John is the way that takes us to the Christ. The writer wanted to give everyone opportunity to understand him. If you develop the Spirit Self from the astral body within you, the wisdom will come to you in the spirit that will help you understand what the Christ is. The Christ himself gave an indication of this. He is hanging on the cross; his mother and his initiate disciple, whom he loves, are standing beside it. The disciple is to give to humanity the wisdom, the insight into the significance of the Christ. Attention is therefore drawn to the mother Sophia with the words: 'Here is our mother, she must be loved.' The spiritualized mother of Jesus is the Gospel itself; she is the wisdom that takes human beings to their most sublime insights. The disciple has given us mother Sophia, that is, he has written the Gospel for us, and for those who explore it this Gospel holds the possibility to get to know Christianity, the origin and goal of this great movement.

The Gospel of John has in it the wisdom of 'God in man', theosophy, and the more human beings devote themselves to the study of this document the more wisdom and enlightenment will come to them from its pages.

QUESTIONS AND ANSWERS

DURING THE LECTURE COURSE GIVEN IN KASSEL ON 16 TO 29 JUNE 1907, BASED ON NOTES TAKEN BY LUDWIG KLEEBERG

Question. Did the Christ rise in the flesh? What is the forgiveness of sins?

Rudolf Steiner. Let me explain the first point in context. The Gospels do not mean that the Christ died for the sins, now we can commit sins, what need is there to make up for them in kamaloka? The only sins that are not forgiven are those against the Holy Ghost; those are the sins that must be atoned through karma if committed in full awareness. The Christ died for the sins caused because human beings also live in other bodies. The sins against the Spirit must be atoned for. Christianity is fully in accord with the law of karma, as we shall see.

How do we explain the genders given to entities and things in animate and inanimate nature? Why do we say the tree (male), the flower (female) and the leaf (neuter) {in German}?

Rudolf Steiner. A mysterious relationship exists among genders throughout the natural world. The gall wasp lives on certain trees. So there is a relationship between the animal and the trees. If we trace this in the devachanic world, we find that wasps and trees are a single whole, like male and female in the world. The separation exists only in the physical world. A kind of sexual relationship thus exists between the animal and the tree. Languages were not created arbitrarily in the primal world but have arisen from the secrets of the world. Certain gender notations derive from relationships in the higher world. Something gender-related thus lives in the (masc.) stone and the (fem.) flower. Changes occurred between sun, moon and earth that also show themselves in the national character of the ancient Germans. In the classical languages the moon is feminine, the sun male. In German it is the other way round. (I did speak of this in Munich when I gave the lectures about the Gospel of John there.)

Is it true, as some say, that Christianity has had its golden age or, as others put it, that Christianity has so far only overcome its childhood diseases, with its golden age still to come? What does the future look like for Christianity?

Rudolf Steiner. So far, Christianity is in its beginnings. Theosophy is meant to help Christianity. More will be said of this.

Are there truly spirits of sublime and most sublime kind that correspond to the gods of the Greeks and Romans? One cannot bear to think that they were an enormous delusion and that the faith of thousands of people was for nothing.

Rudolf Steiner. The mythological figures are images of astral and devachanic spirits, the Greek gods among them. In the astral world, human beings see their inner life as outer life. There were times when humanity was clairvoyant, when people saw the nervous system evolving. It looked like a tree then. This is why they called these powers the world ash. Yggdrasil (I-bearer) was the name of the tree. In the same way Zeus and Prometheus were an astral experience. These are the ordering powers. The dead must have guides, as we have seen. In the ancient mysteries people saw that there were guiding spirits in devachan. Olympus is the true means of expression for 'devachan'. People who say mythologies are 'popular fantasy' are dreamers of the unreal. Legends and folk tales are still created today. The legend of Lady Midday comes from the Slavic peoples. When people are out in the fields and do not go to their homes at midday, a woman appears who asks them three questions. If they cannot answer them, the woman cuts off their heads with a scythe. The legend has come about like this. People go out in the fields to work. Around noon they like to lie down and sleep a little. The sun is burning down and the hot atmosphere causes a dream of Lady Midday's three questions. Anxiety arises. The Sphinx asking its questions is the most sublime form of the Slavonic peoples' Lady Midday. The mythological world arose from past clairvoyance. Some time ago an interesting book by Laistner appeared—*Das Raetsel der Sphinx* (the riddle of the sphinx). The academic world at large ignored it. The legends are explained out of nothing, for popular imagination is nothing but that. The dream world creates myths and at a higher level clairvoyance.

What view is taken of faith healing in theosophy?

Rudolf Steiner. In theosophy, no position is taken with regard to anything. Positive statements are made about things that are known and there is no need to declare any position. No party position is taken. That is what matters. No criticism is made, but things are told. Much is worthy of regard in the world, but much is highly biased. Some things can be done here, but the methods of the spiritual world are not without their dangers if used by lay people. Yes, the Christ did heal. But we must not forget that he healed from the depths of wisdom. Those who become theosophists can do spiritual healing. One only has to extend the spiritual knowledge. The followers of Christian Science are often biased and get very angry when they hear of theosophy. A healing process is often proclaimed though much great damage, which is done in another direction, has been overlooked. You can see dreadful things there. People have been cured by the methods of Christian Science, but something else went parallel to this, which is that someone else got sick or died. There was a direct connection. People should not mess around with this. As you know, according to the New Testament the sickness was transferred to the swine.

What position does theosophy take to Adventists?

Rudolf Steiner. Here a doctrine of Christianity is one-sidedly given preference and held on to fanatically. What they are saying is correct.

But there is a more comprehensive truth. And they harden their minds. Theosophists do not fight them, but people in general do.

How should one take Hebrews 6:4–6? (Epistle of Paul to the Hebrews)

Rudolf Steiner. We must be clear in our minds that the sin against the Holy Ghost has roots that go deep. Human beings are conscious within their astral body. They can sin in the lower bodies. With help, those sins can be taken away. But when we sin in full awareness, outside help will have no effect, for help would be unwise. This can only be balanced out in one's individual karma. This is referred to in the passage, though the German does not really reflect its meaning.

Does one have conscious awareness of previous lives when in kamaloka and devachan?

Rudolf Steiner. This question must be answered with a definite yes. Once a degree of awareness has been gained it stays for good. It is merely pushed into the background in life through the instrument of the body. The initiate can push the instrument back and oversee the lives.

Recall

Rudolf Steiner. Humanity has the advantage of not being able to observe itself. Why do we not remember? Someone said that human beings could not do arithmetic. To prove his case he brought along a four-year-old. After the age of six a child will be able to do sums. Remembering the past is also a matter of time. Why can't it be sooner? Then one should teach the children integral calculus in the first year! One condition has another as a precondition.

You may ask if it might not be better to develop the preconditions for playing the piano in one minute. It is necessary to have no recall because we would not be able to live with the memory. It would be as if someone knew his death. It would paralyse.

Cabbala (Kabbalah)

Rudolf Steiner. This is a specific, methodical way of arriving at certain facts in spiritual science. It is one of the most difficult methods. It is the way in which members of the Hebraic peoples approached the secrets— especially by methodical treatment of signs and numbers and letters. This is not entirely suitable for modern man. It is not possible to understand Spinoza unless one knows the basics of cabbalistics. Those are specific methods, reckoning with letters given numeric values. There's a particular passage in the Book of Revelation. Theologians say that John had no more predicted the future than anyone else, but wrote only of the past, for instance in the case of the Seven Seals. But John had put the truth in signs. People then spoke of earthquakes and the plague of locusts. This is an example of materialistic studies that many think so clever. It also says: 'Here wisdom (Sophia) is needed, for the number of this animal [beast] is the number of a human being—666.' How are we to do that? The scholars heard that letters in certain words are replaced with numbers. So they put the letters corresponding to 600 and 60 and 6. The theologians had a result, and whole libraries were written that should really go on the fire, and they arrived at the name Nero. So John lived after Nero and put it all secretly into the Book of Revelation. The number means Sorat, the adversary of the sun spirit. The sign for this was ⅃, hence 'the horns'. You have to understand what is written there and then you can do history. You can't understand Euclid simply by having good knowledge of classical Greek.

Astral spirits

Rudolf Steiner. In the astral world you meet other spirits just as here you meet people, only more intensely so. The means of communication are of course different.

The dead and we ourselves

Rudolf Steiner. The dead can follow what is going on here. However, no spirit can see me putting out my hand. But there is a power behind the movement; a spiritual counter-image exists for the movement. This the spirits do see.

An influence through dreams is possible, but the human individual must provide the opportunity for this. I could give you examples where the dead have a direct influence on destiny.

The Last Judgement. (Answer given to me {Ludwig Kleeberg} and R. Walkhoff)

Rudolf Steiner. At the end of the present cycle a great judgement will be held, a crisis where the the sheep will be separated from the goats, meaning those who are fit for further development will be separated from those who have to stay behind and go through everything again.

Canals on Mars

Rudolf Steiner. The canals on Mars are an issue in the science of physics. I'll be speaking about the nature of Mars tomorrow. Life takes a different form there. We'll also get an idea of life on Mars tomorrow. Fluids and solids are more evenly distributed in the earlier states of a planet. The earth, too, is fairly regular. Around the North Pole it looks like a reflection of the earth's astral and ether body. This is called the earth's head. Asia is considered to be one hand, and Europe with Africa the other. America looks like the chest, Australia and so on like the extremities. This is also evident in the cultures. The earth's life originates in one pole, like the astral consciousness radiating from the brain. It was possible to see such substantial currents in earlier cosmic bodies. Mars is such a body. Lower animals investigating the human being would also only see nerve strands and have no idea of mind and spirit. All matter reflects the spiritual.

Vegetarianism

Rudolf Steiner. In spiritual science no propaganda is made for vegetarianism. All matter reflects something spiritual. Matter influences human beings. Let me give you two examples (French horn player and printer). It is not contact with matter as such which has an influence but there are much subtler kinds of contact. I could speak about what happens when people fill their mouths with gold. It would go too far. I could tell you how all foods act—how tea makes thoughts volatile, encouraging the presentation of arguments, which is why it is the diplomats' drink. Coffee makes for logical thought. But no propaganda is made for this in occultism. I could tell you various things about the connection between coffee-house and newspaper.

And so it makes a difference if you eat meat or not. Occultists make no crack-brained propaganda. There are plenty of bodies today that cannot do without meat. The question has to be answered in the individual case. People who eat only vegetables do, however, make the path to insight easier for themselves. Meat holds back. The body will be lighter, more efficient in coping more easily with the strains of that path. Meat eaters will tire more quickly. Wanting to follow the path of insight one will need certain sustenance, and this is easier for vegetarians. If your body is able to cope with eating no meat, you will find that you feel greatly relieved in the long run. Vegetarians are also strong in dealing with external influences. You get much more resistant. People grow stronger and fitter for work overall. Those seeking insight will make things very much easier for themselves if able to do without meat. The general trend is that people are more and more doing without food of animal origin. Human beings started by consuming human beings, then animals, and will finally live on vegetables. When physicians say 'animal matter is necessary' this is based on past generations who lived on meat and gave rise to present-day humanity. We should not forget that humanity is evolving. 'And where should the animals go?' people ask. Anyone asking such a question does not know the course of evolution. The animals which we are not eating are moving towards the future. Especially wild creatures are in decline.

Effects of salt

Rudolf Steiner. Salt solidifies. Salt consumption is really one of the most difficult issues in spiritual science. Human beings need salt. A time will come when they no longer need it. The salt issue is one of the first issues to be tackled in the field of nutrition when spiritual science will have more influence in that field. Today people have to develop the right feeling for this. It is a matter of discretion, of tact.

Peace movement

Rudolf Steiner. We can see a decrease in armed conflicts on earth. Before that came a period of horrendous armed struggles. That is how evolution goes. We find ourselves in two streams—one is the spiritual teaching of true Christianity, the brotherhood idea. You do not get anywhere with phrases in this. Associations which put the idea of peace on their programme achieve nothing at all. The theosophical philosophy of life is intended to lead to that idea, and it is the highest degree of spiritual insight which leads to it. Occult knowledge will one day unite all humanity. You cannot have two opinions about the most sublime things. Materialism is responsible for today's strife. Something which some travel agencies do is a symptom. Someone takes people on a guided tour of Italy and rushes them through the galleries, then takes them home again. The rule is that one does not talk about the things that take us to the heights. For when people do talk about them they are in dispute, and the idea is to bring them home feeling satisfied. The day will come when people turn to one and the same insight and this will mean true brotherhood.

The other stream brings egotism to realization. The Atlantean age perished through water, ours will perish in the war of all against all. Only a small group of people who have gained spiritual insight will survive. You have to make distinction between the evolution of souls and that of races. Here it is a matter of races. The bodies perish. Human beings must not cling to their race but move on to a higher level. We are facing a time of major conflicts.

The peace concept is great but impractical. I ask you: does anyone making peace propaganda seriously think that all the opposing interests that exist in the astral world will be swept away? During the Russo-Japanese war it was possible to see in the astral plane that Russians who had died were helping on the Japanese side. Why was that so? Those were noble people who had been influenced by noble ideas and died as martyrs on the gallows or in prison for those ideas. They died in rage and wanting revenge. This rage emerged so powerfully after death that those people fought against their own compatriots. That is how we understand the contrast between the physical and the astral world. One has to encourage the idea of peace, but think about it in a different way. The oppositions that exist in the spiritual world have to be reconciled. Do you want to make peace on earth when there is war in higher worlds?

The Germanic tribes were warriors, for the Egyptians the spiritual world was the most sublime. For the ancient Germans the greatest thing was to die in battle—death in the straw was most inglorious. Initiation also took the form of war. Union with higher things was always presented as union with the female element, among the ancient Germans with the Valkyries. Siegfried, the initiate, united with the Valkyries. The initiation process is presented as warlike. We are still under the after-effects of the Mars state and there will be terrible wars still to come.

Birds

Rudolf Steiner. Birds separated off immediately after the separation of the moon. Their group soul is at a very high level for they have not come down very much into matter.

Planets

Rudolf Steiner. Other planets also go through their earth evolution. The present Mars will one day be earth. Venus has already been earth. The stages were not gone through entirely like those of our earth.

Are clothes a sign of progress or decadence?

Rudolf Steiner. I'll answer this question in a somewhat oblique way. Imagination has grown impoverished, unable to create beautiful garments and only considering things beautiful that have not had things done to them by human beings. It is materialistic to consider only completely natural things beautiful. Paracelsus was mocking this when he said that nature has been taken further in a true medicine, going beyond nature. That is 'natural' in the highest sense.

Reporting, fakirs

Rudolf Steiner. Hume spoke of two boys who saw something but told different stories. Why? One of them had been lying.

A photograph showed a fakir climbing up a tall bamboo rod who tore himself apart at the top, fell down as blood, and vanished. The name was even given at the bottom. But when you read it backwards it said something like this: 'You silly mutt, you're being deceived.' Much is however due to mass suggestion. When someone tells a whole meeting that there is a pillar and someone is climbing up it, this has a significant effect. A small residue also remains of the influence of higher forms of magic.

Many reports can be seen to be based on lies, others on mass suggestion. Suggestion is possible even when fully awake, when an idiot of a schoolmaster teaches something and his students believe it unreservedly. If you study social psychology you'll come across many things. If you go to popular gatherings you'll see the play of the astral powers, bringing about mass suggestion. Ultimately we are dealing with genuinely higher magic.

Connection with the departed

Rudolf Steiner. People who are here can make a connection with the departed if they go through occult training or are initiates, also in dreams if they interpret them correctly. For spiritualists, too, it is not impossible that the dead enter into the sphere of life, though from the theosophical point of view this is not to be recommended because of earthly lust to disturb the dead.

Horse

Rudolf Steiner. A deep relationship exists between man and horse. Look at the old houses of ancient Germans where a horse skull was nailed to the gable. Consider the Trojan Horse, the Four Horses of the Apocalypse, Kalinka, the horse in the Indian mysteries. Going back a long way through evolution we find that animals split off, as the apes split off, and animals remained behind at every level. Man gained higher faculties by this means. If the ape had not split off, man could not have reached the height he has. Today only a last remnant remains of a power from early times—the relationship between man and woman. This came when single-sex nature split up. And there was a connection once with the entities that split off. People sensed the connection between the species splitting off and what they had gained from this. They were indebted to the horses for thinking, the rational mind. This is reflected in the profound legend of the wooden horse, the wiliness of Odysseus. The horse was venerated as a symbol for something to which we owe our rationality. The centaur is connected with the view that man once had horse nature in him.

Last Supper

Rudolf Steiner. The Last Supper is correctly explained in theosophy. The Christ has once been the sun spirit. The words 'He who eats my bread has lifted up his heel against me' must be taken literally. Think of the earth as the body and the Christ as its spirit, and think of the earth evolving over a wide spread of time. The spirit can say of something produced from grains of corn 'That is my body' and to something made from the juices of plants 'That is my blood'. Reality may also lie in these symbols. Anything I am saying about this is very aphoristic. Theosophy brings to light the truth contained in Christianity.

Natural healing methods, sunbaths

Rudolf Steiner. One should never say a method is good or bad in itself. It depends on the human being. Something may be correct in theory but is often used wrongly. Much damage is done by slogans. It is not a matter of encapsulating oneself in slogans and dogmas but of developing better and better insight. You have to know when a sunbath is good and when it is harmful. The best medicine is to have no need of a physician. The ideal is not to take a sunbath but walk in the heat of the sun for half an hour wearing a fur coat. If you manage that your health is good. It is a matter of making oneself into someone who can cope with everything. It is highly individual. Dogmas and views are less important than making the physician truly human. The right methods will then follow. The system must redevelop into recognition for the most competent individual who is independent in his approach to nature, and who always makes a discovery when dealing with a new case. For every case is different.

Sinning against the Holy Ghost

Rudolf Steiner. We can commit sins in different ways. We have the physical, ether and astral body. The I works on the astral body; it engenders Manas. When work is done on the ether body, if you work on your temperament, Buddhi is generated, and work on the physical body leads to Atman. Everything starts from the first. In the present cycle human beings are consciously working only in the astral body. Only an initiand is consciously able to do the other. But humanity must work continually on the astral body. You can only work consciously on the ether body under the guidance of the leader of humanity, especially Christ Jesus. The sins of the ether body are avoided if we go deeply into religion. You will be better in temperament if you follow the Gospels; the Christ died for this. The death in atonement means nothing when it comes to anything human beings can consciously make better, for that becomes part of karma. Sins against the Holy Ghost cannot be forgiven through the death on the cross. They arise because the human being is consciously working in the astral body.

Evidence of reincarnation

Rudolf Steiner. You get a hint in the story of healing the man who had been born blind. The Christ said, 'All this is for the glory of God.' Try for an explanation of this in commonplace Christianity. The man had not sinned in the present life; no punishment there. Nor had his parents sinned; sin passes on through generations. The term 'for the glory' would be better translated as 'that the god may be shown in him'. I do not think that in Christianity one believes in a God who lets a person be born blind so that the Christ may later demonstrate his skill. That would be a terrible way of explaining it. The individual had sinned in an earlier life. That is why he was blind. And doesn't 'God' in the Bible refer to the inmost human being? The Christ himself said 'You are gods'. Remember the saying that the drop of water is part of the ocean.

Then there is the transfiguration. The disciples were 'beyond them-selves', that is they were in devachan; they saw Elijah, Moses and the Christ. The Christ guided the disciples to the higher worlds. When the Christ returned, the disciples said, 'That was due to happen when Elijah comes again.' Jesus said, 'Elijah has come already. He is John. But do not tell anyone until I am come again.' The time will come when the Christ who did say 'I am with you always until the world's end' will come again. It was merely necessary to bring up people so that in one incarnation they would believe this incarnation to be the only one. They then came to love that one life and did not see beyond it. Consider the slave in ancient Egypt working to build the pyramids. He would say to himself, 'Everything you have to suffer now is something you have brought on yourself. You are now preparing your future and will one day be in command just like the one who commands you now. This is only one of many lives.' When the doctrine of reincarnation was popular people would look beyond the one life, feeling that there was a harmony of life. But the great leaders of humanity are the great educators. Man had to see one incarnation where he believed in only one life. And when the Christ comes again people will once again believe in reincarnation. Christianity will continue to exist because it is able to take on new forms all the time, being truth eternal. Humanity needed the lesson of just one incarnation. In theosophy we know that there are relative truths. No one will say the things I am saying today in 2000 years' time. Long ago the Druids taught by telling stories. And we use natural-scientific terms. The theosophical teaching will also vanish, but the truth remains. Reincarnation was well known in esoteric Christianity, but the Christ would not speak of it to the masses.

Basel 1907

Nr. 57

Eintritts=Karte

zum

Vortrags=Cyklus von Herrn Dr. Rudolf Steiner

über das

Johannes=Evangelium

Fräu Alice Kinkel

EMIL BIRKHÄUSER, BASEL.

Bemerkungen.

1. Diese Karte lautet auf den Namen des Teilnehmers und ist nicht übertragbar.

2. Die Vorträge finden in der Aula der oberen Realschule (de Wette=Straße) statt.

3. Es wird regelmäßige Teilnahme an den Vorträgen und pünktliches Erscheinen erwartet.

4. Die Höhe des Beitrages an die Kosten wird dem Ermessen der Teilnehmer anheimgestellt.

298

Admission Ticket

For

Lecture course by Dr Rudolf Steiner

on the

Gospel of John

Frau Alice Kinkel

Please note

1) This ticket is in the name of the person attending and is not transferable.
2) The lectures will be given in the Hall of Obere Realschule (de Wette-Strasse).
3) Regular and punctual attendance is expected.
4) Course members will themselves determine how much to contribute to costs.

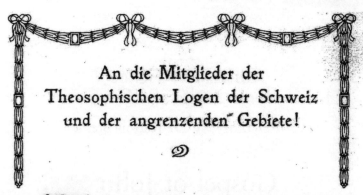

An die Mitglieder der Theosophischen Logen der Schweiz und der angrenzenden Gebiete!

Wir freuen uns, Ihnen mitteilen zu dürfen, dass Herr Dr. R. Steiner vom 16. bis und mit dem 25. November 1907 in Basel einen Vortrags-Zyklus über das

Johannes-Evangelium

abhalten wird.

Wir erlauben uns deshalb, alle unsere theosophischen Freunde herzlich zur Teilnahme an diesem Kursus einzuladen und bitten Sie, im Interesse der vorzunehmenden Organisation uns Ihre Anmeldungen womöglich bis zum 15. Oktober zukommen zu lassen.

Aus dem beigegebenen Programm werden Sie ersehen, dass auf diejenigen, die nur an den Samstag- und Sonntag-Abenden anwesend sein können, Rücksicht genommen worden ist.

Gerne übernehmen wir die Besorgung von Zimmern, wenn uns diesbezügliche Wünsche mitgeteilt werden.

Wer zur Bestreitung der Unkosten beizutragen wünscht, möge seine Beisteuer senden an Herrn S. Hofstetter, 5 Klingelbergstrasse, Basel.

Mit theosophischem Gruss

Loge „Paracelsus" Basel.

To the members of the
Theosophical Lodges in Switzerland
and adjoining areas

We are delighted to inform you that from 16 to 25
November 1907 Dr R. Steiner will be giving a lecture course
on

The Gospel of John

We warmly invite all our theosophical friends to attend the
course. To facilitate organization, please give notification of
your intention to attend by 15 October.

You will see from the enclosed programme that the fact
that some friends will only be able to attend at weekends has
been taken into account.

We'll be happy to arrange accommodation if you let us
know your requirements.

Anyone wishing to contribute to the costs of the course is
requested to send their contribution to Mr S. Hofstetter, 5
Klingelbergstr., Basel.

Theosophically yours

Paracelsus Lodge, Basel

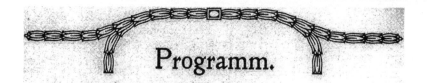

Programm.

Johannes-Evangelium:

Samstag, den 16. November, präzis 8 Uhr   abends
Sonntag, „ 17. „   „ 10 „ 30 morgens

Ansprache von Herrn Dr. R. Steiner und Geselliges Zusammensein:

Sonntag, den 17. November, präzis 3 Uhr 30 mittags

Johannes-Evangelium:

Montag,   den 18. November, präzis 8 Uhr abends
Dienstag,   „ 19.   „   „ 8 „   „
Mittwoch,   „ 20.   „   „ 8 „   „
Donnerstag, „ 21.   „   „ 8 „   „
Freitag,   „ 22.   „   „ 8 „   „

Öffentlicher Vortrag: „Die Naturwissenschaft am Scheidewege"

Samstag, den 23. November, präzis 8 Uhr abends
in der Aula des Museums, Augustinergasse 2.

Geselliges Zusammensein und Fragenbeantwortung:

Sonntag, den 24. November, präzis 7 Uhr abends

Johannes-Evangelium (Schluss):

Montag, den 25. November, präzis 8 Uhr abends.

NB.   Teilnehmer aus dem Elsass machen wir darauf aufmerksam, dass sie
nach den Vorträgen mit dem 9 Uhr 33 abgehenden Zug nach
Mülhausen etc. zurückfahren können.

Programme

Gospel of John

Saturday,	16 November,	8 p.m. precisely
Sunday,	17 November,	10.30 a.m. precisely

Address by Dr R. Steiner and social gathering

On Sunday,	17 November,	3.30 p.m. precisely

Gospel of John

Monday,	18 November,		8 p.m. precisely	
Tuesday,	19	"	8 p.m.	"
Wednesday,	20	"	8 p.m.	"
Thursday,	21	"	8 p.m.	"
Friday,	22	"	8 p.m.	"

Public lecture on Science at the Parting of the Ways

Saturday, 23 November 8 p.m. precisely

In the Hall of the Museum, Augustinergasse 2.

Social Gathering, Questions and Answers

Sunday, 24 November, 7 p.m. precisely

Gospel of John (conclusion)

Monday, 25 November 8 p.m. precisely

N.B. Members from Alsatia may like to know that there is a 9.33 p.m. train to Muehlhausen, etc. for their return home.

Aux Membres
et Amis des Sociétés Théosophiques
de Suisse et des Environs.

ous avons le plaisir de vous communiquer que M. le Dr. R. Steiner de Berlin fera, dans notre ville, du 16 au 25 Novembre inclusivement, une série de conférences, en langue allemande, sur

L'Evangile selon St Jean.

Nous invitons cordialement tous nos amis théosophiques à profiter de ce privilège et nous les prions de nous faire connaître, si possible jusqu'au 15 Octobre, leur participation à ce cours, afin que nous puissions nous organiser en conséquence.

Dans l'élaboration du programme ci-joint, nous avons pris en considération ceux qui, sans pouvoir suivre tout le cours, pourraient néanmoins s'arranger à passer les samedis et dimanches à Bâle.

Nous nous mettons volontiers à la disposition des participants au cours pour retenir des chambres et nous les prions d'exprimer leurs désirs sur le formulaire ci-inclus.

Les personnes désireuses de participer aux frais des conférences voudront bien adresser leurs cotisations à Monsieur S. Hofstetter, 5 Klingelbergstrasse, Bâle.

Loge „Paracelse" Bâle.

French version

NOTES

Text sources: The lectures given in Kassel were originally published in the members' newsletter by Marie Steiner, appearing from 22 February to 18 October 1942. They provided the basis for the first book publication for members of the Anthroposophical Society, part of the Collected Works in German, by Johann Waeger and Hendrik Knobel. Marie Steiner had edited the notes (not very good) she had been given by Mrs Frieda Noll. Johann Waeger and Hendrik Knobel compared the newsletter items with a record written by Ludwig Kleeberg which had been found at a later date, though they adhered largely to the text published by Marie Steiner.

The lectures on the Gospel of John in Basel were taken down by four people, with one of them, Rudolf Hahn, also using shorthand. They compiled an edition which they submitted to Marie Steiner. After some hesitation Marie Steiner agreed for it to go into print, heavily editing the lectures and publishing them in the newsletter from 1 December 1946 to 20 April 1947. They bore the inscription 'Greatly abridged records, not reviewed by the speaker'.

The four members prefaced their efforts 'Based on records written from memory and freely revised.

'Dear reader,

'These pages are mainly intended for people who attended the lectures in Basel. In the interests of the theosophical cause we do not wish and desire this work to be used to spread the thoughts reflected in it, especially as we have not recorded the lectures word for word but given a free rendering of them, so that for this reason alone there will be many objections raised. What is more, Dr Steiner intends to publish the lectures on the Gospel of John himself.

'All we hope to achieve with our work is that some friends who attended the course may have something to remind them of those beautiful November days in Basel. L.S.H.H.E.'

Those initials may represent the following: Lagutt, S.(?); Hahn, Rudolf; Huebner; Edelmann. These lectures also follow the text published in the newsletter.

For the 3rd German edition, some spellings and meanings have been corrected, the Contents page has been revised. The Notes have been extended and Questions and Answers taken down by Ludwig Kleeberg in Kassel added.

Drawings in the text: Based on the sketches in the newsletter, these have been produced by Mrs Hedwig Frey.

Titles: The German title of this volume, *Menschheitsentwicklung und Christus-Erkennnis* (human evolution and finding the Christ), was composed by Johann Waeger and Hendrik Knobel.

Corrections in the text compared to the 2nd German edition—
Lecture of 16 June 1907: '. . . not close their eyes and ears to the questions of our time' replacing '. . . close their eyes and ears to the questions of our time'
Lecture of 17 June 1907: 'so is the physical body differentiated out from the ether body'

1. Richard Wagner (1813–83). Rudolf Steiner repeatedly referred to Richard Wagner's music dramas and his endeavours, both in theory and practice, concerning the 'complete work of art' (a term he created). See Rudolf Steiner's lectures of 22 March 1906 entitled 'Siegfried und die Götterdämmerung' and of 29 March 1906 entitled 'Parsival und Lohengrin' in German collected works vol. 54. Also the lecture of 28 March 1908 on 'Richard Wagner und die Mystik' in German collected works vol. 55 as well as the lecture entitled 'Nietzsches Seelenleben und Richard Wagner. Zur deutschen Weltanschauungsentwicklung der Gegenwart' of 23 March 1916. German collected works vol. 92, *Die okkulten Wahrheiten alter Mythen und Sagen*, includes the four lectures on Richard Wagner available in typescript in English (NSL 175–8, Rudolf Steiner House Library, London).
2. Goethe, *Faust I*, Night 573, tr. David Luke, Oxford University Press, 1987.
3. The name of this individual, not acknowledged to be historic, first became known when The Chymical Wedding of Christian Rosenkreutz, Anno 1459 appeared in German in 1604. According to Rudolf Steiner, the author, Johann Valentin Andreae, was inspired by Christian Rosenkreutz. Steiner referred to Christian Rosenkreutz on many occasions; see also his essays in *A Christian Rosenkreutz Anthology*, tr. P.M. Allen, Floris Books, 1968, and lectures in *Esoteric Christianity and the Mission of Christian Rosenkreutz*, tr. P. Wehrle, Rudolf Steiner Press, London 1984.
4. Judge of the Areopagus, converted to Chrstianity by Paul (Acts, 17:34). Rudolf Steiner referred to him in his writings and in lectures, especially also the assumption that the writings that appeared under his name were written by someone else. In modern history of philosophy it is held that the author used the name as a pseudonym, ascribing his neo-Platonic writings to Dionysius to 'dress them up'. These writings had a powerful influence on the Eastern Orthodox and Roman Catholic Churches and are today ascribed to Pseudo-Dionysius. According to Rudolf Steiner Dionysius the Areopagite led the esoteric Christian school established by Paul. The teachings of this school were only passed on orally until the sixth century, and the head of the school always bore the name Dionysius. So there is an inner connection between the writings of the later Dionysius and Dionysius the Areopagite. See Rudolf Steiner's *The Gospel of St John*, Hamburg, 18–31 May 1908, tr. M.B. Monges, Anthroposophic Press, New York 1940; *Foundations of Esotericism,* tr. V. & J. Compton-Burnett, Rudolf Steiner Press, London 1983; *The Christian Mystery*, tr. A.R. Meuss; Completion Press, Gympie 2000.
5. A passage in the works of Fichte often referred to by Rudolf Steiner. See J.G. Fichte, *Einleitungsvorlesungen in die Wissenschaftslehre* given in Berlin in the autumn of 1813, Bonn 1834: 'Think of a world where all are born blind, so that only objects and the relations between them are known to them which exist for

them through touch. Go among them and talk to them of colours and the other situations that exist only for the eye thanks to light. You'll either be speaking to them about something that does not exist for them, and that is the more fortunate thing for them to tell you; for this will make you perceive your error and stop talking, unless you are able to open their eyes for them. This, I think, should be attainable through the theory of science in the worst case. Or they may want for some reason or other to find a way of making sense of what you are saying: in that case they can only understand it on the basis of what they know from touch: they will want to feel the light and the colours and the other things connected with visibility, thinking they can touch them, imagining they feel things by touch and so lying to themselves about what they call colour. They then misunderstand, twist and misinterpret.'

6. Emil du Bois-Reymond (1818–96), physiologist, Berlin, in his lecture at the 45th congress of German naturalists and physicians on 14 August 1872 in Leipzig, published under the title *Über die Grenzen der Naturerkenntnis*, Leipzig 1872.

7. This passage was checked against the transcriptions which also give the unusual term 'intensive'. Rudolf Steiner probably sought to show that the world does not only have outward dimensions and rich variety but also an inner multiplicity and complexity.

8. Luke 17:21.

9. Theophrastus Paracelsus von Hohenheim (1493–1541). In *Die vierte Defension*.

10. Goethe, *Faust II*, 4666–74, tr. David Luke, Oxford University Press, 1994.

11. Matthew 18:3.

12. Francesco Redi (1626–97), physician and poet. Redi became famous for his experiments to show that maggots do not develop spontaneously in rotting flesh but from eggs laid by flies.

13. J.W. Goethe, *Theory of Colours*. Introduction. The actual quote is: 'The eye owes its existence to the light. Light calls forth an organ from the indifferent animal organs to make it of its own kind, and so the eye develops in the light for the light, letting the inner meet with the outside light.'

14. Rudolf Steiner was probably referring to Darwin's comments in *The Origin of Species*.

15. See Rudolf Steiner's comments in a lecture given in Cologne on 1 December 1906 published in *The Education of the Child*, and his essay on the subject in *Supersensible Knowledge: Anthroposophy as a Demand of the Age*, Anthroposophic Press, New York 1943.

16. Sante de Sanctis (1862–1935), Italian physician, psychologist and psychiatrist.

17. Adalbert von Chamisso (1781–1838), botanist, writer and poet. Wrote a novel about Peter Schlemihl, a man who sold his shadow.

18. See also Rudolf Steiner, *The Mission of the Individual Folk Souls*, Rudolf Steiner Press, London 1970.

19. Fritz Mauthner (1849–1923), novelist, satirist and philosopher now known above all for his critique of language.

20. Vehmic or Feme courts in Westphalia, Germany, with lay judges.

21. See also Rudolf Steiner's lecture on 28 January 1907 in Berlin, *The Lord's Prayer*, Anthroposophic Press, 1970.

22. See Kalmia Bittleston's *The Gospel of Matthew*, Floris Books, Edinburgh 1998.

23. See Note 14.

24. The question has arisen with reference to this passage if it should not be Vulgata rather than Septuagint. This is due to the syntax which would permit the conclusion that the clause 'the standard translation ...' refers to the Septuagint. Today the *Nova Vulgata* is the standard in the Roman Catholic Church.

25. William James (1842–1910), American philosopher and psychologist, co-founder of American pragmatism, wrote: 'The hypothesis here to be defended says that this order of sequence is incorrect, that the one mental state is not immediately induced by the other, that the bodily manifestations must first be interposed between, and that the more rational statement is that we feel sorry because we cry, angry because we strike, afraid because we tremble, and not that we cry, strike or tremble because we are sorry, angry or fearful, as the case may be.' William James in *The Principles of Psychology*, Chapter 25, 'The Emotions', New York 1890.

26. Ludwig Buechner (1824–99), physician, physiologist and philosopher, representing a radical natural-scientific materialism and known for his work *Kraft und Stoff* (energy and matter).

27. See Rudolf Steiner, *Genesis*, Rudolf Steiner Press, Sussex 2002.

28. The Theosophical Society was established by H.P. Blavatsky and H.S. Olcott in 1875.

29. That is what it says in the transcript, which is likely to be a mix-up since one would expect to see bad qualities on the debit and good ones on the credit side.

30. Antoine Fabre d'Olivet (1767–1825), French esotericist and cabbalist. Works: *La langue hebraique restituée*, Paris 1816, *Histoire philosophique du genre humain*, Paris 1824.

31. To be found in the German Collected Works (GA) No. 34.

32. E.g. in *Esoteric Cosmology*, St George Pbs., New York 1978.

33. J.W. Goethe, *Faust II*, 12104–5, tr. David Luke, OUP, 1994.

34. Rudolf Steiner was probably referring to *Three Essays on Haeckel and Karma*, Theosophical Pub. Co., London 1914.

35. Manvantara (Sanskrit) means a stage of development where life unfolds outwardly.

36. John 8:12.

37. Thomas Henry Huxley (1825–95), English zoologist and palaeontologist. Coined the term 'agnostic'. Vehemently stood for Darwin's theory of evolution, though critical of some aspects. The statement referred to here appears in his *Physiography*, Chapter 13.

38. Theodor Arldt, 'Das Atlantic Problem', in *Kosmos*, Stuttgart 1905, S. 295–302.

39. Plato, *Critias* and *Timaeus*.

40. Genesis 9:13, 14, 16.

41. One set of notes has 'animals' instead of 'life forms' or 'entities'.

42. Genesis 1:2.

43. Genesis 2:7.
44. See Note 9.
45. Peter Rosegger (1843–1918), Austrian writer to whom Rudolf Steiner referred on various occasions.
46. Ludwig Anzengruber (1839–1918), Viennese dramatist and writer. Rudolf Steiner wrote about him and Rosegger in *Biographien und biographische Skizzen 1894–1905*, S. 94 (not in English).
47. 'Another day out for a walk with Anzengruber. We chatted about the work of a writer and subjects for writers. I said that Anzengruber must have lived in Upper Bavaria or at least have had much to do with Upper Bavarian farmers. The figures in his writings were very characteristic of the type. He put his pince-nez on his angular nose and said, "Upper Bavaria? No, I've actually never had any dealings with farmers. At least not close ones." Noting my amazement, "I don't need that. Just need to see someone like that from a distance, hear a few ordinary words, observe some gesture he makes, and I know the chap inside out." "Strange!" "My dear friend," he said, "you know this yourself. All outward opportunities and occasions are merely midwives. The writer has to give birth out of himself. Farmers, pah! I'm a city person! But if I am able, as you say, to write better about country than city people, then that must be in the blood. Or in some bone or other, like inherited gout. On my father's side the family used to be Upper Austrian country people. Well, and such things have their echoes." ' Peter Rosegger's Collected Works, vol. 36.
48. Genesis 2:7.
49. See Augustine, *Retractationes* I.1.ch. XIII: 'The Christian religion, as it is called today, existed in antiquity and was there in the beginnings of the human race, and when the Christ came in the flesh the true religion, existing already, was given the name Christian.' See also *De civitate Dei* VIII, 9.
50. Matthew 13:16.
51. Rudolf Steiner referred to those words in several lectures. It is given in the Bible as 'Eli, Eli, lama sabachthani!' (Matthew 27:46 and Mark 15:34), translated (wrongly according to Rudolf Steiner) as 'My God, my God, why have you forsaken me?' See *The Gospel of St Matthew* (CW 123), *An Esoteric Cosmology* (CW 94) *and Original Impulses for the Science of the Spirit* (CW 96).
52. Luke 14:26.
53. 1 John 1:1.
54. John 13:18.
55. Goethe's Scientific Writings vol. 3, Introduction. With introductions and explanations by Rudolf Steiner. As Steiner has written there, the verse goes back to Jakob Boehme.
56. Goethe, *Faust II*, 12104, tr. David Luke, OUP, 1994.
57. Goethe, *Faust I*, Night, 501, tr. David Luke, OUP, 1994.
58. This is an image frequently given by Rudolf Steiner. Plato spoke of it when describing the origin of the world in *Timaeus* (Ch. 8 and 9, 34b–37c). In a book in his library, Vincenz Knauer's *Die Hauptprobleme der Philosophie in ihrer Entwicklung und ihrer theilweisen Loesung von Thales bis Robert Hamerling*, Rudolf Steiner firmly marked the following passage: 'The myth in *Timaeus* tells us

that God made this world soul lie across the universe in the shape of a cross, with the world body stretched upon it.'

59. See Note 3.

60. As representative of a 'hermetic' society, the physician and poet Kortum from Bochum, Germany, published an appeal on 8 October 1796 inviting people seeking the Philosophers' Stone, alchemists and chemists, to share their knowledge, so that it might be deepened in further research. It is interesting to note that he believed the Stone to be anthracite. See also Willy Bein, *Der Stein der Weisen und die Kunst Gold zu waschen. Irrtum und Erkenntnis der Elemente, mitgeteilt nach den Quellen der Vergangenheit und Gegenwart*, Voigt-laender Quellenbeucher, Band 88, Leipzig 1915.

61. J.W. Goethe, *Westoestlicher Diwan*, notes and treatises.

62. Eduard von Hartmann (1842–1906), philosopher. His *Philosophy of the Unconscious* published in Berlin in 1869, *The Unconscious from the Point of View of Physiology and the Theory of Descent* in 1872, the second edition in 1877, giving his name as the author.

63. Oscar Schmidt (1823–86), significant zoologist in his day in Vienna, Jena, Cracow, Graz and Strasbourg. One of the early protagonists of Darwin's theory of evolution.

64. See Note 34.

65. Rowland Hill (1795–1879), completely reformed British postal system.

66. See Max Kemmerich, *Kultur-Kuriosa*, Munich 1909.

67. See Note 26.

68. Jakob Moleschott (1822–93), physiologist and materialistic philosopher. See Rudolf Steiner's *The Riddles of Philosophy*, also with regard to Buechner and Vogt.

69. Karl Vogt (1817–95), professor of geology and zoology in Giesen, protagonist of materialism and convinced follower of Darwin; known as Ape-Vogt.

70. Rudolf Wagner (1805–64), zoologist and physiologist. On the dispute between Vogt and Wagner, see Karl Vogt's *Koehlerglaube und Wissenschaft. Eine Streitschrift gegen Hofrat Rudolf Wagner in Goettingen*, 2nd edition, Giessen 1855. See also Rudolf Steiner's *The Riddles of Philosophy*.

71. See Note 4.

72. Goethe, *Faust II*, 6861 ff.: 'When we live long, we learn a thing / Or two, nothing surprises any more. / I have, in my long years of wandering, / Seen crystallized humanity before.'

73. Goethe, Faust I, 1740. See also Rudolf Steiner's *The Occult Significance of Blood*, Rudolf Steiner Press, London 1967.

74. See Note 55.

75. Rudolf Steiner regarded Pythagoras as a philosopher who was still able to draw on the sources of mystery wisdom, changing them into concepts. See Rudolf Steiner's *Christianity as Mystical Fact* and *The Riddles of Philosophy*.

76. See L. Kuhlenbeck, *Der Occultismus der nordamerikanischen Indianer* (native American occultism), Leipzig 1896.

77. See Ernst Haeckel, *Natürliche Schöpfungsgeschichte*, published in Berlin in 1868, and translated into English as *The History of Creation* in 1876.

78. See Note 58.

79. John 8:58.
    [Kalmia Bittleston's translation: Before Abraham was
                                                  I
                                                  I AM   ]
80. See also Rudolf Steiner, *The Temple Legend*, Rudolf Steiner Press, London 1987.

RUDOLF STEINER'S COLLECTED WORKS

The German Edition of Rudolf Steiner's Collected Works (the *Gesamtausgabe* [GA] published by Rudolf Steiner Verlag, Dornach, Switzerland) presently runs to 354 titles, organized either by type of work (written or spoken), chronology, audience (public or other), or subject (education, art, etc.). For ease of comparison, the Collected Works in English [CW] follows the German organization exactly. A complete listing of the CWs follows with literal translations of the German titles. Other than in the case of the books published in his lifetime, titles were rarely given by Rudolf Steiner himself, and were often provided by the editors of the German editions. The titles in English are not necessarily the same as the German; and, indeed, over the past seventy-five years have frequently been different, with the same book sometimes appearing under different titles.

For ease of identification and to avoid confusion, we suggest that readers looking for a title should do so by CW number. Because the work of creating the Collected Works of Rudolf Steiner is an ongoing process, with new titles being published every year, we have not indicated in this listing which books are presently available. To find out what titles in the Collected Works are currently in print, please check our website at www.rudolfsteinerpress.com (or www.steinerbooks.org for US readers).

Written Work

CW 1	Goethe: Natural-Scientific Writings, Introduction, with Footnotes and Explanations in the text by Rudolf Steiner
CW 2	Outlines of an Epistemology of the Goethean World View, with Special Consideration of Schiller
CW 3	Truth and Science
CW 4	The Philosophy of Freedom
CW 4a	Documents to 'The Philosophy of Freedom'
CW 5	Friedrich Nietzsche, A Fighter against His Time
CW 6	Goethe's Worldview
CW 6a	Now in CW 30
CW 7	Mysticism at the Dawn of Modern Spiritual Life and Its Relationship with Modern Worldviews
CW 8	Christianity as Mystical Fact and the Mysteries of Antiquity
CW 9	Theosophy: An Introduction into Supersensible World Knowledge and Human Purpose
CW 10	How Does One Attain Knowledge of Higher Worlds?
CW 11	From the Akasha-Chronicle

Public Lectures

Lectures to the Members of the Anthroposophical Society

CW 266/1   From the Contents of the Esoteric Lessons. Volume 1: 1904–1909. Notes from Memory of Participants. Meditation texts from the notes of Rudolf Steiner
CW 266/2   From the Contents of the Esoteric Lessons. Volume 2: 1910–1912. Notes from Memory of Participants
CW 266/3   From the Contents of the Esoteric Lessons. Volume 3: 1913, 1914 and 1920–1923. Notes from Memory of Participants. Meditation texts from the notes of Rudolf Steiner
CW 267   Soul-Exercises: Vol. 1: Exercises with Word and Image Meditations for the Methodological Development of Higher Powers of Knowledge, 1904–1924
CW 268   Soul-Exercises: Vol. 2: Mantric Verses, 1903–1925
CW 269   Ritual Texts for the Celebration of the Free Christian Religious Instruction. The Collected Verses for Teachers and Students of the Waldorf School
CW 270   Esoteric Instructions for the First Class of the School for Spiritual Science at the Goetheanum 1924, 4 Volumes
CW 271   Art and Knowledge of Art. Foundations of a New Aesthetic
CW 272   Spiritual-Scientific Commentary on Goethe's 'Faust' in Two Volumes. Vol. 1: Faust, the Striving Human Being
CW 273   Spiritual-Scientific Commentary on Goethe's 'Faust' in Two Volumes. Vol. 2: The Faust-Problem
CW 274   Addresses for the Christmas Plays from the Old Folk Traditions
CW 275   Art in the Light of Mystery-Wisdom
CW 276   The Artistic in Its Mission in the World. The Genius of Language. The World of Self-Revealing Radiant Appearances—Anthroposophy and Art. Anthroposophy and Poetry
CW 277   Eurythmy. The Revelation of the Speaking Soul
CW 277a   The Origin and Development of Eurythmy
CW 278   Eurythmy as Visible Song
CW 279   Eurythmy as Visible Speech
CW 280   The Method and Nature of Speech Formation
CW 281   The Art of Recitation and Declamation
CW 282   Speech Formation and Dramatic Art
CW 283   The Nature of Things Musical and the Experience of Tone in the Human Being
CW 284/285 Images of Occult Seals and Pillars. The Munich Congress of Whitsun 1907 and Its Consequences
CW 286   Paths to a New Style of Architecture. 'And the Building Becomes Human'
CW 287   The Building at Dornach as a Symbol of Historical Becoming and an Artistic Transformation Impulse
CW 288   Style-Forms in the Living Organic
CW 289   The Building-Idea of the Goetheanum: Lectures with Slides from the Years 1920–1921
CW 290   The Building-Idea of the Goetheanum: Lectures with Slides from the Years 1920–1921

SIGNIFICANT EVENTS IN THE LIFE OF RUDOLF STEINER

1829:   June 23: birth of Johann Steiner (1829–1910)—Rudolf Steiner's father—in Geras, Lower Austria.

1834:   May 8: birth of Franciska Blie (1834–1918)—Rudolf Steiner's mother—in Horn, Lower Austria. 'My father and mother were both children of the glorious Lower Austrian forest district north of the Danube.'

1860:   May 16: marriage of Johann Steiner and Franciska Blie.

1861:   February 25: birth of *Rudolf Joseph Lorenz Steiner* in Kraljevec, Croatia, near the border with Hungary, where Johann Steiner works as a telegrapher for the South Austria Railroad. Rudolf Steiner is baptized two days later, February 27, the date usually given as his birthday.

1862:   Summer: the family moves to Mödling, Lower Austria.

1863:   The family moves to Pottschach, Lower Austria, near the Styrian border, where Johann Steiner becomes stationmaster. 'The view stretched to the mountains ... majestic peaks in the distance and the sweet charm of nature in the immediate surroundings.'

1864:   November 15: birth of Rudolf Steiner's sister, Leopoldine (d. November 1, 1927). She will become a seamstress and live with her parents for the rest of her life.

1866:   July 28: birth of Rudolf Steiner's deaf-mute brother, Gustav (d. May 1, 1941).

1867:   Rudolf Steiner enters the village school. Following a disagreement between his father and the schoolmaster, whose wife falsely accused the boy of causing a commotion, Rudolf Steiner is taken out of school and taught at home.

1868:   A critical experience. Unknown to the family, an aunt dies in a distant town. Sitting in the station waiting room, Rudolf Steiner sees her 'form,' which speaks to him, asking for help. 'Beginning with this experience, a new soul life began in the boy, one in which not only the outer trees and mountains spoke to him, but also the worlds that lay behind them. From this moment on, the boy began to live with the spirits of nature ...'

1869:   The family moves to the peaceful, rural village of Neudörfl, near Wiener-Neustadt in present-day Austria. Rudolf Steiner attends the village school. Because of the 'unorthodoxy' of his writing and spelling, he has to do 'extra lessons.'

1870:   Through a book lent to him by his tutor, he discovers geometry: 'To grasp something purely in the spirit brought me inner happiness. I know that I first learned happiness through geometry.' The same tutor allows him to draw, while other students still struggle with their reading and writing. 'An artistic element' thus enters his education.

1871: Though his parents are not religious, Rudolf Steiner becomes a 'church child,' a favourite of the priest, who was 'an exceptional character.' 'Up to the age of ten or eleven, among those I came to know, he was far and away the most significant.' Among other things, he introduces Steiner to Copernican, heliocentric cosmology. As an altar boy, Rudolf Steiner serves at Masses, funerals, and Corpus Christi processions. At year's end, after an incident in which he escapes a thrashing, his father forbids him to go to church.

1872: Rudolf Steiner transfers to grammar school in Wiener-Neustadt, a five-mile walk from home, which must be done in all weathers.

1873–75: Through his teachers and on his own, Rudolf Steiner has many wonderful experiences with science and mathematics. Outside school, he teaches himself analytic geometry, trigonometry, differential equations, and calculus.

1876: Rudolf Steiner begins tutoring other students. He learns bookbinding from his father. He also teaches himself stenography.

1877: Rudolf Steiner discovers Kant's *Critique of Pure Reason*, which he reads and rereads. He also discovers and reads von Rotteck's *World History*.

1878: He studies extensively in contemporary psychology and philosophy.

1879: Rudolf Steiner graduates from high school with honours. His father is transferred to Inzersdorf, near Vienna. He uses his first visit to Vienna 'to purchase a great number of philosophy books'—Kant, Fichte, Schelling, and Hegel, as well as numerous histories of philosophy. His aim: to find a path from the 'I' to nature.

October 1879–1883: Rudolf Steiner attends the Technical College in Vienna—to study mathematics, chemistry, physics, mineralogy, botany, zoology, biology, geology, and mechanics—with a scholarship. He also attends lectures in history and literature, while avidly reading philosophy on his own. His two favourite professors are Karl Julius Schröer (German language and literature) and Edmund Reitlinger (physics). He also audits lectures by Robert Zimmermann on aesthetics and Franz Brentano on philosophy. During this year he begins his friendship with Moritz Zitter (1861–1921), who will help support him financially when he is in Berlin.

1880: Rudolf Steiner attends lectures on Schiller and Goethe by Karl Julius Schröer, who becomes his mentor. Also 'through a remarkable combination of circumstances,' he meets Felix Koguzki, a 'herb gatherer' and healer, who could 'see deeply into the secrets of nature.' Rudolf Steiner will meet and study with this 'emissary of the Master' throughout his time in Vienna.

1881: January: '... I didn't sleep a wink. I was busy with philosophical problems until about 12:30 a.m. Then, finally, I threw myself down on my couch. All my striving during the previous year had been to research whether the following statement by Schelling was true or not: *Within everyone dwells a secret, marvelous capacity to draw back from the stream of time—out of the self clothed in all that comes to us from outside—into our innermost being and there, in the immutable form of the Eternal, to look into ourselves.* I believe, and I am still quite certain of it, that I discovered this capacity in myself; I had long had an inkling of it. Now the whole of idealist philosophy stood before me in modified form. What's a sleepless night compared to that!'

    Rudolf Steiner begins communicating with leading thinkers of the day, who send him books in return, which he reads eagerly.

July: 'I am not one of those who dives into the day like an animal in human form. I pursue a quite specific goal, an idealistic aim—knowledge of the truth! This cannot be done offhandedly. It requires the greatest striving in the world, free of all egotism, and equally of all resignation.'

August: Steiner puts down on paper for the first time thoughts for a 'Philosophy of Freedom.' 'The striving for the absolute: this human yearning is freedom.' He also seeks to outline a 'peasant philosophy,' describing what the worldview of a 'peasant'—one who lives close to the earth and the old ways—really is.

1881–1882: Felix Koguzki, the herb gatherer, reveals himself to be the envoy of another, higher initiatory personality, who instructs Rudolf Steiner to penetrate Fichte's philosophy and to master modern scientific thinking as a preparation for right entry into the spirit. This 'Master' also teaches him the double (evolutionary and involutionary) nature of time.

1882:   Through the offices of Karl Julius Schröer, Rudolf Steiner is asked by Joseph Kürschner to edit Goethe's scientific works for the *Deutschen National-Literatur* edition. He writes 'A Possible Critique of Atomistic Concepts' and sends it to Friedrich Theodor Vischer.

1883:   Rudolf Steiner completes his college studies and begins work on the Goethe project.

1884:   First volume of Goethe's *Scientific Writings* (CW 1) appears (March). He lectures on Goethe and Lessing, and Goethe's approach to science. In July, he enters the household of Ladislaus and Pauline Specht as tutor to the four Specht boys. He will live there until 1890. At this time, he meets Josef Breuer (1842–1925), the co-author with Sigmund Freud of *Studies in Hysteria*, who is the Specht family doctor.

1885:   While continuing to edit Goethe's writings, Rudolf Steiner reads deeply in contemporary philosophy (Eduard von Hartmann, Johannes Volkelt, and Richard Wahle, among others).

1886:   May: Rudolf Steiner sends Kürschner the manuscript of *Outlines of Goethe's Theory of Knowledge* (CW 2), which appears in October, and which he sends out widely. He also meets the poet Marie Eugenie Delle Grazie and writes 'Nature and Our Ideals' for her. He attends her salon, where he meets many priests, theologians, and philosophers, who will become his friends. Meanwhile, the director of the Goethe Archive in Weimar requests his collaboration with the *Sophien* edition of Goethe's works, particularly the writings on colour.

1887:   At the beginning of the year, Rudolf Steiner is very sick. As the year progresses and his health improves, he becomes increasingly 'a man of letters,' lecturing, writing essays, and taking part in Austrian cultural life. In August–September, the second volume of Goethe's *Scientific Writings* appears.

1888:   January–July: Rudolf Steiner assumes editorship of the 'German Weekly' (*Deutsche Wochenschrift*). He begins lecturing more intensively, giving, for example, a lecture titled 'Goethe as Father of a New Aesthetics.' He meets and becomes soul friends with Friedrich Eckstein (1861–1939), a vegetarian, philosopher of symbolism, alchemist, and musician, who will introduce him to various spiritual currents (including Theosophy) and with whom he will meditate and interpret esoteric and alchemical texts.

1889:   Rudolf Steiner first reads Nietzsche (*Beyond Good and Evil*). He encounters Theosophy again and learns of Madame Blavatsky in the Theosophical circle around Marie Lang (1858–1934). Here he also meets well-known figures of Austrian life, as well as esoteric figures like the occultist Franz Hartmann and Karl Leinigen-Billigen (translator of C.G. Harrison's *The Transcendental Universe*). During this period, Steiner first reads A.P. Sinnett's *Esoteric Buddhism* and Mabel Collins's *Light on the Path*. He also begins travelling, visiting Budapest, Weimar, and Berlin (where he meets philosopher Eduard von Hartmann).

1890:   Rudolf Steiner finishes volume 3 of Goethe's scientific writings. He begins his doctoral dissertation, which will become *Truth and Science* (CW 3). He also meets the poet and feminist Rosa Mayreder (1858–1938), with whom he can exchange his most intimate thoughts. In September, Rudolf Steiner moves to Weimar to work in the Goethe-Schiller Archive.

1891:   Volume 3 of the Kürschner edition of Goethe appears. Meanwhile, Rudolf Steiner edits Goethe's studies in mineralogy and scientific writings for the *Sophien* edition. He meets Ludwig Laistner of the Cotta Publishing Company, who asks for a book on the basic question of metaphysics. From this will result, ultimately, *The Philosophy of Freedom* (CW 4), which will be published not by Cotta but by Emil Felber. In October, Rudolf Steiner takes the oral exam for a doctorate in philosophy, mathematics, and mechanics at Rostock University, receiving his doctorate on the twenty-sixth. In November, he gives his first lecture on Goethe's 'Fairy Tale' in Vienna.

1892:   Rudolf Steiner continues work at the Goethe-Schiller Archive and on his *Philosophy of Freedom. Truth and Science*, his doctoral dissertation, is published. Steiner undertakes to write introductions to books on Schopenhauer and Jean Paul for Cotta. At year's end, he finds lodging with Anna Eunike, née Schulz (1853–1911), a widow with four daughters and a son. He also develops a friendship with Otto Erich Hartleben (1864–1905) with whom he shares literary interests.

1893:   Rudolf Steiner begins his habit of producing many reviews and articles. In March, he gives a lecture titled 'Hypnotism, with Reference to Spiritism.' In September, volume 4 of the Kürschner edition is completed. In November, *The Philosophy of Freedom* appears. This year, too, he meets John Henry Mackay (1864–1933), the anarchist, and Max Stirner, a scholar and biographer.

1894:   Rudolf Steiner meets Elisabeth Förster Nietzsche, the philosopher's sister, and begins to read Nietzsche in earnest, beginning with the as yet unpublished *Antichrist*. He also meets Ernst Haeckel (1834–1919). In the fall, he begins to write *Nietzsche, A Fighter against His Time* (CW 5).

1895:   May, *Nietzsche, A Fighter against His Time* appears.

1896:   January 22: Rudolf Steiner sees Friedrich Nietzsche for the first and only time. Moves between the Nietzsche and the Goethe-Schiller Archives, where he completes his work before year's end. He falls out with Elisabeth Förster Nietzsche, thus ending his association with the Nietzsche Archive.

1897:   Rudolf Steiner finishes the manuscript of *Goethe's Worldview* (CW 6). He moves to Berlin with Anna Eunike and begins editorship of the *Magazin für Literatur*. From now on, Steiner will write countless reviews, literary and philosophical articles, and so on. He begins lecturing at the 'Free Literary Society.' In September, he attends the Zionist Congress in Basel. He sides with Dreyfus in the Dreyfus affair.

1898:   Rudolf Steiner is very active as an editor in the political, artistic, and theatrical life of Berlin. He becomes friendly with John Henry Mackay and poet Ludwig Jacobowski (1868–1900). He joins Jacobowski's circle of writers, artists, and scientists—'The Coming Ones' (*Die Kommenden*)—and contributes lectures to the group until 1903. He also lectures at the 'League for College Pedagogy.' He writes an article for Goethe's sesquicentennial, 'Goethe's Secret Revelation,' on the 'Fairy Tale of the Green Snake and the Beautiful Lily.'

1898–99:   'This was a trying time for my soul as I looked at Christianity. . . . I was able to progress only by contemplating, by means of spiritual perception, the evolution of Christianity. . . . Conscious knowledge of real Christianity began to dawn in me around the turn of the century. This seed continued to develop. My soul trial occurred shortly before the beginning of the twentieth century. It was decisive for my soul's development that I stood spiritually before the Mystery of Golgotha in a deep and solemn celebration of knowledge.'

1899:   Rudolf Steiner begins teaching and giving lectures and lecture cycles at the Workers' College, founded by Wilhelm Liebknecht (1826–1900). He will continue to do so until 1904. Writes: *Literature and Spiritual Life in the Nineteenth Century; Individualism in Philosophy*; *Haeckel and His Opponents; Poetry in the Present;* and begins what will become (fifteen years later) *The Riddles of Philosophy* (CW 18). He also meets many artists and writers, including Käthe Kollwitz, Stefan Zweig, and Rainer Maria Rilke. On October 31, he marries Anna Eunike.

1900:   'I thought that the turn of the century must bring humanity a new light. It seemed to me that the separation of human thinking and willing from the spirit had peaked. A turn or reversal of direction in human evolution seemed to me a necessity.' Rudolf Steiner finishes *World and Life Views in the Nineteenth Century* (the second part of what will become *The Riddles of Philosophy*) and dedicates it to Ernst Haeckel. It is published in March. He continues lecturing at *Die Kommenden*, whose leadership he assumes after the death of Jacobowski. Also, he gives the Gutenberg Jubilee lecture before 7,000 typesetters and printers. In September, Rudolf Steiner is invited by Count and Countess Brockdorff to lecture in the Theosophical Library. His first lecture is on Nietzsche. His second lecture is titled 'Goethe's Secret Revelation.' October 6, he begins a lecture cycle on the mystics that will become *Mystics after Modernism* (CW 7). November-December: 'Marie von Sivers appears in the audience....' Also in November, Steiner gives his first lecture at the Giordano Bruno Bund (where he will continue to lecture until May, 1905). He speaks on Bruno and modern Rome, focusing on the importance of the philosophy of Thomas Aquinas as monism.

1901: In continual financial straits, Rudolf Steiner's early friends Moritz Zitter and Rosa Mayreder help support him. In October, he begins the lecture cycle *Christianity as Mystical Fact* (CW 8) at the Theosophical Library. In November, he gives his first 'Theosophical lecture' on Goethe's 'Fairy Tale' in Hamburg at the invitation of Wilhelm Hubbe-Schleiden. He also attends a gathering to celebrate the founding of the Theosophical Society at Count and Countess Brockdorff's. He gives a lecture cycle, 'From Buddha to Christ,' for the circle of the *Kommenden*. November 17, Marie von Sivers asks Rudolf Steiner if Theosophy needs a Western-Christian spiritual movement (to complement Theosophy's Eastern emphasis). 'The question was posed. Now, following spiritual laws, I could begin to give an answer....' In December, Rudolf Steiner writes his first article for a Theosophical publication. At year's end, the Brockdorffs and possibly Wilhelm Hubbe-Schleiden ask Rudolf Steiner to join the Theosophical Society and undertake the leadership of the German section. Rudolf Steiner agrees, on the condition that Marie von Sivers (then in Italy) work with him.

1902: Beginning in January, Rudolf Steiner attends the opening of the Workers' School in Spandau with Rosa Luxemburg (1870–1919). January 17, Rudolf Steiner joins the Theosophical Society. In April, he is asked to become general secretary of the German Section of the Theosophical Society, and works on preparations for its founding. In July, he visits London for a Theosophical congress. He meets Bertram Keightly, G.R.S. Mead, A.P. Sinnett, and Annie Besant, among others. In September, *Christianity as Mystical Fact* appears. In October, Rudolf Steiner gives his first public lecture on Theosophy ('Monism and Theosophy') to about three hundred people at the Giordano Bruno Bund. On October 19–21, the German Section of the Theosophical Society has its first meeting; Rudolf Steiner is the general secretary, and Annie Besant attends. Steiner lectures on practical karma studies. On October 23, Annie Besant inducts Rudolf Steiner into the Esoteric School of the Theosophical Society. On October 25, Steiner begins a weekly series of lectures: 'The Field of Theosophy.' During this year, Rudolf Steiner also first meets Ita Wegman (1876–1943), who will become his close collaborator in his final years.

1903: Rudolf Steiner holds about 300 lectures and seminars. In May, the first issue of the periodical *Luzifer* appears. In June, Rudolf Steiner visits

London for the first meeting of the Federation of the European Sections of the Theosophical Society, where he meets Colonel Olcott. He begins to write *Theosophy* (CW 9).

1904: Rudolf Steiner continues lecturing at the Workers' College and elsewhere (about 90 lectures), while lecturing intensively all over Germany among Theosophists (about 140 lectures). In February, he meets Carl Unger (1878–1929), who will become a member of the board of the Anthroposophical Society (1913). In March, he meets Michael Bauer (1871–1929), a Christian mystic, who will also be on the board. In May, *Theosophy* appears, with the dedication: 'To the spirit of Giordano Bruno.' Rudolf Steiner and Marie von Sivers visit London for meetings with Annie Besant. June: Rudolf Steiner and Marie von Sivers attend the meeting of the Federation of European Sections of the Theosophical Society in Amsterdam. In July, Steiner begins the articles in *Luzifer-Gnosis* that will become *How to Know Higher Worlds* (CW 10) and *Cosmic Memory* (CW 11). In September, Annie Besant visits Germany. In December, Steiner lectures on Freemasonry. He mentions the High Grade Masonry derived from John Yarker and represented by Theodore Reuss and Karl Kellner as a blank slate 'into which a good image could be placed.'

1905: This year, Steiner ends his non-Theosophical lecturing activity. Supported by Marie von Sivers, his Theosophical lecturing—both in public and in the Theosophical Society—increases significantly: 'The German Theosophical Movement is of exceptional importance.' Steiner recommends reading, among others, Fichte, Jakob Boehme, and Angelus Silesius. He begins to introduce Christian themes into Theosophy. He also begins to work with doctors (Felix Peipers and Ludwig Noll). In July, he is in London for the Federation of European Sections, where he attends a lecture by Annie Besant: 'I have seldom seen Mrs. Besant speak in so inward and heartfelt a manner....' 'Through Mrs. Besant I have found the way to H.P. Blavatsky.' September to October, he gives a course of thirty-one lectures for a small group of esoteric students. In October, the annual meeting of the German Section of the Theosophical Society, which still remains very small, takes place. Rudolf Steiner reports membership has risen from 121 to 377 members. In November, seeking to establish esoteric 'continuity,' Rudolf Steiner and Marie von Sivers participate in a 'Memphis-Misraim' Masonic ceremony. They pay forty-five marks for membership. 'Yesterday, you saw how little remains of former esoteric institutions.' 'We are dealing only with a "framework"... for the present, nothing lies behind it. The occult powers have completely withdrawn.'

1906: Expansion of Theosophical work. Rudolf Steiner gives about 245 lectures, only 44 of which take place in Berlin. Cycles are given in Paris, Leipzig, Stuttgart, and Munich. Esoteric work also intensifies. Rudolf Steiner begins writing *An Outline of Esoteric Science* (CW 13). In January, Rudolf Steiner receives permission (a patent) from the Great Orient of the Scottish A & A Thirty-Three Degree Rite of the Order of the Ancient

Freemasons of the Memphis-Misraim Rite to direct a chapter under the name 'Mystica Aeterna.' This will become the 'Cognitive-Ritual Section' (also called 'Misraim Service') of the Esoteric School. (See: *Freemasonry and Ritual Work: The Misraim Service*, CW 265). During this time, Steiner also meets Albert Schweitzer. In May, he is in Paris, where he visits Edouard Schuré. Many Russians attend his lectures (including Konstantin Balmont, Dimitri Mereszkovski, Zinaida Hippius, and Maximilian Woloshin). He attends the General Meeting of the European Federation of the Theosophical Society, at which Col. Olcott is present for the last time. He spends the year's end in Venice and Rome, where he writes and works on his translation of H.P. Blavatsky's *Key to Theosophy*.

1907: Further expansion of the German Theosophical Movement according to the Rosicrucian directive to 'introduce spirit into the world'—in education, in social questions, in art, and in science. In February, Col. Olcott dies in Adyar. Before he dies, Olcott indicates that 'the Masters' wish Annie Besant to succeed him: much politicking ensues. Rudolf Steiner supports Besant's candidacy. April-May: preparations for the Congress of the Federation of European Sections of the Theosophical Society—the great, watershed Whitsun 'Munich Congress,' attended by Annie Besant and others. Steiner decides to separate Eastern and Western (Christian-Rosicrucian) esoteric schools. He takes his esoteric school out of the Theosophical Society (Besant and Rudolf Steiner are 'in harmony' on this). Steiner makes his first lecture tours to Austria and Hungary. That summer, he is in Italy. In September, he visits Edouard Schuré, who will write the introduction to the French edition of *Christianity as Mystical Fact* in Barr, Alsace. Rudolf Steiner writes the autobiographical statement known as the 'Barr Document.' In *Luzifer-Gnosis*, 'The Education of the Child' appears.

1908: The movement grows (membership: 1,150). Lecturing expands. Steiner makes his first extended lecture tour to Holland and Scandinavia, as well as visits to Naples and Sicily. Themes: St. John's Gospel, the Apocalypse, Egypt, science, philosophy, and logic. *Luzifer-Gnosis* ceases publication. In Berlin, Marie von Sivers (with Johanna Mücke (1864–1949) forms the *Philosophisch-Theosophisch* (after 1915 *Philosophisch-Anthroposophisch*) *Verlag* to publish Steiner's work. Steiner gives lecture cycles titled *The Gospel of St. John* (CW 103) and *The Apocalypse* (104).

1909: *An Outline of Esoteric Science* appears. Lecturing and travel continues. Rudolf Steiner's spiritual research expands to include the polarity of Lucifer and Ahriman; the work of great individualities in history; the Maitreya Buddha and the Bodhisattvas; spiritual economy (CW 109); the work of the spiritual hierarchies in heaven and on earth (CW 110). He also deepens and intensifies his research into the Gospels, giving lectures on the Gospel of St. Luke (CW 114) with the first mention of two Jesus children. Meets and becomes friends with Christian Morgenstern (1871–1914). In April, he lays the foundation stone for the Malsch model—the building that will lead to the first Goetheanum. In May, the International Congress of the Federation of European Sections of the

Theosophical Society takes place in Budapest. Rudolf Steiner receives the Subba Row medal for *How to Know Higher Worlds*. During this time, Charles W. Leadbeater discovers Jiddu Krishnamurti (1895–1986) and proclaims him the future 'world teacher,' the bearer of the Maitreya Buddha and the 'reappearing Christ.' In October, Steiner delivers seminal lectures on 'anthroposophy,' which he will try, unsuccessfully, to rework over the next years into the unfinished work, *Anthroposophy (A Fragment)* (CW 45).

1910: New themes: *The Reappearance of Christ in the Etheric* (CW 118); *The Fifth Gospel; The Mission of Folk Souls* (CW 121); *Occult History* (CW 126); the evolving development of etheric cognitive capacities. Rudolf Steiner continues his Gospel research with *The Gospel of St. Matthew* (CW 123). In January, his father dies. In April, he takes a month-long trip to Italy, including Rome, Monte Cassino, and Sicily. He also visits Scandinavia again. July–August, he writes the first mystery drama, *The Portal of Initiation* (CW 14). In November, he gives 'psychosophy' lectures. In December, he submits 'On the Psychological Foundations and Episte-mological Framework of Theosophy' to the International Philosophical Congress in Bologna.

1911: The crisis in the Theosophical Society deepens. In January, 'The Order of the Rising Sun,' which will soon become 'The Order of the Star in the East,' is founded for the coming world teacher, Krishnamurti. At the same time, Marie von Sivers, Rudolf Steiner's co-worker, falls ill. Fewer lectures are given, but important new ground is broken. In Prague, in March, Steiner meets Franz Kafka (1883–1924) and Hugo Bergmann (1883-1975). In April, he delivers his paper to the Philosophical Con-gress. He writes the second mystery drama, *The Soul's Probation* (CW 14). Also, while Marie von Sivers is convalescing, Rudolf Steiner begins work on *Calendar 1912/1913*, which will contain the 'Calendar of the Soul' meditations. On March 19, Anna (Eunike) Steiner dies. In September, Rudolf Steiner visits Einsiedeln, birthplace of Paracelsus. In December, Friedrich Rittelmeyer, future founder of the Christian Community, meets Rudolf Steiner. The *Johannes-Bauverein*, the 'building committee,' which would lead to the first Goetheanum (first planned for Munich), is also founded, and a preliminary committee for the founding of an indepen-dent association is created that, in the following year, will become the Anthroposophical Society. Important lecture cycles include *Occult Phy-siology* (CW 128); *Wonders of the World* (CW 129); *From Jesus to Christ* (CW 131). Other themes: esoteric Christianity; Christian Rosenkreutz; the spiritual guidance of humanity; the sense world and the world of the spirit.

1912: Despite the ongoing, now increasing crisis in the Theosophical Society, much is accomplished: *Calendar 1912/1913* is published; eurythmy is created; both the third mystery drama, *The Guardian of the Threshold* (CW 14) and *A Way of Self-Knowledge* (CW 16) are written. New (or renewed) themes included life between death and rebirth and karma and reincarnation. Other lecture cycles: *Spiritual Beings in the Heavenly Bodies and in the Kingdoms of Nature* (CW 136); *The Human Being in the Light of Occultism, Theosophy, and Philosophy* (CW 137); *The Gospel of St. Mark* (CW 139); and *The Bhagavad Gita and the Epistles of Paul* (CW 142). On May 8, Rudolf Steiner celebrates White Lotus Day, H.P. Blavatsky's death day, which he had faithfully observed for the past decade, for the last time. In August, Rudolf Steiner suggests the 'independent association' be called the 'Anthroposophical Society.' In September, the first eurythmy course takes place. In October, Rudolf Steiner declines recognition of a Theosophical Society lodge dedicated to the Star of the East and decides to expel all Theosophical Society members belonging to the order. Also, with Marie von Sivers, he first visits Dornach, near Basel, Switzerland, and they stand on the hill where the Goetheanum will be built. In November, a Theosophical Society lodge is opened by direct mandate from Adyar (Annie Besant). In December, a meeting of the German section occurs at which it is decided that belonging to the Order of the Star of the East is incompatible with membership in the Theosophical Society. December 28: informal founding of the Anthroposophical Society in Berlin.

1913:   Expulsion of the German section from the Theosophical Society. February 2–3: Foundation meeting of the Anthroposophical Society. Board members include: Marie von Sivers, Michael Bauer, and Carl Unger. September 20: Laying of the foundation stone for the *Johannes Bau* (Goetheanum) in Dornach. Building begins immediately. The third mystery drama, *The Soul's Awakening* (CW 14), is completed. Also: *The Threshold of the Spiritual World* (CW 147). Lecture cycles include: *The Bhagavad Gita and the Epistles of Paul* and *The Esoteric Meaning of the Bhagavad Gita* (CW 146), which the Russian philosopher Nikolai Berdyaev attends; *The Mysteries of the East and of Christianity* (CW 144); *The Effects of Esoteric Development* (CW 145); and *The Fifth Gospel* (CW 148). In May, Rudolf Steiner is in London and Paris, where anthroposophical work continues.

1914:   Building continues on the *Johannes Bau* (Goetheanum) in Dornach, with artists and co-workers from seventeen nations. The general assembly of the Anthroposophical Society takes place. In May, Rudolf Steiner visits Paris, as well as Chartres Cathedral. June 28: assassination in Sarajevo ('Now the catastrophe has happened!'). August 1: War is declared. Rudolf Steiner returns to Germany from Dornach—he will travel back and forth. He writes the last chapter of *The Riddles of Philosophy*. Lecture cycles include: *Human and Cosmic Thought* (CW 151); *Inner Being of Humanity between Death and a New Birth* (CW 153); *Occult Reading and Occult Hearing* (CW 156). December 24: marriage of Rudolf Steiner and Marie von Sivers.

1915:   Building continues. Life after death becomes a major theme, also art. Writes: *Thoughts during a Time of War* (CW 24). Lectures include: *The Secret of Death* (CW 159); *The Uniting of Humanity through the Christ Impulse* (CW 165).

1916:   Rudolf Steiner begins work with Edith Maryon (1872–1924) on the

274   *   TRUE KNOWLEDGE OF THE CHRIST

sculpture 'The Representative of Humanity' ('The Group'—Christ, Lucifer, and Ahriman). He also works with the alchemist Alexander von Bernus on the quarterly *Das Reich*. He writes *The Riddle of Humanity* (CW 20). Lectures include: *Necessity and Freedom in World History and Human Action* (CW 166); *Past and Present in the Human Spirit* (CW 167); *The Karma of Vocation* (CW 172); *The Karma of Untruthfulness* (CW 173).

1917:   Russian Revolution. The U.S. enters the war. Building continues. Rudolf Steiner delineates the idea of the 'threefold nature of the human being' (in a public lecture March 15) and the 'threefold nature of the social organism' (hammered out in May-June with the help of Otto von Lerchenfeld and Ludwig Polzer-Hoditz in the form of two documents titled *Memoranda*, which were distributed in high places). August–September: Rudolf Steiner writes *The Riddles of the Soul* (CW 20). Also: commentary on 'The Chymical Wedding of Christian Rosenkreutz' for Alexander Bernus (*Das Reich*). Lectures include: *The Karma of Materialism* (CW 176); *The Spiritual Background of the Outer World: The Fall of the Spirits of Darkness* (CW 177).

1918:   March 18: peace treaty of Brest-Litovsk—'Now everything will truly enter chaos! What is needed is cultural renewal.' June: Rudolf Steiner visits Karlstein (Grail) Castle outside Prague. Lecture cycle: *From Symptom to Reality in Modern History* (CW 185). In mid-November, Emil Molt, of the Waldorf-Astoria Cigarette Company, has the idea of founding a school for his workers' children.

1919:   Focus on the threefold social organism: tireless travel, countless lectures, meetings, and publications. At the same time, a new public stage of Anthroposophy emerges as cultural renewal begins. The coming years will see initiatives in pedagogy, medicine, pharmacology, and agriculture. January 27: threefold meeting: ' We must first of all, with the money we have, found free schools that can bring people what they need.' February: first public eurythmy performance in Zurich. Also: 'Appeal to the German People' (CW 24), circulated March 6 as a newspaper insert. In April, *Towards Social Renewal* (CW 23) appears— 'perhaps the most widely read of all books on politics appearing since the war.' Rudolf Steiner is asked to undertake the 'direction and leadership' of the school founded by the Waldorf-Astoria Company. Rudolf Steiner begins to talk about the 'renewal' of education. May 30: a building is selected and purchased for the future Waldorf School. August–September, Rudolf Steiner gives a lecture course for Waldorf teachers, *The Foundations of Human Experience (Study of Man)* (CW 293). September 7: Opening of the first Waldorf School. December (into January): first science course, the *Light Course* (CW 320).

1920:   The Waldorf School flourishes. New threefold initiatives. Founding of limited companies *Der Kommende Tag* and *Futurum A.G.* to infuse spiritual values into the economic realm. Rudolf Steiner also focuses on the sciences. Lectures: *Introducing Anthroposophical Medicine* (CW 312); *The Warmth Course* (CW 321); *The Boundaries of Natural Science* (CW 322); *The Redemption of Thinking* (CW 74). February: Johannes Werner

Klein—later a co-founder of the Christian Community—asks Rudolf Steiner about the possibility of a 'religious renewal,' a 'Johannine church.' In March, Rudolf Steiner gives the first course for doctors and medical students. In April, a divinity student asks Rudolf Steiner a second time about the possibility of religious renewal. September 27–October 16: anthroposophical 'university course.' December: lectures titled *The Search for the New Isis* (CW 202).

1921:   Rudolf Steiner continues his intensive work on cultural renewal, including the uphill battle for the threefold social order. 'University' arts, scientific, theological, and medical courses include: *The Astronomy Course* (CW 323); *Observation, Mathematics, and Scientific Experiment* (CW 324); the *Second Medical Course* (CW 313); *Colour*. In June and September-October, Rudolf Steiner also gives the first two 'priests' courses' (CW 342 and 343). The 'youth movement' gains momentum. Magazines are founded: *Die Drei* (January), and—under the editorship of Albert Steffen (1884–1963)—the weekly, *Das Goetheanum* (August). In February–March, Rudolf Steiner takes his first trip outside Germany since the war (Holland). On April 7, Steiner receives a letter regarding 'religious renewal,' and May 22–23, he agrees to address the question in a practical way. In June, the Klinical-Therapeutic Institute opens in Arlesheim under the direction of Dr. Ita Wegman. In August, the Chemical-Pharmaceutical Laboratory opens in Arlesheim (Oskar Schmiedel and Ita Wegman are directors). The Clinical Therapeutic Institute is inaugurated in Stuttgart (Dr. Ludwig Noll is director); also the Research Laboratory in Dornach (Ehrenfried Pfeiffer and Günther Wachsmuth are directors). In November–December, Rudolf Steiner visits Norway.

1922:   The first half of the year involves very active public lecturing (thousands attend); in the second half, Rudolf Steiner begins to withdraw and turn toward the Society—'The Society is asleep.' It is 'too weak' to do what is asked of it. The businesses—*Der Kommende Tag* and *Futurum A.G.*—fail. In January, with the help of an agent, Steiner undertakes a twelve-city German lecture tour, accompanied by eurythmy performances. In two weeks he speaks to more than 2,000 people. In April, he gives a 'university course' in The Hague. He also visits England. In June, he is in Vienna for the East–West Congress. In August–September, he is back in England for the Oxford Conference on Education. Returning to Dornach, he gives the lectures *Philosophy, Cosmology, and Religion* (CW 215), and gives the third priests' course (CW 344). On September 16, The Christian Community is founded. In October–November, Steiner is in Holland and England. He also speaks to the youth: *The Youth Course* (CW 217). In December, Steiner gives lectures titled *The Origins of Natural Science* (CW 326), and *Humanity and the World of Stars: The Spiritual Communion of Humanity* (CW 219). December 31: Fire at the Goetheanum, which is destroyed.

1923:   Despite the fire, Rudolf Steiner continues his work unabated. A very hard year. Internal dispersion, dissension, and apathy abound. There is conflict—between old and new visions—within the Society. A wake-up call is needed, and Rudolf Steiner responds with renewed lecturing vitality. His focus: the spiritual context of human life; initiation science; the course of the year; and community building. As a foundation for an artistic school, he creates a series of pastel sketches. Lecture cycles: *The Anthroposophical Movement; Initiation Science* (CW 227) (in England at the Penmaenmawr Summer School); *The Four Seasons and the Archangels* (CW 229); *Harmony of the Creative Word* (CW 230); *The Supersensible Human* (CW 231), given in Holland for the founding of the Dutch society. On November 10, in response to the failed Hitler-Ludendorff putsch in Munich, Steiner closes his Berlin residence and moves the *Philosophisch-Anthroposophisch Verlag* (Press) to Dornach. On December 9, Steiner begins the serialization of his *Autobiography: The Course of My Life* (CW 28) in *Das Goetheanum*. It will continue to appear weekly, without a break, until his death. Late December–early January: Rudolf Steiner re-founds the Anthroposophical Society (about 12,000 members internationally) and takes over its leadership. The new board members are: Marie Steiner, Ita Wegman, Albert Steffen, Elisabeth Vreede, and Günther Wachsmuth. (See *The Christmas Meeting for the Founding of the General Anthroposophical Society*, CW 260). Accompanying lectures: *Mystery Knowledge and Mystery Centres* (CW 232); *World History in the Light of Anthroposophy* (CW 233). December 25: the Foundation Stone is laid (in the hearts of members) in the form of the 'Foundation Stone Meditation.'

1924: January 1: having founded the Anthroposophical Society and taken over its leadership, Rudolf Steiner has the task of 'reforming' it. The process begins with a weekly newssheet ('What's Happening in the Anthroposophical Society') in which Rudolf Steiner's 'Letters to Members' and 'Anthroposophical Leading Thoughts' appear (CW 26). The next step is the creation of a new esoteric class, the 'first class' of the 'University of Spiritual Science' (which was to have been followed, had Rudolf Steiner lived longer, by two more advanced classes). Then comes a new language for Anthroposophy—practical, phenomenological, and direct; and Rudolf Steiner creates the model for the second Goetheanum. He begins the series of extensive 'karma' lectures (CW 235–40); and finally, responding to needs, he creates two new initiatives: biodynamic agriculture and curative education. After the middle of the year, rumours begin to circulate regarding Steiner's health. Lectures: January–February, *Anthroposophy* (CW 234); February: *Tone Eurythmy* (CW 278); June: *The Agriculture Course* (CW 327); June–July: *Speech Eurythmy* (CW 279); *Curative Education* (CW 317); August: (England, 'Second International Summer School'), *Initiation Consciousness: True and False Paths in Spiritual Investigation* (CW 243); September: *Pastoral Medicine* (CW 318). On September 26, for the first time, Rudolf Steiner cancels a lecture. On September 28, he gives his last lecture. On September 29, he withdraws to his studio in the carpenter's shop; now he is definitively ill. Cared for by Ita Wegman, he continues working, however, and writing the weekly installments of his *Autobiography* and *Letters to the Members/Leading Thoughts* (CW 26).

1925:   Rudolf Steiner, while continuing to work, continues to weaken. He finishes *Extending Practical Medicine* (CW 27) with Ita Wegman.

On March 30, around ten in the morning, Rudolf Steiner dies.

INDEX